Politics,

RL

RUSSIA IN TRANSITION:

Politics, Privatisation and Inequality

by

David Lane
(Editor)

Longman
London and New York

Addison Wesley Longman Limited
Edinburgh Gate
Harlow, Essex CM20 2JE, England
and Associated Companies throughout the world.

Published in the United States of America
by Addison Wesley Longman Publishing, New York

First published 1995
Second impression 1996
ISBN 0 582 275660 PPR

British Library Cataloguing-in-Publication Data

A catalogue record for this book is
available from the British Library

Learning Resources
Centre

Library of Congress Cataloging-in-Publication Data

Russia in transition / by David Lane (editor).
   p. cm.
  Includes bibliographical references (p.) and index.
  ISBN 0–582–27566–0 (U.K.)
   1. Russia (Federation)—Social conditions—1991– —Congresses.
2. Russia (Federation)—Economic conditions—1991– —Congresses.
3. Russia (Federation)—Politics and government—1991– —Congresses.
I. Lane, David Stuart.
HN530.2.A8R865 1995   95–18239
306′.0947—dc20   CIP

set in 9pt Times by 5

Produced through Longman Malaysia, GPS

CONTENTS

PREFACE

The book is the outcome of a conference held in Cambridge in December 1994. In addition to the authors of the following chapters, the conference was enlivened by the presence of Professor Andrei Zdravomyslov, Professor John Scott, Ms Nirwal Pawar, Professor Peter Frank, Dr Ian Gough, Dr Peter McMylor, Professor Herman van der Wusten, Dr Geoffrey Ingham, Ms Sarah Caro, Mr Mark Knackstedt, Ms Liz Gray, Dr Tatiana Dudina and Ms Carolina Zincone. I am indebted to the Economic and Social Research Council who, through the East–West initiative, provided finance and to Emmanuel College for their support.

LIST OF CONTRIBUTORS

Simon Clarke is Professor of Sociology and a member of the Centre for Comparative Labour Studies, University of Warwick. With Peter Fairbrother and his Russian collaborators he has been researching the restructuring of industrial enterprises, labour organisation and the worker's movement in Russia since 1990. The current focuses of this research are the restructuring of the Russian coal-mining industry and the restructuring of employment and the development of labour markets.

Veronika Kabalina is Senior Researcher at the Centre for Comparative Social, Economic and Political Studies, IMEMO, Moscow. Her main research activity is in the areas of industrial relations and management strategy in privatised enterprises.

Irina Y. Kuzes pursued graduate study at the Institute of Urban Planning in Moscow and is a lecturer at the Institute of Architecture (Moscow) and a correspondent with the journal *Znanie – Sila*. She is co-author (with Lynn Nelson) of *Property to the People: The Struggle for Radical Economic Reform in Russia* (1994) and *Radical Reform in Yeltsin's Russia: Political, Economic and Social Dimensions* (forthcoming 1995). She held an appointment as a visiting researcher at Virginia Commonwealth University from 1992 to 1994.

David Lane studied at the Universities of Birmingham and Oxford and is currently Reader in Sociology and Fellow of Emmanuel College, Cambridge University. He has written extensively on socialism, social stratification and political power. His recent books include *Soviet Society Under Perestroika* (2nd edition 1992), *Russia in Flux* (editor, 1993). Supported by the British Economic and Social Research Council, he is currently researching into the structure and composition of elites in the former USSR and contemporary Russia.

Nick Manning studied at the Universities of Cambridge, York, and Kent. He is Reader in Social Policy at the University of Kent. His publications include, with Vic George, *Socialism, Social Welfare and the Soviet Union* (1980), with Bob Deacon and others, *The New Eastern Europe: social policy, past, present, and future* (1992). He is currently writing up an ESRC-funded study of social movements in Russia and Eastern Europe, and starting a new project to examine Russian employment and social policy up to 1998.

Alastair McAuley is a Reader in Economics at the University of Essex. He is a leading specialist on the former Soviet economy and has recently acted as a consultant to the World Bank in both Russia and Uzbekistan. His work focuses upon two topics: income inequality and the labour market under central planning and during the transition; regional policy and regional development under socialism. His publications include *Economic Welfare in the Soviet Union* (1979), 'The economic transition in Eastern Europe: employment, income distribution and the social security net' *Oxford*

Review of Economic Policy 7 (4) (December 1991) and 'The Economic Consequences of Soviet disintegration' *Soviet Economy* 7 (3) (July–September 1991).

Ellen Mickiewicz is Director of the DeWitt Wallace Center for Communications and Journalism and is James R. Shepley Professor of Public Policy at Duke University. She is also a Fellow of the Carter Center and Director of the Commission on Radio and Television Policy, a multilateral non-governmental organisation, chaired by the former President Jimmy Carter and Eduard Sagalaev, President of the independent broadcast television channel TV6, in Moscow. She is currently writing a book on television and democratisation at the end of the Soviet period and in post-Soviet Russia. Recent work has included a study of television and elections in Russia and public opinion and political change. She is the author of *Split Signals: Television and Politics in the Soviet Union* (winner of the National Association of Broadcasters' Book of the Year award), and a number of other books and articles.

Lynn D. Nelson is a Professor of Sociology at Virginia Commonwealth University. He is co-author (with Irina Kuzes) of *Property to the People: The Struggle for Radical Economic Reform in Russia* (1994) and *Radical Reform in Yeltsin's Russia: Political, Economic and Social Dimensions* (forthcoming 1995). He has been a visiting fellow at Harvard University's Russian Research Centre and has held a Fulbright lectureship in the Soviet Union.

Cameron Ross is a Lecturer at Dundee University, and he collaborated on a research project on political elites in the Soviet Union and contemporary Russia. He has taught previously at the College of William and Mary in Virginia, and Oberlin College in Ohio. His publications include *Local Government in the Soviet Union* (St Martin's Press, 1987) and 'Party–state relations', in *Executive Power and Soviet Politics: The Rise and Decline of the Soviet State* (ed. Eugene Huskey, 1992).

Wendy Slater served as regional editor on the Soviet Union, CIS, and Eastern Europe at CIRCA, Cambridge, for *Keesing's Record of World Events*, and as a research analyst on Russian domestic politics for Radio Free Europe/Radio Liberty Research Institute in Munich. She has worked as a freelance writer and translator. She is currently researching into the Russian Right at the University of Cambridge.

Graham Smith is Director of the Post-Soviet States Research Programme and Fellow, Sidney Sussex College, and Lecturer in the Department of Geography, University of Cambridge. His main interests are in nationalism and the ethnic policies of the post-Soviet states. Recent books in the area include *Planned Development in the Socialist World* (1989), *The Nationalities Question in the Soviet Union* (1990), *The Baltic States. The National Self-Determination of Estonia, Latvia and Lithuania* (1994) and *Federalism. The Multi-ethnic Challenge* (1995).

Stephen White is Professor of Politics and a member of the Institute of Russian and East European Studies at the University of Glasgow. Currently President of the British Association for Slavonic and East European Studies, he also edits *Coexistence* and the *Journal of Communist Studies and Transition Politics*. His recent publications include *After Gorbachev* (1993, with others), *The Politics of Transition* (1993, with others), *Developments in Russian and Post-Soviet Politics*, and *Russia Goes Dry: Alcohol, Society and the Policy Process* (1995).

Stephen Whitefield is a Fellow in Politics at Pembroke College, Oxford. His publications include: *Industrial Power and the Soviet State* (1993) and, as editor and contributor, *The New Institutional Architecture of Eastern Europe* (1993). The chapter in the current volume is part of a wider research project on the bases of political competition in post-communist Eastern Europe. Among his other publications on this subject are (with Geoffrey Evans) 'The Russian election of 1993: public opinion and the transition experience', *Post-Soviet Affairs*, 10 (1994), 38–40; 'Identifying the bases of party competition in Eastern Europe', *British Journal of Political Science*, 23 (1993), 521–48; 'The politics and economics of democratic commitment', *British Journal of Political Science*, forthcoming 1995.

Matthew Wyman is Lecturer in Russian Politics at Keele University. Previously, he has worked as a research associate on Glasgow University's ESRC-funded project on 'Public Opinion and Democratic Consolidation in Russia and Eastern Europe'. He has published articles on Russian elections and political culture and is currently working on a monograph on *Public Opinion in Post-communist Russia*.

Olga Zdravomyslova is a Senior Research Fellow of the Institute of Socio-Economic Population Studies of the Russian Academy of Sciences, Moscow. She is one of the co-ordinators (with Marina Arutiunian) of the *Family: East–West* project. She is currently working on gender socialisation in the period of transition in Russia.

INTRODUCTION

David Lane

By 1991, the Soviet Union was in terminal disintegration. Its republics had declared their own sovereignty. In June 1990, Yeltsin had become leader of the Parliament of the Russian Republic and declared its laws to have precedence over those of the USSR. In August 1991, in an attempt to halt the disintegration of the Soviet system, a state of emergency was declared by the State Committee for the State of Emergency. This was a bid to replace Mikhail Gorbachev as President of the USSR. Ironically, Gorbachev's rival, Boris Nikolaevich Yeltsin, rallied around the Parliament of the Russian Federation and declared the state of emergency illegal. The attempted coup failed but it effectively ended Gorbachev's rule and with it any hope of reviving the USSR.

Between August and December 1991, when the hammer and sickle was finally hauled down from the Kremlin, when Gorbachev resigned as President and when the USSR was disbanded as a state, the institutions of the USSR were brought under the control of the government of the Russian Federation and its President, Yeltsin. In the first chapter of this book we have defined this as a successful counter-coup. In August, the Council of Ministers of the Russian Republic declared its right to take over the ministries and departments of the USSR, and the Russian Prime Minister, Ivan Silaev, appointed his own ministers to take control of the USSR government. In September the USSR Congress of People's Deputies dissolved itself. Effectively the Parliament of the Russian Republic assumed control over the institutions of the USSR in its territory. In December, the Supreme Soviet of the Russian Federation took over the property previously subordinate to the USSR and Russia's President replaced the Soviet President. One by one the other republics of the USSR declared their independence.

On 1 January 1992, the Russian Federation was recognised by the United Nations as the legal successor state to the USSR. The symbols of the Soviet state, its flag, anthem, ideology and institutions were all repudiated by the new Russian government and its President. The policy of the Russian leadership under Yeltsin was to shift conclusively away from the organic type of polity, economy and society characteristic of Soviet communism. The major thrust of the reform leadership was to create a pluralist polity and society. This involved the creation of boundaries between polity, economy and society: a multi-party competitive political system, a market economy based on privatised enterprises and autonomous social groups in 'civil society'. These internal changes entailed a major reorientation in the position of Russia in the world economy and political order. The international network of communist states, and its military alliance, the Warsaw Pact, was terminated and replaced with an open political and economic frontier to the West. In this pluralistic and polymorphic setting the new leadership had to shape a new nation.

Russia entered an era of transition: by this we mean a period of change, a passage from one set of circumstances, institutions, values and ways of doing things. We do not imply that 'transition' involves a predetermined route from state socialism to capitalism. The objectives of the political leadership of Russia have been defined above; such ambitions contain ambiguities and contradictions, they are opposed by many people, they have to be implemented in the context of established values, traditions and institutions. We do not imply that the leadership will succeed, we do not presume that the 'transition' has only one outcome, we do not assume that forces within the leadership or in society will not deflect policy to achieve different ends or different combinations of ends.

Discarding the Soviet system was easier done than finding a viable model to replace it. Indeed, the major theme of this book are the difficulties faced by the reform leadership in its attempt to move to a liberal market society. In the first and fourth chapters David Lane and Cameron Ross remind us that the reform leadership of President Yeltsin was under challenge by an opposition; he came to power only on the barest majority of votes. His support, both in the country and in the Parliament has come disproportionately from the professional classes (the intelligentsia). The major obstacle to reform has been the legacies of the past: not only the institutions of state socialism but also the values of Russia which have been mediated by the communist political and economic order. Lane and Ross demonstrate in their chapter on elites that the reform leadership has been successful in cutting off the head of the old administration, but here and in other chapters we are reminded that it is much more difficult to replace the administrative system and those who have benefited from it.

The new leaders have struggled to define a political system with a strong presidential power, multiple competitive parties, and an independent legislature set in a federal framework. Instability has been endemic. In the struggle of the republics against the hegemony of the USSR under Gorbachev, the movements for radical reform legitimised the interests of the localities against the centre and this was proved to be a two-edged sword. Yeltsin supported the demands for autonomy of the ethno-republics to undermine Gorbachev. However, following the constitution of Russia as a sovereign state, the regions and republics have begun to assert their own autonomy against the centre. Graham Smith defines the problem of maintaining the integrity of the emergent Russian state against the self-interest of the federal units – graphically illustrated in 1995 by the civil war in Chechnia. Federation without federalism has resulted. Spatially Russia has been fragmented, the party system has failed to provide a political anchor. The pluralist system of political parties, which in the stable Western societies evolved over more than a hundred years, cannot be replicated overnight in Russia. Stephen White illustrates the lack of identification and confidence between voters and parties. Russian government is characterised as 'a party system without parties' and hence a conduit between government and society is lacking. At the apex of politics, leadership takes on an individualistic character and in the country it becomes segmented geographically and institutionally. Endemic political instability ensues.

The legacy of Soviet Communism prevails in values which are opposed to aspects of reform: this is particularly so with respect to the privatisation of property. Lane and Ross in their study of voting in the Russian Parliament illustrate this principled division. Division is not only in terms of personalities but ideological groupings with respect to the pace and scope of privatisation and marketisation and to the role of Parliament and President. The social divisions in support for and opposition to the reform process are studied by Stephen Whitefield who, distinguishing between normative and evaluative attitudes to reform, emphasises the regional differences in perspective. He shows that in a normative sense, support for reform, particularly democracy, is positive. However, the reformers are not more 'democratic' than the opponents of reform, and anti-reformers are often more in favour of liberal values such as freedom of speech and association. The evaluation of reform has been mixed, depending on its success or failure: privatisation is universally perceived as having progressed badly. The confusion and incompatibilities of reform policies are mirrored in popular attitudes to reform.

The legacy of the past is also apparent in the position of women. Here, however, 'the past' refers not only to Soviet values but also to traditional Russian attitudes which predate the Soviet period. Indeed, Soviet culture was infused with the traditional culture of Russia. Wendy Slater and Olga Zdravomyslova both emphasise the ways in which patriarchy is being established. Women are not only excluded from participation in the political elites and executive positions, but increasingly a dominant ideology is being asserted stressing their traditional position as mothers and home-makers. Here Zdravomyslova points to a major difference with the West: Russian women have a cultural tradition which strongly values their family and home-centred role.

Privatisation of public assets is a major process of the period of transition. It is not merely concerned with the effective ownership and control of material assets but has important political and social ramifications. In contrast to 'transitions' from authoritarianism in the southern European states where, for example, private property and a bourgeoisie were already deeply embedded, in Russia a bourgeois class has had to be created. Privatisation then is multi-functional: its purpose is not only to change the legitimate ownership and control of assets, it seeks also to create a propertied class with a stake in the system and concurrently to support a new entrepreneurial class. These functions often conflict. Lynn Nelson and Irina Kuzes argue that independent entrepreneurial activity has not been supported by the government, rather the state bureaucracy has been reconstituted in a different form. They point out that the initial political process weakened state control to enable the 'hidden hand' of the market to work and it also had the effect of allowing the criminalisation of the process of privatisation. Regional and local interests are able to assert their hegemony in the shaping of economic reforms and control over property.

This argument is taken up by Simon Clarke who sees privatisation as an attempt by the state to restore control over the economy through a new juridical framework. However, interests at the micro level in the form of managers in the enterprise have asserted their own interests. He affirms that the first stage of a 'managerial revolution' is in progress. Privatisation of the ownership of assets, he argues, is a formal process which does not give control to the owner but allows the management to benefit from enhanced salaries and other forms of advantage. Rather than developing a competitive market economy, there is a tendency for the systemic relations of the previous state system to reestablish themselves in new forms. A major conflict is presented between the centre with the industrial ministries (discussed also from an elite position by Lane and Ross) seeking to reestablish their hegemony, and the regional authorities pursuing local monopolisation. Fraud, theft and deception are hallmarks of privatisation in the localities.

Study of the contemporary media illustrates the conflicting forces at work at the top of the system of political power. Ellen Mickiewicz analyses three sources of political influence over the control of the mass media: the central state, the local political elites and independently financed institutions. Here again the interaction of competing elites is expressed through struggle for control. The clash of commercial and political interests as well as new and old values are manifested through these different channels. These contradictions between Russian/Soviet values and those of commercialism, Western mass culture and commercial advertising indicate the immense problems involved in the creation of a national identity; the fragmentation of the television media and its linkages to political interests retard the development of a democratic political system. The reaction to cultural 'contamination' and to the indiscriminate adoption of Western, especially American, political values and cultural symbols takes the form of a nationalist backlash. The commercial and political emphasis on individualism undermines a collective sense of national self-determination and gives an ideological legitimacy to the local ethno-national interests discussed in the chapter by Graham Smith.

The social consequences of reform are detailed by Alastair McAuley and Nick Manning. Economically, the initial impact of the introduction of the market and the collapse of the Soviet command system have been a disaster for most of the population of Russia. While, politically, the population has gained in freedom of expression, organisation and movement, disorder has accompanied transition. Gross national income has declined significantly; it has been accompanied by hyperinflation and a large increase in income differentiation. McAuley documents the rise of a wealthy class and the growth of poverty and homelessness: one example – the 'ultra poor' rose from 2.9 per cent of the population in 1990 to 27.1 per cent in 1992. Children, women and the old bear the brunt of poverty. At the other end of the income scale, the number of rich and very rich have greatly increased.

The welfare state was one of the major achievements of Soviet power: it provided at least a basic minimum for the population and was comprehensive in delivery of services. The process of transition has intensified the need for social support. Inflation, unemployment, privatisation of housing, the growth of poverty and homelessness, on the one side, and the underfunding of the public sector in general and social services in particular, on the other, have led to a dramatic decline in the provision of social services, documented in Nick Manning's chapter. The privatisation of the health service and underfunding in the public sector has led to a significant increase in illness and to a rise in mortality rates. In education, privatisation and the introduction of fee-paying education after nine years favours the rich. Manning cogently argues that social policy is moving away from the social democratic tradition towards a 'corporatist' policy. A greater market-linked access to the delivery of services is taking place. The consequence is that not only will income and wealth become more unevenly distributed, but also such stratification will be paralleled in the welfare sector.

The effects of the movement to the market and the destruction of state planning have led to a reduction in the level of industrial production and to greater inequality. This is the economic side to reform; on the political side, some argue that all are winners in the sense that choice and freedom of expression and movement have immeasurably increased for all. However, the research in this book indicates that there is a realisation that some are net 'winners' as a consequence of the transition and others are 'losers'. The former are those who have been able to start or develop their own business, the young whose yearning for a Western culture has been fulfilled and who are able to compete more successfully in the market. Winners include those who had authority under state socialism and were astute enough to abandon their commitment to socialism under Gorbachev, others have been able to make private capital out of their previous public position. The losers are the old living on pensions or savings, those on low wages (particularly women employees), those dependent on social security and transfer payments – children have done particularly badly.

Freedom signifies choice and diversity and the market system also implies uncertainty. All are now subject to levels of uncertainty unknown under state socialism. It is the poor, those with lower levels of education, those with inferior qualifications, those living in the countryside, those whose vision of society emphasises public virtues rather than private gains, who have lost out in the present stage of transition. The movement for radical reform, however, has another aspect: it is a concern for democracy. The articulation of the interests of the losers not only through the institutions of politics but also by local political interests may yet frustrate and possibly reverse the move to marketisation. Unless the movement to privatisation and marketisation can be performed more effectively and efficiently than hitherto, democratisation may yet defeat it. Paradoxically, the movement for democratic reform – in its policy to marketise, to privatise assets and to create a propertied bourgeois class – may be forced to adopt some of the restrictive political features of state socialism in order to achieve it. The call for democracy may well legitimise those who seek a return to traditional Russian (and Soviet) values and to the dominant role of the state in providing employment, welfare state supports and limitation to radical reform. Democracy and marketisation may be incompatible objectives in Russian conditions.

Part One

THE POLITICS OF TRANSITION

Chapter 1

FROM SOVIET GOVERNMENT TO PRESIDENTIAL RULE

David Lane and Cameron Ross

The government of the USSR differed significantly from that of Western parlia-mentary government. Unlike the latter, which was pluralistic in substance with competing parties and a division of powers, the former was based on an organic system of government. A key role was played by the Communist Party of the Soviet Union, which was a ruling party; under its general direction functioned a government bureaucracy (the Council of Ministers) and elected soviets of people's deputies. This was a federal system of government with a division of powers between the USSR and the republics. Under the leadership of Mikhail Gorbachev, major changes took place: the role of the Party was weakened, the soviets were endowed with greater authority and the office of the presidency (at both the USSR and republican levels) was instituted.[1] Popular competitive elections involving a choice of candidates were introduced giving legitimacy to the legislature (the Congresses of People's Deputies and Supreme Soviets). The President of the USSR (the position occupied by Gorbachev) was not directly elected by popular vote, but by the Congress of People's Deputies. In some of the republics, however, direct popular election did occur and in Russia, Gorbachev's rival, Boris Yeltsin, was so elected. Shifting authority to the soviets strengthened the position of the republican governments *vis-à-vis* that of the USSR and a struggle for power ensued between them.

The attempted coup of August 1991 led by the State Committee for the State of Emergency was a decisive turning point in the history of the Soviet Union. Its participants had all been appointed to positions of authority by Gorbachev, and many of the leading politicians in the USSR presidency, the Council of Ministers and the USSR Supreme Soviet supported the actions of the State Committee. In defusing the attempted coup, Yeltsin turned the tables on Gorbachev. He and his supporters, clustered around the institutions of the Russian Republic (then the Russian Federative Socialist Republic or RSFSR), conducted what was in effect a successful counter-coup. They not only dismissed the leadership of the government of the USSR and effectively deposed its President, Gorbachev, but assumed control over the activities of the government of the USSR. There followed an interim government largely appointed by Yeltsin, which ruled the USSR until 25 December 1991 when Gorbachev resigned as President and the USSR was disbanded. In this chapter we outline how this transformation took place, consider the major institutions which were set up to replace the Soviet ones and the conflict which ensued between them.

1.   For a detailed account of the changes under Gorbachev see David Lane, *Soviet Society under Perestroika*, Routledge, London, 1992, chapter 3.

The Russian Congress of People's Deputies and Supreme Soviet

One of the major components in Gorbachev's policy of *perestroika* was the revival of the soviets. In order to secure legitimacy for his policies, which were blocked by entrenched interests in the Council of Ministers and in the executive of the Communist Party of the Soviet Union, he saw in the soviets an arena in which political change could be more easily secured from below. He instituted contested elections which entailed the absence of communist control over the selection of candidates. He also sanctioned open voting and the formation of groups and factions (*fraktsiia*) in the Parliament. These later became the source of the nascent independent party organisations. In the process of political change leading to the collapse of the USSR, no other single institution played a greater role than the parliaments (as the congresses and soviets began to be called). They not only aggregated political demands but articulated a policy in opposition to the domination of the USSR's political institutions.

While the election and subsequent politics of the USSR Congress of People's Deputies and Supreme Soviet have been the focus of much scholarly and political attention, it was the legislative body of the RSFSR (then known as the Russian Republic) from which the Parliament of the Russian Federation was to be derived. The major thrust for, and legitimacy of, political change came from the Parliament of the RSFSR. The leadership of Yeltsin and the organisation of forces around the parliamentary buildings against the powers of the State Committee for the State of Emergency in August 1991 effectively sealed the fate of the rule of Gorbachev and led to the collapse of the USSR.

Election of Yeltsin as Chair of the Supreme Soviet

At the first session of the Congress on 24 May 1990, after two rounds of voting, Yeltsin was narrowly elected Chair of the Supreme Soviet, In the first round, Yeltsin competed against Vladimir Morokin (senior lecturer at the Kazan Aviation Institute) and Ivan Polozkov (Chair of the Krasnodar Krai Soviet and a leading member of the newly formed Russian Communist Party) but neither candidate secured the majority of votes required (531). (For short biographical descriptions of the major personalities see Appendix.) Yeltsin received 497 votes, Polozkov 473, and Morokin 32. Polozkov and Morokin then dropped out of the contest. In the second round Yeltsin was challenged by Aleksandr Vlasov (the chairman of the RSFSR Council of Ministers) and Valentin Tsoi (chairman of the board of the Ekspa State Cooperative Enterprise). Yeltsin won the election with 535 votes (only four more than required), Vlasov received 467 and Tsoi 11.[2] This electoral success, it must be borne in mind, preceded the election of Yeltsin as President of the RSFSR – an event which took place on 12 June of the following year. The size of these votes, however, remind us that Yeltsin from the outset commanded the authority of only a small majority of the Congress deputies.

---

2. Martin McCauley (ed.) *Directory of Russian MPs: People's Deputies of the Supreme Soviet of Russia–Russian Federation*, Longman, London, 1992, p. viii.

While the political institutions in the Russian Republic were similar to those in the USSR, there was one very important exception. The election of the President in Russia was to be by direct popular vote, whereas in the USSR, the election was by the Congress of People's Deputies. This gave the President of the Russian Republic a direct authority from the people – a fact that later was used to legitimate presidential authority. Following election, the President of Russia consequently gave up the post of Chair of the Supreme Soviet.

New elections for the Chair of the Supreme Soviet took place at the 5th Congress in the summer and autumn of 1991. Once again there was a fierce contest and several rounds of voting. The two main contenders were Ruslan Khasbulatov, who was at the time the First Deputy Chairman of the Parliament, and Sergei Baburin, a leading member of the political faction 'Rossiia'. Elections in July failed to provide a clear winner, with Khasbulatov receiving 409 votes and Baburin 412. Khasbulatov was appointed Acting Chairman until new elections could be held in the autumn.

The Congress reconvened on 10 October 1991 in a highly charged atmosphere after the events of the attempted August coup. Five candidates stood for election (Khasbulatov, Baburin, Iurii Slobodkin, Mikhail Chelnokov and Il'ia Konstantinov) but this time Khasbulatov was able to win outright – benefiting from his positive stand during the events of August, where he played a major role in defending the Parliament.[3]

Political Parties, Factions and Groups

As the deputies had been elected in competitive conditions, their political affiliation to parties and political groups took on a different significance to the pre-Gorbachev elections. But it has to be borne in mind that, at the time of the 1990 elections, party formation was extremely weak. Technically, parties were not registered and therefore could not contest elections. However, many deputies stood on the basis of 'platforms' (e.g. 'Democratic platform' of the CPSU, 'Marxist–Leninist' platform) and indicated in their election address their political viewpoint.

After the election in 1990, members of the CPSU still overwhelmingly dominated the Congress. There were 920 members of the CPSU (86.7 per cent) and Komsomol members made up another 0.5 per cent. However, 'party members' were not one unitary group and were distinguished by factional membership, the major factions being Marxist Platform, Communists of Russia and Communists for Democracy. Moreover, by 16 August 1991, just before the failed coup and the dissolution of the CPSU, Party membership was in decline and Party allegiance of the deputies had fallen to 767 or 71.8 per cent. In 1990, there were just 20 deputies who declared their membership of other political parties. By October 1991, eight members declared for the Republican Party of the Russian Federation, four were Social Democrats, three were members of the Democratic Party of Russia and three of the Free Democratic

---

3. The results of the voting was as follows: Khasbulatov 559, Baburin 274, Slobodkin 42, Chelnokov 20, Konstantinov, 20. The fifth Congress also ratified the election of Sergei Filatov as First Deputy Chair of the Parliament and Iurii Voronin, Vladimir Shumeiko, and Iurii Iarov as deputy chairs. Martin McCauley, *op. cit.* 1992, pp. xvii–xviii.

Party of Russia, only two were Constitutional Democrats and one was a member of the People's Party (Narodnaia partiia) of Russia.[4]

One of the reasons why the struggle between the legislative and the executive branches in Russia became so acute was the absence of strong disciplined parties in the Parliament and an almost total divide between the Parliament and the government. Elections in 1990 took place before parties had had the opportunity to develop, and the hundreds of tiny parties that had emerged had no parliamentary presence. With the exception of Civic Union, and later Russia's Choice, none of the parties were given representation in Yeltsin's government. Within the Parliament most of the deputies had no strong allegiance to any party and informal factions and political groups quickly dominated the life of the Congress.

These groups after the elections had an official status: to qualify as a registered political faction, 50 members had to declare their allegiance to the group. By October 1991, there were 14 political factions (*politicheskie fraktsii*) and 13 other groups set up claiming to defend professional and regional interests. In the Congress in May 1992, 850 of the deputies (81 per cent) were members of political factions or groups.[5]

A Council of Political Factions was formed, headed by Vladimir Novikov, to coordinate the activities of the factions. According to the regulations of the Congress, each deputy was allowed to enter into only one political association but there were no such restrictions for professional and regional groups. As discussed below, this rule was not adhered to.

Table 1.1 charts the rise (and in some cases the fall) of the political factions in Parliament between October 1991 and February 1993. By far the largest faction in 1991 was that of the Communists of Russia with 357 deputies, and this was followed by the rural communist Agrarian Union which had 111 deputies. Aleksandr Rutskoi's Communists for Democracy numbered 96. By October 1991, Democratic Russia had lost a substantial number of deputies – falling from nearly 200 in March to only 69 and the other major democratic faction, the Radical Democrats, had even fewer (55). Democratic Russia had played a vital role in the 1990 elections, enabling a number of reformers to win seats in the Parliament. It was also a major force in helping Yeltsin become the Chairman of the Parliament in May 1990 and members of Democratic Russia were important allies in Yeltsin's successful campaign to become Russian President in June 1991. Rutskoi's Communists for Democracy split the CPSU vote in the Parliament and, in March 1991, saved Yeltsin from being pushed out of office in a vote of no confidence. Partly for this reason, and also to bring in the votes of the military–industrial complex, Yeltsin chose Rutskoi – then co-chair of the Civic Union – as his candidate for Vice-President in the summer of 1991.

4. 'Piatyi (Vneocherednoi) S'ezd Narodnykh Deputatov RSFSR. – Parlamentskomu Korrespondentu', prilozhenie k informatsionnomu biulleteniu, *Parlamentskaia Nedelia*, Part 1, 16 May 1990–1 October 1991, pp. 1–287, esp. pp. 11–12.
5. For details of factions and their membership, see Vladimir Pribylovskii *Politicheskie Fraktsii i Deputatskie Gruppy Rossiiskogo Parlamenta* (Informatsionno-Ekspertnaia Gruppa 'Panorama', Moscow, May 1992), and the update of this work, *Politicheskie Fraktsii i Deputatiskie Gruppy Rossiiskogo Parlamenta* ('Panorama', Moscow, March 1993).

Table 1.1 **Factions in the Congress October 1991–February 1993**

	Oct 91 (N)	May 92 (N)	Feb 93 (N)
Agrarian Union (RU)	111	149	129
Non-Party Deputies†	55	43	–
Democratic Russia (CR)	69	73	49
Communists for Democracy*	96	–	–
Free Russia (DC)	–	66	55
Communists of Russia (RU)	357	59	67
Social Democrats and Republicans**	52	–	–
Left Centre (Levyi tsentr) (DC)	65	68	62
Fatherland (Otchizna) (RU)	70	54	51
Industrial Union (CS)			
(Soiuz promyshlennikov)	58	73	52
Radical Democrats (CR)	55	47	50
Russian Union	51	–	–
Rossiia (RU)	74	54	55
Change-New Politics (Smena) (CS)	51	44	53
Sovereignty and Equality (DC)	50	73	49
Workers' Union of Russia*** (CS)	–	41	53
Motherland (Rodina) (DC)	–	–	52
Consensus for the Sake of Progress			
(Soglasie radi progressa) (CR)	–	–	53

CR = Coalition for Reform (Koalitsiia reform)
DC = Democratic Centre (Demokraticheskii tsentr)
CS = Creative Strength (Sozidatel'nye sily)
RU = Russian Unity (Rossiiskoe edinstvo)
*Communists for Democracy changed their name to Free Russia in December 1991.
**From December 1991–May 1992 United Faction: Social Democratic Party/Republican Party
– Left Centre. From 1993 Left Centre – Collaboration. (Levyi tsentr – Sotrudnichestvo)
***From 1993 Workers' Union, Reform Without Shock.
†There were 36 members of the Non-Party Faction in February 1993 but this was below the
required 50 to register as a faction.
Source: Vladimir Pribylovskii *Politicheskie Fraktsii i Deputatiskie Gruppy Rossiiskogo Parlamenta*
(Panorama, Moskva, March 1993) p. 2 and pp. 31–87.

By May 1992, there were 13 factions in the Congress. Communists of Russia saw
the most dramatic change falling from 357 in 1991 to 59. Rutskoi's Communists
for Democracy, which had changed its name to Free Russia in December 1991,
fell from 96 to 66. This left the Agrarian Union as the largest faction with 149
members. Democratic Russia increased slightly from 69 to 73 members and the
Radical Democrats were down from 55 to 47.

By February 1993, there were 15 factions. The Agrarian Union maintained its
status as the largest with 129 members. Communists of Russia's membership was

up slightly to 67 and it was now the second largest faction in the Congress. Both Democratic Russia and the Radical Democrats were down to 49 and 50 respectively, and Free Russia numbered 55.

One must be cautious, however, in interpreting the politics of the Russian Congress on the basis of factions for it soon became apparent that some deputies belonged to more than one faction. One deputy (Viktor Dedegkaev) even belonged to four, and discipline was very weak within the factions. The voting behaviour of the factions will be examined in chapter 4 which shall show that political factions divided the members, often on ideological lines.

By the beginning of 1993 in the Congress of People's Deputies these factions had formed four broad political blocs each containing from two to five factions:

1 *Coalition for Reform* (CR) – Supporters of Egor Gaidar, 221 members in the Congress with deputies from the factions: Democratic Russia, Radical Democrats, Consensus for the Sake of Progress, and other individual members. (Approximately 50 members in the Supreme Soviet.)

2 *Democratic Centre* (DC) – Reformist Centre – approximately 200 in the Congress included: Left Centre-Collaboration, Free Russia, Sovereignty and Equality. (Approximately 80 in the Supreme Soviet.)

3 *Creative Strength* (CS) (Sozidatel'nye sily) – the conservative centre, or constructive opposition, 150 deputies in Congress, included: Workers' Union, Reform Without Shock, Smena, and the Industrial Union. (Approximately 50 in the Supreme Soviet.)

4 *Russian Unity* (RU) Communist–nationalist opposition to president and government – 300 deputies from factions: Rossiia, Communists of Russia, Agrarian Union, Fatherland, and the group Civic Society (with approximately 60 in the Supreme Soviet). Almost all involved in Russian Unity were also members of the National Salvation Front.

In June 1992, Civic Union was formed from members of the Congress and non-parliamentary groups. The Democratic Party of Russia (headed by Nikolai Travkin), People's Party of Free Russia (Rutskoi) and the All Russian Union – Renewal (Arkadii Volskii and Aleksandr Vladislavlev) joined with the factions 'Smena' and 'Rodina'.

Both the reformers (groups 1 and 2 above) and their opponents (groups 3 and 4), a combination of communists and nationalists (sometimes referred to as a 'Red–Brown alliance'), were unable to muster the two-thirds of the votes necessary to make changes to the Constitution or to push forward radical policies one way or the other. By 1993, the Parliament was deadlocked even though the conservatives often commanded a plurality or majority of votes.

On 14 December 1992 there was a general reregistration which was designed to prevent deputies from belonging to more than one faction. This led to a situation where the Non-Party Deputies and Civic Society did not have the necessary 50 deputies and they lost their status as factions. The factions Left Centre and Collaboration escaped this fate by merging. As a result of the registration of 14 December 1992, there were 14 factions.

The emerging conflict between President and Parliament: 1991–1993

The Russian Federation from the time of its separation from the USSR had two pillars of administration and decision-making. The presidency, the state ministries and committees and the Parliament (Congress and Supreme Soviet). After the euphoria following the overthrow of the USSR and the establishment of the Russian Federation as an independent state, divisions became clear between the President and the Parliament over their areas of jurisdiction and responsibility. The President's office had its own personnel in the form of a cabinet and presidential advisers and, from the inception of the Russian state, the President claimed supreme power, a position increasingly contested by many in the Supreme Soviet.

At the 5th Congress of People's Deputies in October 1991, Yeltsin was able to win support for his policies of radical economic and political reforms and he gained the approval of the deputies to rule by decree for the period of one year. This was agreed by a vote of 575 (53.6 per cent) of the deputies with 266 (24.8 per cent) voting against, 58 (5.4 per cent) abstaining and 173 (16.1 per cent) not voting.[6] Executive power at this time therefore was clearly taken by the President, and from the outset the Russian Parliament lacked authority. Yeltsin was given a free hand to appoint members of his new government without requiring ratification from the deputies. On 30 September, Silaev had resigned as RSFSR Prime Minister and the Russian government was without a chair until 6 November, when Yeltsin, in a series of decrees, named himself head of the government and made sweeping changes to the structure of the executive. Over the period November–December 1991, Yeltsin dismissed 20 members of the RSFSR Council of Ministers, including five deputy chairs.[7]

In November he was able to replace these officials with five new deputy chairs, all of whom were strong supporters of radical economic and political reforms. Thus, Gennadii Burbulis who held the post of State Secretary in the Russian Presidency also became a First Deputy Chairman in the Russian government. He was made responsible for the general organisation of the work of the government and for the policy areas of foreign affairs, media and the judiciary. Egor Gaidar was brought in to take responsibility for economic reform.[8]

6. See voting figures on the resolution, *Adopting in principle the draft by the Drafting Committee*, 1.11.91, 'To adopt, in principle, the draft Resolution on organisation of the executive branch in the period of the radical economic reform' (Bull. N21, 11/1/91, p. 16), introduced by the Drafting Committee.

7. See Decree of President Yeltsin 'O Chlenakh Byvshevo Soveta Ministrov RSFSR', of 5 December 1991 in *Vedomosti RSFSR*, No. 50, 1991 p. 2034.

8. The following deputy chairs were also appointed: Mikhail Poltoranin (information and mass media), Sergei Shakhrai (legal affairs), Aleksandr Shokhin (social affairs). Other reformers who entered the government were Petr Aven (Minister for Foreign Economic Relations), Boris Saltykov (Minister of Science and Technical Policy), Vladimir Lopukhin, Minister of Fuel and Energy. Yeltsin took personal charge of the Ministries of Defence, Internal Affairs and the State Committee for Security. For details of distribution of duties of chairs of RSFSR Government see RSFSR Presidential Decree, 6 November, 'On the Organisation of the Work of the RSFSR Government under the Conditions of Economic Reform', *TASS* 6 November 1991, translated in *FBIS* No. 216, 7 November 1991, pp. 49–51.

The 'Law on the RSFSR President', which was adopted in April 1991, gave Yeltsin similar powers to the former USSR President which combined aspects of the American and French presidential systems. In Article Six, the President was given the right to 'direct the activity of the RSFSR Council of Ministers' and in Articles Four and Five to appoint the Prime Minister with 'the Supreme Soviet's assent', and appoint and release from duty other ministers and chairs of state committees. Article Nine also stated that the President headed the RSFSR Security Council.[9]

By the time of the formation of the Russian Republic in 1992, rather than a parliamentary democracy, a strong presidential power characterised the government of Russia. Yeltsin was President, Prime Minister, Chair of the State Council, Chair of the Security Council, and Minister of Defence. This formal legal power of Yeltsin, however, has to be seen in the context of other political forces in the new republic. In addition to the President and his staff, two other major structural forces were emerging which were to shape Russian politics in its formative period. First was the government bureaucracy in the Russian Republic and second, the nascent Russian Parliament.

While Yeltsin was able to make new appointments to the top posts, this did not put an end to the interests of the government bureaucracy. The governing elite of new Russian Republic still contained many former officials from the USSR and RSFSR governments, the CPSU, and Gorbachev's presidency. (We discuss in detail the background and continuity of the executive elite in Chapter 4.)

Another weakness of the President's position was of Yeltsin's own making. His power to appoint state officials without the formal approval of Parliament was accepted when he was pitted against Gorbachev and the government of the USSR; however, when his actions adversely affected the interests of members of the Russian Parliament, his formal powers were called into question.   ·

During the period 1991–93, the political weight of the Russian Congress of People's Deputies (called hereafter the Russian Congress) and Supreme Soviet shifted in favour of the communists and nationalists against the forces of radical reform. By 1993, umbrella reform movements (such as the Movement for Democratic Reform and Civic Union) had broken down and fragmented and Yeltsin was no longer able to command a regular majority in the legislature. The idea of a 'presidential party' in support of Yeltsin, which Burbulis had been charged with creating, fell by the wayside as politics became more polarised. The Chairman of the Supreme Soviet, Khasbulatov, once a trusted colleague of Yeltsin's (he had been the first deputy chair of the RSFSR Supreme Soviet when Yeltsin was chair) and a strong supporter of economic reform, increasingly moved into opposition against the President in the period after the August events.

At the heart of the struggle was the question of whether Russia was to have a presidential or parliamentary system and who was to control the executive. There were also policy issues at stake, with Yeltsin supporting radical market reforms and privatisation while strong factions in the Parliament sought to limit and slow down these changes – especially as conditions deteriorated. Khasbulatov wanted to

---

9.   See *Sovetskaia Rossiia*, 30 April 1991, p. 1 translated in *FBIS* 1 May 1991, pp. 57–58.

create a strong parliamentary system, having real control over the government and restricting the President's powers. Yeltsin's policy, on the contrary, was to form an executive presidency with powers to appoint the Prime Minister and chief members of the Cabinet with as little interference from the Parliament as possible.

Policy

Behind these political positions arose different attitudes about the course of reform in the Russian Republic, with Yeltsin being associated with a more radical reform policy including privatisation and greater accommodation to the interests of the Western states and international organisations such as the World Bank. Many of Yeltsin's opponents in Parliament, on the other hand, sought to preserve much of state industry, a high level of welfare benefits, and a more independent policy in international relations.

Back in December 1990, the 2nd Russian Congress had overwhelmingly endorsed Prime Minister Silaev's programme of economic reform which called for a programme of economic stabilisation and the development of a market economy in Russia: 835 (77.9 per cent) of the deputies voted for Silaev's programme and only 41 (3.8 per cent) opposed this measure. (Details of this and other votes cited in this chapter are given below in Chapter 4.) Undoubtedly Yeltsin gained support for these radical reforms as part of his continuing struggle against the hegemony of the USSR and its President. In the winter of 1990, Gorbachev moved away from the forces of radical reform. He abandoned the 'Shatalin' 500-day economic plan, which would have moved the USSR rapidly to a market economy, and began openly to court members of the military and security forces. By voting for Silaev's economic programme, the deputies of the Russian Federation were showing their defiance of the USSR Government and were striking a blow for Russian independence.[10]

Nevertheless, in two further parliamentary debates in December 1990, the deputies showed that although they favoured a general move to the market they were still strongly divided over the question of privatisation. Thus, one amendment, tabled by deputy Sergei Iushenkov, which proclaimed the 'sanctity and inviolability of private property' was soundly defeated by a vote of 650 (60.6 per cent) against, with only 283 (26.4 per cent) voting for the motion.[11] A compromise draft introduced by Viktor Belov with regard to the privatisation of land 'subject to control by local soviets' was also defeated, although by a smaller margin. Here 552 (51.5 per cent) voted against and 379 (35.4 per cent) were in favour of the motion.[12]

Russian politics changed dramatically after the collapse of the USSR when divisions within the Russian Parliament began to crystallise as new political factions

10. 'The Resolution on Silaev's report on the RSFSR Council of Ministers activities with regard to economic stabilisation and conversion to market economy' 07.12.90 (Bull. N. 16, 12/7/90, p. 6).
11. See S.N. Iushenkov's amendment to Article 10, which proclaims the principle of 'sanctity and inviolability of private property' (Bull. N. 24, 12/12/90, p. 19).
12. See 'Alternative Draft by Belov', which in essence admits private property in land for the development of agricultural production, subject to control by local soviets (Bull. N. 24, 12/12/90, p. 23).

were formed and deputies took a stand in favour of or against Gaidar's policy of 'shock therapy'.

By the summer of 1992 Yeltsin's popularity was starting to wane as Gaidar's economic reforms began to make themselves felt. Over the period 1990–94 GNP declined by an incredible 40 per cent. From as early as January 1992, when Gaidar's policy of 'price liberalisation' began, members of the government were subjected to verbal abuse by deputies and calls for the government to resign became almost a daily occurrence. In the first month of price liberalisation, prices rose by 460 per cent, and each month after that there were increases of 20–25 per cent, giving an annual inflation rate in 1992 of 2,600 per cent. These price increases struck hardest at those sections of the population on fixed incomes, such as pensioners, and also those who had savings. According to the Russian Centre for Economic Reform, 37 per cent of Russia's 150 million people were living in poverty (see also Chapter 10 below).

Lacking formal parliamentary approval made it more difficult for Yeltsin's ministers, Gaidar and his team, to push through these unpopular market reforms. At the 6th Congress in April 1992, members of the government came under such fierce attack that they walked out of the Congress and threatened to resign.

Parliament versus President

These policy divisions led to political conflict, not only on the floor of the Parliament but also within the presidential office. Of particular importance was the opposition to Yeltsin of Vice-President Rutskoi who had been chosen by Yeltsin to stand for election in June 1991. Rutskoi had been an officer in Afghanistan and later as a member of the RSFSR Supreme Soviet had formed the Communists for Democracy faction in the RSFSR Congress of People's Deputies. But he was opposed to price liberalisation and as early as January 1992 he joined forces with Khasbulatov, giving support to those who called for the government's resignation. In February 1992 Yeltsin struck back and, in a manner somewhat reminiscent of Gorbachev's downgrading of Egor Ligachev, demoted Rutskoi, removing him from his post in charge of defence conversion and placing him in control of agricultural reform.[13] On 1 September 1993 Yeltsin dismissed Rutskoi from his post and on 21 September the President dissolved the Parliament. In retaliation, the Parliament declared the President's actions unconstitutional and appointed Rutskoi as President.

Back at the Seventh Congress of People's Deputies in December 1992, when Yeltsin's executive powers came to an end, a fierce battle took place between President and Parliament for control over the government. Two measures were introduced to censure the government and impeach the President. They were rejected even though the motion had received solid support from the deputies. Ivan Fedoseev's motion to impeach the President was supported by 352 votes (32.8 per cent) with

13. See Yeltsin's Presidential Decree 'On the duties and powers of the Russian Federation Vice-President', of 26 February 1992, *BBC Summary of World Broadcasts* p. 1329 B/4, 'Yeltsin Decree on Vice-President's Powers', *Rossiiskaia Gazeta*, 4 March 1992.

428 deputies (39.9 per cent) voting against and 77 (7.2 per cent) abstaining, while 215 (20.1 per cent) did not vote.[14] Deputy Gennadii Saenko's proposal to include a question of confidence in the government into the agenda of the Congress received a plurality of votes but not a majority.[15] However, the Congress did succeed in passing a new Law on the Council of Ministers, on 22 December, which stripped the President of his right to appoint the heads of the ministries of defence, foreign affairs, security and internal affairs without the Supreme Soviet's approval.

Yeltsin also had to sacrifice Prime Minister Gaidar and other key liberals in his government in order to maintain control. Viktor Chernomyrdin, a representative of the industrial lobby in the Parliament, replaced Gaidar as Prime Minister. However, in a compromise deal worked out behind the scenes between Yeltsin, Khasbulatov and Valerii Zorkin (Chair of the Constitutional Court), the President won the right to hold a referendum. This would give the people the opportunity to approve a new constitution which was to be drafted by the Parliament.

After the 7th Congress, Yeltsin followed a dual policy: he continued to bring new people into the government and to broaden its political base, but he also went on the political offensive, transferring power from the government to the presidency. Yeltsin created new parallel executive bodies in the presidency which bypassed both the Parliament and government. Such policies here remind us of Gorbachev's attempts to move power from the Party to the state. After the 28th Party Congress, it will be recalled, Gorbachev fatally weakened the Politburo and Central Committee and transferred leading state officials in the Politburo over to his Presidential Council. However, Gorbachev was not able to maintain control over the security forces and this ultimately led to the attempted coup against him in August 1991. Perhaps learning from this lesson, on 7 July Yeltsin created a more powerful Security Council under the presidency.

The existing Security Council, which had largely been a consultative body, was upgraded to a fully fledged executive agency with powers of control over the ministries of defence, internal affairs, security and foreign affairs. The Security Council quickly became branded as a new Russian Politburo and Yeltsin's policies were likened to Gorbachev's attempts to bypass both the Party and the Parliament with his creation of an executive presidency in March 1990. By bringing the security ministries under the presidency, Yeltsin was formally in a strong position to maintain his position against any threat to his station by the Parliament.

Between December 1992 and October 1993, President and Parliament each accused the other of usurping power and violating the Russian Constitution. Rival drafts of the new Russian Constitution only heightened this conflict, leading to a

14. See 'On constitutionality of the President's actions', Deputy I.V. Fedoseev's proposal, 'to include into the agenda debate on the Congress of People's Deputies of the Russian Federation requesting the Constitutional Court of the [RF] to submit a conclusion on conformity of actions and decisions of President of the [RF] Boris Nikolaevich Yeltsin to the Constitution of the [RF], which conclusion should serve as foundation for impeaching him . . .'. Votes on the agenda are adopted by 521 votes. (Bull. 1, p. 5) 1.12.92.
15. The results were as follows: those in favour 423 (39.5 per cent), against 357 (33.3 per cent), abstaining 54 (5.0 per cent), not voting 238 (22.2 per cent). 'On expressing confidence in the Government' (Bull. 1, p. 17) 1.12.92.

stalemate between Parliament and executive that ended only after Yeltsin dissolved the Parliament on 21 September 1993.

On 20 March, in a television address to the nation, Yeltsin announced the introduction of 'special rule' and decreed that his authority was above that of the Congress.[16] This led to deputies calling for the impeachment of the President. After further tense negotiations between the President, Khasbulatov, and Zorkin, Yeltsin backed down from introducing 'special rule' but instead insisted on going ahead with the planned referendum.

At the 9th Extraordinary Congress at the end of March 1993, 70 per cent of the deputies present voted to impeach the President, but this did not make up the required two-thirds of the total membership of the Congress. In the vote on the procedures and questions for the referendum, which took place on 27 March, 621 (57.9 per cent) of the deputies voted in favour of holding a referendum (on 25 April), 223 (20.8 per cent) voted against this form of conducting the election, 36 (3.4 per cent) abstained and 192 (17.9 per cent) did not vote.[17] There were four issues to be decided by the referendum: a vote of confidence in the President, a vote of confidence in the President's socio-economic programme, a vote to decide if there should be elections for the Russian President in 1993 (before the end of Yeltsin's term in office), and finally a vote to decide if there should be elections ahead of schedule for a new Parliament. For the motions to be passed would require the support of the majority of the electorate and not just of those who voted. Later the Constitutional Court ruled that only the last two questions would require a majority of the electorate and that the first two would pass if they gained a majority of the votes cast in the election.

The results of the referendum held on 25 April 1993 came as a surprise to Yeltsin's opponents and were a narrow formal victory for the President. Thus, of those who voted, 58.1 per cent declared their confidence in the President and 52.9 per cent endorsed his socio-economic programme. But he failed to gain enough votes to call for early parliamentary elections. Also the results were compromised by a relatively low turnout with only 64.6 per cent voting.

The problem of drafting a new Russian Constitution continued to be deadlocked in a stalemate with Congress and presidency producing competing drafts favouring either a parliamentary or presidential system. Both sides began to seek the support of the heads of the republics and regions in the Russian Federation – promising them more powers if they backed their particular versions of the Constitution. In 1992, Yeltsin had created a Council of Heads of Republics and in 1993 he formed yet another consultative body – a Council of Heads of Administrations which included *ex officio* membership of republics and regional heads of government.

16. For an excellent discussion of the struggle between Parliament and executive see the following works by Alexander Rahr: 'The Roots of the Power Struggle', *RFE/RL Research Report*, 2 (20), 14 May 1993, pp. 9–15 and 'The Rise and Fall of Ruslan Khasbulatov', *RFE/RL Research Report*, 2 (24), 11 June 1993, pp. 12–16.
17. The draft is being adopted in principle. It sets the referendum, for 25 April with four questions (Bull. 4, p. 5) 27.03.93. (Voting data given in Vote 10 Table 4.3 below in Chapter 4.)

In July, Yeltsin attempted to bypass the Parliament by creating a 'Constitutional Conference' charged with drawing up yet another version of the Constitution. But Khasbulatov and leading parliamentarians declared it invalid.

The dissolution of the Congress of People's Deputies

From July 1993 until Yeltsin's decree suspending the Congress on 21 September, relations deteriorated between the legislature and executive even further. In June, a majority of deputies in the parliament voted against the government's privatisation programme and threats were made to oust members of Yeltsin's government who were charged with corruption. Khasbulatov and Rutskoi began to form a 'shadow government' in the Parliament and to create links between the Parliament and military and security forces. Weapons were stockpiled in the Parliament building and many of its leaders prepared for military action.

In 1993 the Supreme Soviet declared its own alternative 'shadow' government ministers. Key figures here included Vladimir Achalov, a former commander of the USSR Airborne Forces and a USSR Deputy Defence Minister, who was appointed Minister of Defence. Former Russian Security Minister, Viktor Barannikov, dismissed by Yeltsin on charges of corruption, took over as the Parliament's security chief, and likewise the former Russian Minister of Internal Affairs, Andrei Dunaev, took charge of that portfolio in the Parliament. Another member of the shadow government was the head of the Russian Communist Workers' Party, General Albert Makashov.

By a Decree of President Yeltsin, on 1 September 1993, Vice-President Rutskoi and First Deputy Chair of the Russian Government Vladimir Shumeiko were temporarily 'suspended from the performance of their duties'. Both had been accused of corruption, and Yeltsin used this as an excuse to dismiss Rutskoi. Constitutionally, it was highly doubtful whether Yeltsin had the right to abolish the vice-presidency. Not surprisingly, on 3 September, the Supreme Soviet retaliated and suspended the part of the presidential decree that related to Rutskoi's dismissal. As relations worsened between Parliament and President, compromises, which are the essence of parliamentary government, became fewer and a mood of confrontation arose. As head of the legislature, Khasbulatov claimed authority over the Russian Central Bank and the courts. Khasbulatov also had under his command a 5,000-strong parliamentary guard. To enforce Parliament's will they were ordered to secure several buildings in the capital, including the publishing house Izvestiia, on the grounds that they came under the jurisdiction of the Parliament. These detachments were later disbanded by a Yeltsin decree which was enforced by his own special 'Alfa' combat unit.

Finally, by a Decree of the President of the Russian Federation,[18] Yeltsin dissolved the Parliament and called for elections for a new State Duma to be held on 12 December.[19] On the evening of 21 September at a press conference in the parliamentary building, the White House, Rutskoi declared himself Russian

18. No. 1400 'On stage-by-stage constitutional reform in the Russian Federation', of 21 September. See *Rossiiskie Vesti*, 22 September 1993, p. 1, translated in *CDPSP* XLV (38), 20 October 1993, pp. 1–4.
19. Ibid.

President and Khasbulatov announced the following appointments: Barannikov as Minister of Security, Achalov as Minister of Defence and Dunaev as Minister of Internal Affairs. The next morning, 22 September, Khasbulatov signed a decree which stated that, 'In accordance with Art. 121.6 of the Constitution of the Russian Federation/Russia, the powers of B.N. Yeltsin as President of the Russian Federation are terminated as of 8 p.m. on 21 September 1993'. On the same day a resolution of the Parliament appointed Rutskoi President. The Constitutional Court also ruled that Yeltsin's decree dissolving Parliament was unconstitutional.[20]

Storming the White House

From Yeltsin's viewpoint, all possibilities for compromise with the Parliament had been exhausted. On Sunday 12 September, Yeltsin held a meeting at his dacha with his ministers of defence, interior, security, and foreign affairs. All of these top officials backed Yeltsin's plan to take over the parliamentary building, the White House. On 13 September, Prime Minister Chernomyrdin (just back from a trip to the United States) also agreed that there was no other way out of the impasse.

As Yeltsin notes:

> By occupying the White House, we would resolve several problems at once: we would deprive the dissolved Supreme Soviet of a headquarters from which to coordinate all the opposition's moves, and we would prevent it from reconvening. Without the White House, the rebel deputies would turn into a handful of loudmouths. What were six hundred people compared to the whole population of Moscow? No one would listen to them.[21]

However, Yeltsin's original plan to storm the White House on Sunday 19 September, when the building would be empty, was soon abandoned when it became apparent that Khasbulatov and Rutskoi had learned of Yeltsin's plan and had called on all their supporters immediately to occupy the building. It was decided that the decree abolishing the Parliament would have to be postponed until 21 September, by which time Yeltsin was faced with a hostile group of deputies, and other supporters who refused to leave the building.

Between 21 September and the military operation against the Parliament on 4 October, attempts to mediate a settlement by Aleksi II, the Russian Patriarch, broke down. On 23 September a group from the Parliament attempted to seize the former headquarters of the CIS armed forces. An OMON (international security troops) squad had to be called out to protect the building and two people were killed in the incident. Up until this point the encirclement of the White House had been purely symbolic. People were free to enter and leave the building. On 24 September, however, Yeltsin ordered a full-scale blockade, and he gave the parliamentarians an ultimatum to leave the building by 4 October. It was still possible to leave the White House but no one was permitted to enter. Yeltsin also ordered that all of the Parliament's communications, electricity, heat, and water supplies be turned off.

20. For these decrees and rulings, see *Rossiiskaia Gazeta*, 23 September, p. 2, translated in *CDPSP*, XLV (38), 20 October 1993, p. 6.
21. Boris Yeltsin, *The View From the Kremlin*, Harper Collins, London, 1994, p. 247.

On the day before Yeltsin's ultimatum, Sunday 3 October, Khasbulatov and Rutskoi, misjudging the level of support they commanded in the country and among the armed forces, called on their supporters to leave the White House and take over the Ostankino Television Station and the Moscow mayor's office. Before long the police surrounding the Parliament were beaten back and battles were under way at the Television Centre, the mayor's office, and the ITAR-TASS building. Khasbulatov and Rutskoi emboldened by these first successes called for the rebellion to proceed even further:

> Dear Friends! The victory is not yet final, armed units under the leadership of commanders who have sold out may still be flung at you. They are supported by Yeltsin's underlings and stooges. Be vigilant and stand firm. We appeal to all collectives, to all citizens of our motherland: do not obey the criminal decrees of the Yeltsinites. Unite around the lawfully elected government bodies – the Soviets of People's Deputies. We call on soldiers of the Russian Army and Navy: display civic courage, preserve your military honour in loyalty to the Constitution, support the concrete deeds of popular power and the law. Russia will be grateful to you and will give genuine patriots the deserved appreciation.[22]

Yeltsin called for assistance from Viktor Erin, the head of interior security police, and to Defence Minister Pavel Grachev who assured him that troops had been ordered into the city to squash the uprising. But it soon became clear that there were in fact no troops in Moscow and that they had stopped their advance on the outskirts of the city at the Moscow Ring Road. As Yeltsin admitted, 'I saw that the army, despite all the assurances of the defence minister, for some reason was not able to come quickly to Moscow's defence and fight the rebels. The forces of the interior minister turned out to be insufficient for waging combat in the capital against such heavily armed rebels.'[23]

It was clear that the army had become highly politicised and divided. Yeltsin realised that he would have to take control of the situation and persuade the army to defend the President. He succeeded.

At 7 a.m. on Monday 4 October, tanks began to fire on the White House and by 4.30 p.m. virtually the entire leadership of the Parliament (including Khasbulatov and Rutskoi) had been arrested and taken to Lefortovo Prison. Approximately 144 people had been killed. The battle between the Parliament and the presidency had ended with a victory for Yeltsin.[24] Presidential power rather than parliamentary rule was to become dominant in the Russian Federation.

After his victory, Yeltsin banned those parties and groups implicated in the rebellion, such as the National Salvation Front, the Russian Communist Workers' Party, Russian National Unity and those groups in the army such as the Officer's Union and Shield. Members of these groups and individuals arrested in connection with the uprising were not permitted to take part in the 12 December elections. The President was soon accused of using his control over the media to censor opposition

---

22. Yeltsin, *ibid*, p. 286.
23. Yeltsin, *ibid*, p. 276.
24. In February 1994, Rutskoi, Khasbulatov, General Makashev and about a dozen other leaders of the rebellion were given an amnesty and released from prison.

parties and to promote Gaidar's new party, Russia's Choice. A two-week state of emergency was declared in Moscow under which 90,000 people were arrested and a further 10,000 Caucasian traders and refugees expelled from the city.[25]

The 12 December 1993 elections

On 12 December 1993, elections took place for the new 628-member Russian Federal Assembly and the people were asked to give their support to a new Russian Constitution. The Parliament was divided into two chambers: an upper chamber, the Federation Council (178 members) which consists of two deputies from each of Russia's 89 republics and regions, and a lower chamber, the State Duma (450 members). Elections to the State Duma were divided into 225 seats filled on the basis of party lists, and 225 seats filled by elections in single member territorial districts. Electors were thus given four separate ballots, one for the upper house, two for the lower house, and another to decide on the Constitution.

The results of the election came as a shock to the pro-market liberal democratic parties. Although Russia's Choice came top with 96 seats in the Duma, the three main opposition parties gained an impressive 182 seats. Vladimir Zhirinovskii's nationalist Liberal Democratic Party came second with 70 seats. In the 1991 presidential elections about six million Russians had voted for Zhirinovskii and that number had now risen to approximately 15 million. Third and fourth places went to the Communist Party of Russia (65 seats) and the Agrarian Party of Russia (47). The four pro-reform blocs of Russia's Choice (96), the Iavlinskii–Boldyrev–Lukin bloc (33), the Party of Russian Unity and Concord (27), and the Russian Movement for Democratic Reform (8) gained a total of 164 seats. Civic Union, which had previously been the dominant centrist force in the country, won only 18 seats.[26]

However, in the elections for individuals rather than those chosen from party lists, Zhirinovskii's supporters came second to Russia's Choice: the latter gaining 56 seats compared to the former's 11. Overall, the elections perpetuated the political hostility between a more traditionally oriented Parliament and a more market and capitalist-based policy of the President.

A new executive presidency

The President also secured the passage by popular vote of the new Constitution which legitimated his powers (58.4 per cent of those who voted voting in favour).[27] A new executive presidency was created which had effectively diminished the role of the Parliament and allowed Yeltsin to rule by decree. Under the new Constitution the President determines the basic guidelines of the state's domestic and foreign policy

---

25. Wendy Slater, 'Russia: the return of authoritarian government?', *RFE/RL Research Report*, 3 (1), 7 January 1994, p. 25.
26. Vera Tolz, 'Russia's parliamentary elections: what happened and why', *RFE/RL Research Report*, 3 (2), 14 January 1994, pp. 1, 3.
27. However, recent reports have revealed that turnout at the elections, and the referendum on the constitution, was only 46 per cent (see *ITAR-TASS*, 5 May 1994).

(Article 80). The President is the supreme commander in chief of the Armed Forces (Article 87), forms and heads the Russian Security Council, appoints and removes the high command of the armed forces and approves the military doctrine of the Russian Federation. The President also submits to the Federation Council candidates to the office of justices of the Constitutional Court, Supreme Court, Superior Court of Arbitration and also the candidate for General Prosecutor (Article 83).

It is extremely difficult for the Parliament to impeach the President. This right is given to the Federation Council. But for this to take place a charge of treason or other grave crime would have to be filed against the President by at least one-third of the members of the State Duma. These charges would then have to be upheld by the Supreme Court and supported by the votes of two-thirds of the members of each chamber (Article 93).

The President also has the right to appoint the Chair of the Government with the consent of the State Duma, but if the Duma turns down the presidential candidate for Prime Minister three times the President may dissolve the Duma and schedule new elections (Article 111). Moreover, if the State Duma declares a vote of no confidence in the government, the President can either announce the dismissal of the government or disagree with the decision of the Duma. If the Duma declares a second vote of no confidence in the government within three months, the President can choose either to dismiss the government or dissolve the Duma instead, and call for new elections (Article 117).

The Duma is not the only body vested with legislative initiative; this is also granted to the President, the Federation Council, the government, local legislative bodies, the Constitutional Court, Supreme Court and Supreme Court of Arbitration (Article 104). Also for some legislative policies the Duma must consider the views of the government before it drafts its legislation. This applies to 'draft laws on the introduction or abolition of taxes . . . and other draft laws envisaging expenditure funded out of the state budget' which 'can only be submitted when the government's findings are known' (Article 104). The upper chamber and the President can both veto legislation passed by the Duma. The veto of the upper chamber can only be overturned if two-thirds of the deputies of the Duma vote against it. For the President's veto to be overturned two-thirds of the votes of deputies in both chambers of the Parliament are necessary (Articles 105 and 107).

The Russian President has undoubtedly emerged victorious from his struggle with the Parliament. Whether such legal authority may represent effective power, however, has yet to be resolved.

Conclusion

During the last days of the Soviet Union, the Parliament of the RSFSR led by Boris Yeltsin was fairly united in its struggle for sovereignty and economic and political reform. With the establishment of statehood, however, the perennial questions of politics arose: which institutions and interests would be supreme? Would conciliation through a parliamentary type of democracy with an elected President replace the leadership of the CPSU? The development of political competition and the proposals for reform created conditions which led to stalemate in the relationship between the forces of government and radical reform around the President and the more heterogeneous interests represented in the Parliament. While earlier there had been unanimous support for the economic reforms of Silaev, the deteriorating economic conditions associated with the rise of market reforms led to opposition from factions organised in the Parliament. Divisions soon arose over the ownership and control of property and the style of Yeltsin's administration.

The perennial problem of the need for firm action on the part of the President in conditions of economic turmoil, on the one hand, and the promises for parliamentary democracy to replace the centralism of the Soviet past, on the other, led increasingly to conflict between President and government. Whereas in Western democracies this relationship has been resolved through centuries of mutual adjustment, in Russia the time-scale was much shorter. The scale of the transition to the market and to changes in property relations exacerbated the political conflicts. While the Russian Parliament moved towards the formation of groups and factions which successfully articulated different policies, compromise with the President was not achieved. In Russia there continued to function a dual system of power, with the executive and Parliament contesting for power. As Gaidar's programme of privatisation and marketisation began to take effect and inflation soared, Yeltsin found it increasingly difficult to command a majority in the Parliament. Isolated from the factional struggles within the Parliament, and unable to create a strong presidential party, the President was increasingly forced to turn to the executive and to force through measures by presidential decree. By 1993 he had alienated not only the conservatives in the Parliament but also many reformers, as he strove to bypass the legislature and to place power in presidential bodies such as the Security Council. His ideological opponents by 1993 were the dominant force in the Parliament but they could not muster the two-thirds of the votes necessary to impeach the President or to make major constitutional changes. The dissolution of the Parliament was both a sign of Yeltsin's strength and weakness. The resulting presidential power created by the December 1993 elections and the ratification of a new Russian Constitution turned into a major victory for Yeltsin. Presidential power, in some ways not unlike Soviet power before it, triumphed – at least constitutionally.[28]

28. The authors acknowledge the support of the British ESRC East–West Initiative in carrying out this work.

Chapter 2

THE ETHNO-POLITICS OF FEDERATION WITHOUT FEDERALISM

Graham Smith

Russia is unique amongst the post-communist states in opting for a federal structure. Yet having declared its choice of federation as central to its state-building project, the New Russia has been faced with belligerent ethno-republics who question Moscow's commitment to a federal principle that provides a scale of home rule compatible with their regional aspirations. This has not only resulted in a number of the ethno-republics placing their own self-interests before those of the federation as a whole but also, as in the case of Chechnia, of an unwillingness to participate in the federal arrangement altogether. Consequently, the type of federalisation that Russia is pursuing raises the question of whether it is capable of affecting the country's successful transition towards democracy while keeping itself territorially intact.

Despite the introduction in December 1993 of a federal constitution, there are doubts as to whether Russia can legitimately claim to be a federation based on democratic principles. On the one hand, it contains many of the features generally associated with a federation.[1] First, representation is preponderantly territorial. Russia comprises 88 territories, 32 of which are based on ethnic criteria, namely 21 ethno-republics and 11 autonomous territories, the remainder on the basis of non-ethnic criteria[2] (Fig. 2.1). Second, territorial representation is secured on at least two sub-national levels, namely 'local' and 'regional government'. Third, regional units are incorporated electorally into the decision procedure of the national centre. This is secured through representation in both the upper (Federation Council) and lower (State Duma) chambers of the Federal Assembly. On the other hand, as Roeder notes,[3] the move towards presidential rule following the September 1993 coup, and the increasing powers that the President has secured in relation to both the Federal Assembly and over regional and local governments, signals the building blocks of centralised autocracy rather than of a democratic federation. In particular, some of

1. See P. King 'Federation and representation', in M. Burgess and A. Gagnon (eds) *Comparative Federalism and Federation. Competing Traditions and Future Directions*, Harvester, New York, 1993, pp. 94–101.
2. The Russian Federation comprises the following hierarchy of territorial units: at the top are 21 ethnically based republics (or ethno-republics) which includes Chechnia whose declaration of independent statehood has not been recognised by either Russia or by the international community. The remaining 68 units have been granted fewer powers than the republics: 57 are non-ethnically based regions, comprising 49 *oblasts*, six *krais* (territories), and two 'federal' cities (Moscow and St Petersburg); and 10 ethnically based autonomous districts and one national *okrug* (Jewish Autonomous Okrug).
3. P. Roeder 'Varieties of Post-Soviet Authoritarian Regimes', *Post-Soviet Affairs*, 10 (1), 1994, pp. 61–101.

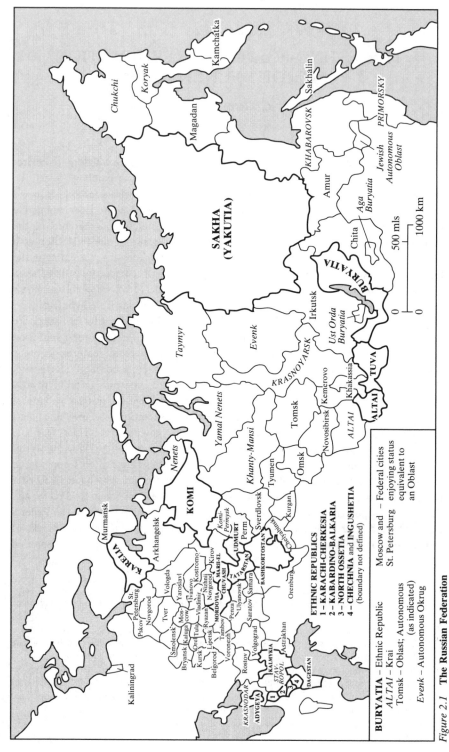

Figure 2.1 **The Russian Federation**

the distinctive executive functions of the federation, as secured by the President, do not derive from entrenchment of regional representation at the centre through a national legislature. Moreover, to qualify legitimately as a federation, regional autonomy should be constitutionally guaranteed; the centre should not have the judicial right to abolish, amend or to redefine the federation's regional units. It is precisely because of such shortcomings that Russia might at best be more appropriately labelled a highly centralised federation.

The problem, however, does not end with whether Russia's institutional structures, procedures and conventions fulfil the formal credentials of a federal democracy. As experiences elsewhere show, for a federation as a particular organisational form of governance to work successfully, it also requires a set of socially held values and beliefs predicated on an understanding that unity through diversity is best reflected in federation. This is what is often referred to as federalism or a federal society.[4] For a federation to endure, it also requires a social commitment to the federal idea in which regional identities are held to be simultaneously national and local in scope. Moreover, as Burgess notes:

> The genius of federation lies in its infinite capacity to accommodate and reconcile the competing and sometimes conflicting array of diversities having political salience within a state. Toleration, respect, compromise, bargaining and mutual recognition are its watchwords and 'union' combined simultaneously with 'autonomy' its hallmark.[5]

Underpinning the weakness in Russia of a federal idea based on 'checks and balances' is the problem that pluralist democracy has had little opportunity to develop either at the centre or in the regions. As a recent presidential working paper on Russia's regional problems noted, 'Russia needs to create an environment capable of sustaining and stimulating the democratic process, a sort of school of democracy for the whole of Russian society'.[6]

The making of the Russian Federation

That support for federation is weakly developed has much to do with the way in which the notion of federalism retains a pejorative meaning within the ethno-republics, associated with Soviet rule. As former autonomous republics within what was commonly labelled 'the facade of Soviet federalism', the peoples of Russia's present day ethno-republics were provided with little autonomy over their regional affairs, far less than even the former union republics of Ukraine, Armenia or Moldova. In some

---

4. For a fuller discussion of the distinction between federation and federalism, see G. Smith 'Mapping the federal condition. Ideology, political practice and social justice', in G. Smith (ed.) *Federalism. The Multi-ethnic Challenge*, Longman, London, 1995.
5. M. Burgess 'Federalism and federation. A reappraisal', in M. Burgess and A. Gagnon (eds) *Comparative Federalism and Federation. Competing Traditions and Future Directions*, Harvester, 1993, p. 7.
6. A. Livshits, A. Novikov and L. Smirnyagin *A Regional Strategy for Russia. Discussion Document* (Moscow, Presidential Working Paper on Regional Problems), 1994, p. 16.

respects the autonomous republics possessed features more attributable to 'internal colonies'.[7]

The first of these features is limited regional autonomy. Although Russia's autonomous republics were provided with a limited degree of more control over their administrative and cultural affairs than the other regions of Russia, this was more than checked by the functions that its disproportionately large Russian personnel played as part of a local Party–state machine accountable only to central interests. Local cultural rights were more heavily restricted than in the union republics (e.g. language rights, amenities for native schooling), with their peoples receiving much of their education in the Russian language. They also had fewer publications per head of population in their local languages than the non-Russian union republic-based nationalities. In short, they were subjected to a scale of political and cultural Russification far greater than that experienced by the union republics. Such were the consequences of Russification that on the eve of the dissolution of the Soviet Union nearly half of Karelians and a quarter of Komis, Udmurts, Mari, Karachis and Cherkess spoke Russian as their native tongue.[8]

A second feature is primary resource-based, core-dependent economies. Moscow practised a policy of regional economic interdependency throughout its republics. Within Russia's own ethno-republics, regional overspecialisation was characteristically linked to the exploitation of local primary resources which structured the nature of the local regional economy and resulted in a far greater degree of limited and dependent development than in the Union republics. Such a policy of regional specialisation was in effect tantamount to a form of economic colonialism in which the resources of the ethno-republics were heavily exploited for the benefit of nationally determined economic priorities, often with far-reaching local environmental consequences.

Another feature is limited social stratification. As a consequence of their specialist forms of development, the indigenous peoples of Russia's ethno-republics remained concentrated in primary economic activities with only a small native urban middle class. More specialist urban positions tended to be filled by Russian immigrants, a settlement process linked in part to the exploitation of their natural resources. Thus within each ethno-republic, a detectable ethnic division of labour existed in which the native populations remained dependent on the primary economic sector, whereas Russians were more likely to be found in more specialist managerial, technical and administrative positions in the cities.[9]

A fourth feature relates to lower living standards. Due to their general under-development, living standards in Russia's ethno-republics were among the lowest in the Soviet federation, a legacy which has continued into the post-Soviet period.

---

7. The notion of internal or federal colonialism is developed in G. Smith *Planned Development in the Socialist World*, Cambridge University Press, Cambridge, 1989, chapter 3 and in G. Smith 'The Soviet Federation. From corporatist to crisis politics', in M. Chisholm and D. Smith (eds) *Shared Space. Divided Space. Essays on Conflict and Territorial Organisation* Unwin Hyman, London, 1990, pp. 84–105.
8. Language data from 'Gosudarstvennyi Komitet SSSR Po Statistike Soobshchaet', *Natsional'nyi sostav naselenia* (Moscow), 1991, Vol. 11.
9. Yu.V. Arutunyan *et al. Russkie, Etnosotsiologicheskie Ocherki* Nauka, Moscow, 1992.

Thus despite a commitment by the Soviet state to regional equalisation, inter-regional disparities persisted, with below national average levels of income still evident in Chechnia, Ingushetia, North Ossetia, Dagestan, Kabardino-Balkaria, Mari-El, Mordovia and Kalmykia.[10]

For the architects of the New Russia, a more democratised federal arrangement was held up as a new beginning in relations between the centre and its ethno-republics. For Russia's first President, Boris Yeltsin, such a redesignated federal arrangement held a number of attractions. First, in the transition to securing Russian statehood (1990–91), Yeltsin saw in supporting the autonomist demands of Russia's ethno-republics a way of strengthening his own power base and of undermining Gorbachev's position as President of the Soviet Union. Thus Yeltsin openly encouraged Russia's own ethno-republics to declare themselves as sovereign entities with greater political powers. And in return, several of the ethno-republics boycotted Gorbachev's last minute referendum in 1991 to keep the Soviet Union together. By so doing the ethno-republics signalled their support for Yeltsin and for the establishment of an independent Russia. Second, federalisation offered a way of speeding up Moscow's commitment to the country's democratisation. By 1990, Yeltsin argued that the only way Russia could be effectively democratised was by restructuring the country 'from below' in which the various ethno-republics should have whatever powers they wished.[11] Finally, a federal arrangement was envisaged as a territorial strategy to prevent the break-up of Russia. By arguing that the ethno-republics should be granted substantive powers over the running of their own regional affairs, Yeltsin was in effect attempting to prevent the centre from becoming the focus of increasing frustration and animosity. Through adopting an accommodationist line, Yeltsin was in effect trying to deflect support for secession, thus sandbagging the territorial preservation of the new Russia.

Having secured the support of the ethno-republics in the transition towards the establishment of a Russian state, the issue of sovereignty necessarily raised the question of what exact form the Soviet federation should take. Two main schools of thought emerged. Firstly, there was the so-called Rumiantsev Plan of November 1990. Rather than viewing federation as based on an ethnic principle, the Parliament's Constitutional Commission, headed by Oleg Rumiantsev, proposed instead that Russia should move towards the establishment of a German *Länder*-type system in which 50 or so non-ethnically based territorial units would be created. It was a proposal designed to ensure the equality of citizen rights between the regions, and that some citizen-regions, because of their ethnic credentials, would not receive more privileges than others. Accordingly, the former Russian *oblasts* (regions) were to be transformed into republics, ensuring that citizens, irrespective of where they lived (in whatever region of Russia) would be entitled to the same rights. The other proposal, adopted by the Presidium of the Supreme Soviet of the Russian Federation in January 1992, favoured drawing a distinction between the ethno-republics and the regions, albeit as a stop-gap measure. It drew a distinction between those republics and regions based on ethnic criteria which, it was argued, should have the right to

10. Current levels of national income for the republics are drawn from *Izvestiia*, 4 July 1992.
11. *Literaturnaia Gazeta*, 15 August 1990.

their own constitutions and laws, form their own governments and have automatic representation in federal bodies, and those non-ethnic regions and minor ethnic districts, which, while having the right to their own charters and to form their own legislatures, should not have a right to their own constitution.[12]

What in effect these proposals reflected was a tension between the ethno-republics and the non-ethnic regions. While the former were outraged at the Rumiantsev Plan to deny special status and to acknowledge their cultural difference, the latter took exception to the decision of the Supreme Soviet to in effect create two classes of citizens: those who live in a federation (ethno-republics) and those who had to abide by the rules of a unitary state (non-ethno-republics). It was, however, the ethno-republics that managed to secure the high ground in part because they had already seized the initiative in declaring for themselves the sovereignty that Moscow had formally failed to deliver. Fearing that secession would follow from any constitutional proposals by Moscow which took away the territorial privileges that the ethno-republics had already secured, the centre relented. The outcome was the Federal Treaty of 31 March 1992 which only two of the 21 ethno-republics, Tatarstan and Chechnia, refused to sign. As a consequence, the ethno-republics were granted a scale of rights, including ownership over their natural resources, which were not granted to the regions.

Following further constitutional wrangles and revisions, the new federal treaty became the basis in December 1993 of Russia's new Constitution.[13] The new Constitution was, however, widely considered within the ethno-republics as an abrogation of many of the autonomous rights previously embodied in the Federal Treaty; consequently, the electorate in only 12 of the 21 republics voted in the constitutional referendum in favour of the Federal Constitution.[14]

The new Russian Constitution falls short of the scale of sovereignty that many of the ethno-republics had originally envisaged. Although the Constitution accepts the principle of self-determination for nations, this is in effect nullified by Article 4 which ensures the territorial integrity and inviolability of the Russian Federation, so pre-empting secession. Thus striking at the heart of this tension between the centre and the ethno-republics is the omission from the federal constitution of the right of the ethno-republics to secede, if they so wish, from the Federation, a right which was built in to the original 1992 Federal Treaty.[15] This, as the ethno-republics see it, is the abrogation of the basic right of nations to practise, if they so want, the right of national self-determination, a right which, at least in theory, was even available during Soviet rule to the union republics. Compared with federations in late modern democracies, the federal constitution also contravenes a basic given that central

12. E. Teague 'Centre-Periphery Relations in the Russian federation', in R. Szporluk (ed.) *National Identity and Ethnicity in Russia and the New States of Eurasia*, Westview Press, Boulder, Colorado, 1994, pp. 21–57.
13. The December 1993 Constitution was printed in *Rossiiskaia Gazeta*, 25 December 1993.
14. The Chechen republic did not participate in the December 1993 referendum. In a further eight republics, the draft constitution was either rejected, or following the agreed electoral procedures, was invalid (at least 50 per cent of the electorate had to go to the polls for the referendum to be valid).
15. *Rossiiskaia Gazeta*, 18 March 1992.

authorities may not unilaterally redefine the powers of regional governments. In the Constitution of the Russian Federation, the President has been given both powers of judicial review (i.e. to suspend acts issued by the executive bodies in Russia's provinces) and of arbitration between federal and local bodies or between constituent members of the federation. Indeed, some ethno-republics, notably Bashkortostan, Tatarstan, Sakha and Tuva, in adopting their own local constitutions, have in the process proclaimed the supremacy of their own republic laws over Russia's federal laws, thus violating the new Constitution which forbids republics and regions within the Federation to pass legislation that contradicts the country's basic law.

The new federal politics

Russia's transition from initially signalling the construction of a decentralised federation to one in which power has become more centralised but largely ineffective in the republics and regions threatens to undermine federal stability, raising the possibility of fragmentation. Three arenas of tension have emerged as central: the precarious relationship between federation and democracy, centre–regional economic relations, and issues of local cultural rights and autonomy.

Federation and democracy

While Russia has declared its commitment to federation as a building block for democracy, the republics criticise Moscow for increasingly practising the 'dictate of the centre', Yeltsin's dismissal of the Russian Parliament in October 1993 and its replacement with rule for three months by presidential decree was widely interpreted in the provinces as symptomatic of the weakness of the centre's commitment to a federal democracy. The fear is that Russia, given its historically centralising impulse, is sliding back towards a centralised authoritarianism in which it will become a federation only in name. In part, however, centralised control is also a response by Moscow to strong centrifugal pressures from the republics and regions.

According to Tarlton's seminal essay on federalism, in polities where localities differ in terms of a range of criteria from the national state in general (e.g. ethnicity, language, economic development), 'relieving the tensions and discord . . . requires not further recognition of diversity and their protection in the complicated processes of ever increasing federalisation, but rather increased coordination and coercion from the centralising authorities in the system'.[16] Tarlton was clearly concerned, as indeed is Moscow, that 'when diversity predominates, the "secessionist potential" of the system is high and unity would require control to overcome disruptive, centrifugal tendencies and forces'.[17]

As a counterweight, many centralists in Moscow have called for a 'harsh federation', with greater dependence of the ethno-republics and regions on the centre, insisting that without a strong centre it will be impossible to effect Russia's successful transition

16. C. Tarlton 'Symmetry and asymmetry as elements of federalism. A theoretical speculation', *The Journal of Politics*, Vol. 27, 1965, p. 874.
17. *Ibid*, p. 875.

towards market prosperity.[18] This view is not only put forward by the nationalist-right but also by some democrats who argue that it is only by the centre taking a stronger lead that economic reform will succeed.[19] Indeed, within certain spheres of federal politics, centre-building strategies to 'contain ethno-regionalism' are already apparent. This has included re-emphasising the need for bilingualism within the ethno-republics through playing up the importance of the Russian language as a factor in inter-regional communication. More starkly, however, it has involved the re-employment of coercive measures. These have included the threatened use of economic sanctions against wayward republics, most notably against Tatarstan in 1991–93 following that republic's reluctance to sign the New Federal Treaty, to arming local Russian-based pro-federal organisations against nationalist-secessionist movements in the North Caucasus. Without doubt, however, the extent to which the centre is willing to go in order to secure federal control is best demonstrated by its decision to send Russian troops into the secessionist republic of Chechnia in December 1994 on a scale of military intervention unprecedented since the Soviet occupation of Afghanistan 15 years earlier.

Yet the centre, sensitive to the potential disruption of locally based nationalisms, has allowed the ethno-republics more leeway in managing their own affairs than in the federation's other regions. This is particularly notable with regard to central appointments at the provincial level. In contrast to the other regional units, the ethno-republics have been exempted from the central executive imposing the appointment of key administrative officials accountable only to the President, and are allowed to determine their own systems of government and to elect their leading officials, including their heads of state. Consequently, Moscow appears willing to practise a form of asymmetrical federalism in which the potentially most problematic localities are paradoxically allowed the most flexibility. Unsurprisingly, such differentiated practices have not been without their critics. The Russian regions argue that not only is the appointment of 'regional administrators' undermining local democratic self-government but that as a consequence of such a centralist practice, they are being discriminated against compared to what is regarded as 'privileged ethnic minorities'.[20]

It would, however, be mistaken to assume that despite the calls for greater democracy through regional autonomy, within the ethno-republics democracy is necessarily high on their own agendas. As experiences elsewhere show, it is a mistake to claim that the desire for local accountability automatically leads to greater local democracy. There is, after all, no basis in political theory for claiming that smaller territorial units would be more hospitable to democratic politics. In Russia and its provinces, because civil society is still at an embryonic stage of development, pressures to counter locally centralising impulses are weak. This is in part demonstrated by the alarmingly low levels of participation in local elections. Thus in the 1994 elections in Russia's regions, turnout was so low that the results in a number of places were declared invalid as they failed to attract the necessary 25 per cent of eligible voters to

18. The term 'harsh federation' was coined by R. Sakwa *Russia. Politics and Society*, Routledge, London, 1993.
19. *Rossiiskaia Gazeta*, 14 March 1993.
20. *Literaturnaia Gazeta*, No. 16, 1994, p. 11.

the polls.[21] In some ethno-republics, such as Mordovia and Kalmykia, authoritarian trends are already evident. In these *de facto* sovereign states, conservative-minded leaders, many of whom were in power during the late Soviet period, are able to justify semi-authoritarian rule by claiming that it provides both social stability and economic direction in times of political uncertainty. Furthermore, these political leaders are also willing and able to play the nationalist card to justify their actions based on the logic that it is only through a strong and united 'regional-state' that local interests will be protected against encroachment from the centre and from the anarchy of the market place.

Centre–local economic relations

The nature of economic relations between the centre and the localities has occupied much of the federal agenda. Three problems in particular have dominated. First, there is the problem of geo-economic fragmentation. Seven decades of centrally directed economic coordination between the regions has given way to the anarchy of regional autarky. Adjusting from being a component part of a centrally planned economy, in which each republic and region was told what to produce and where market niches were guaranteed as part of the process of central planning, has proven extremely painful. One symptom has been the breakdown of inter-regional trade, exacerbated by dramatic falls in regional production. Responding to this, the regions have tended to pursue their own economic self-interests. This has ranged from introducing protectionist measures such as quotas on the export of consumer goods to some regions even going so far as to print their own local currencies.[22]

Second, there is the issue of at what level – the central, the local state or the macro-regional – politicians can most effectively secure for the localities the successful transition to the market. For its part, the centre has provided little in the way of effective economic policies for the regions, including policies that minimalise disruption in the supply and demand for commodities between the regions. Indeed, with the exception of the brief period of the 1992 reform-minded government of Egor Gaidar, which identified economic decentralisation as crucial to securing market reform, there has been little direction from the centre. The chaos of this transition to market exchange has meant that the centre has been singled out by the ethno-republics and regions for failing to provide effective leadership in order to minimalise the scale of economic disruption. As Hughes notes, 'the centre has been devoid of a policy for the regionalisation of reform'.[23]

It is at the level of the local state (republics and regions) where much of the initiative for economic change is occurring. Through taking greater control over policies affecting their economies, the localities see such a strategy as also central to using their own resources to the advantage of revitalising their local economies.

21. J. Wishnevsky 'Problems of Russia's Regional Leadership', *RFE/RL Research Report*, 3 (19), 1994, pp. 6–13.
22. *Literaturnaia Gazeta*, 28 October 1993.
23. J. Hughes 'Regionalism in Russia. The rise and fall of the Siberian Agreement', *Europe–Asia Studies*, 46 (7), 1994, p. 1138.

Although such policies have gone hand in hand with a commitment to achieving a successful transition to market economies, local political elites in many of the ethno-republics, aware of having to strike a balance between engaging in structural adjustment and continuing to secure the support of their constituents, have been reluctant to move too fast for fear that too radical a policy would undermine their authority within the locality. Consequently many local leaders continue to seek maximum subsidies from the federal government for their public sector heavy industry, so postponing decisions that would lead to factory closures and large-scale local unemployment.[24]

Other ethno-republics have pursued a more radical set of economic policies, combined with local initiatives tailored towards finding a market niche for their locality within the global economy. One republic at the forefront is the south-western republic of Kalmykia. In order to escape from being one of the poorest and least economically viable of Russia's republics, Kalmykia has introduced a far-reaching programme of market liberalisation designed to restructure its economy from its specialist export-dependency on agriculture and other primary products to one based on greater economic diversification through establishing a range of competitive manufacturing-based industries. It is a programme for economic renewal which plans to rely on outside capital investment through tax-free incentives, and which is designed to end the republic's dependency on economic subsidies from Moscow.[25] It is, however, also a developmental strategy that combines a commitment to rapid economic growth with the idea of the strong local state, one in which securing economic growth takes precedence over promoting a pluralist democracy.

Rather than simply pursuing a 'going it alone course', most of the ethno-republics and regions have initiated a macro-regional strategy of local state cooperation for economic development. This has entailed the formation of geo-economic power blocs, based on mutual economic self-interests. Amongst the most influential and archetypical of the eight geo-economic power blocs to emerge is that of Siberia whose membership includes all 19 of its regions and ethno-republics. Declared into existence in November 1990, the Siberian Agreement (*Sibirskoe Soglashenie*) was set up as a means of coordinating the region's economic reform as well as providing a stronger territorial power base for securing shared interests in relation to greater local allocative control over the wealth generated by the region's vast storehouse of natural resources. By July 1992 a charter stating the fundamental principles underlying the regional organisation was ratified by its members. In accepting its political authority, Moscow in effect paved the way not only for a more effective Siberian lobby but also for the formation of other geo-economic power blocs along the lines adopted by the Siberian Agreement. Although this Agreement has not been without its own inter-regional tensions, most notably between the largest and economically most powerful of the ethno-republics, Sakha, and the rest, the Agreement has gone some way to facilitating cooperation over a number of issues, notably of how best to utilise

24. P. Hanson 'The Centre versus the Periphery in Russian Economic Policy', *RFE/RL Research Report*, 3 (17), 1994, pp. 23–28.
25. V. Tolz 'Russia's Kalmyk Republic follows its own course', *RFE/RL Research Report*, 3 (19), 1993, pp. 6–13.

Siberia's raw material potential for the region's more balanced development and of how best to sell Siberia as a place for global investment.[26]

Finally, centre–local economic relations have been plagued by the question of fiscal federalism, of what contribution the ethno-republics and regions should make to the federal budget and of how that budget's resources should be redistributed, both sectorally and regionally. For its part, the centre is seen as demanding too much in terms of fiscal revenue from impoverished localities while in return for the increased burden of fiscal responsibilities, the ethno-republics and regions feel that they are not receiving their fair dues from the federal budget. With large sums having to be allocated to the federal budget, it is argued, the ethno-republics and regions have had to cut back on much-needed local public spending, be it on economic investment or social welfare, acting as a brake in stimulating local development. What however has emerged as a particular focus of contention concerning fiscal budgetary policy is the way in which the republics and regions are increasingly in competition with one another for scarce federal resources.

The benefits that accrue to the ethno-republics from such redistributive policies, it would seem, are not always based on considerations of regional equity or need but rather on geo-politics. Indeed those ethno-republics who under the federal arrangement are allowed to retain a larger proportion of their locally collected taxes, are also receiving the largest subsidies from the centre. Thus only 10 per cent of federal transfers in 1992–93 were being directed to the poorer ethno-republics and regions, whereas the remaining 90 per cent were being allocated to the richer and potentially more geo-politically problematic republics, notably Sakha, Bashkortostan and Tatarstan. Thus Sakha received well over five times the national average, Bashkortostan double the national average, and Tatarstan a third more than the national average.[27]

Local cultural autonomy and citizenship rights

Relations between the centre and the ethno-republics are also being shaped by issues of cultural rights in which the ethnic republics want to reclaim their local identities through promoting their own national languages, national cultures and religions. There is widespread concern within the ethno-republics over such claims in the constitution that in the new Russia what should take precedence 'is the individual and his (sic) inalienable rights' and that collective rights, such as ethnic, linguistic or religious rights, are of secondary importance.[28] The ethno-republics therefore remain suspicious of Moscow's commitment to a federal Russia in which their rights as ethnic citizens are not considered as paramount.

Instituting what the ethno-republics regard as their right to be culturally different is interpreted as contrary to a federal structure in which a strong and regionally insensitive centre may be keen to re-establish its own cultural hegemony through again reinstituting policies of Russification. This is especially worrying given the

26. For a fuller discussion of the Siberian Agreement, see Hughes *op. cit.*, 1994.
27. *Moskovskie Novosti*, No. 28, July 1993, p. 2.
28. *Rossiiskaia Gazeta*, 13 June 1993.

sizeable Russian presence in the ethno-republics and the fear that local Russians may again be used as agents of centrally initiated policies of Russification. Thus in the republic of Tatarstan there is concern among many Tatars, following their government signing of the February 1994 Federal Treaty with Russia, which in effect ended Tatarstan's three-year period of *de facto* political independence, that the way is now open for the republic's political and cultural Russification. They fear that the cultural practices of the republic's two-fifths Russian population, centred on the Orthodox Church and the Russian language, may provide a building block for marginalising the Tatar culture.

In promoting local-national cultures, however, many ethno-republics have also been accused by the centre of initiating an overly nationalistic form of cultural dominance, of even moving towards creating local ethnocracies. This has fuelled tensions between indigenous peoples and local Russians and as a consequence many Russians, fearful of their future, have left in large numbers.[29] It is a fear not without substance. A handful of ethno-republics have even gone so far as to propose a definition of local citizenship in which the right to participate in republic elections would be open only to those who are of the local-indigenous nationality.[30] In some republics, where the dominant local culture is Islamic, the fear of the establishment of a fundamentalist state is also causing concern amongst local Russians, notably in the Muslim republics of Bashkortostan and Tatarstan, although Islamic fundamentalism still remains very much on the margins of local political life.[31]

Russia at the crossroads: empire rebuilding, federation or secession

Centralising strategies of coping with an ethno-regionally diverse federal union have only fuelled concern within the ethno-republics. The Chechen crisis, in particular, and Moscow's handling of it, has again raised widespread concern both within the ethno-republics and elsewhere in Russia over whether federation and democracy are compatible.[32] Yet it would seem that, with few exceptions, the ethno-republics still view themselves as having a political stake in securing a more federalist Russia rather than pursuing the secessionist path. In a show of regional solidarity against Moscow's handling of the Chechen crisis, the seven Central Russian republics noted that the way forward was to 'try to influence federal policy and to reverse current (undemocratic) trends'.[33]

Even if secessionist policies were to gain increasing support, it should not be assumed that fragmentation is somehow preordained. For one thing, secession could be managed 'from above' by a coercive state: after all, the totalitarian state of the Soviet Union successfully contained ethno-regional dissent within its vast multi-ethnic empire for seven decades. Such a scenario, however, would see federation

29. *Izvestiia*, 4 July 1992, p. 3.
30. *Literaturnaia Gazeta*, 21 May 1992.
31. M. Broxup 'Tatarstan and the Tatars', in G. Smith (ed.) *The Nationalities Question in the Post-Soviet States*, Longman, London, 1995.
32. *Rossiiskaia Gazeta*, 4 and 5 January 1995.
33. *Komsomolskaia Pravda*, 5 January 1995.

being replaced by empire rebuilding. For another thing, it would be shortsighted to accept the argument that because the political and economic turmoil following the 1917 Revolution led to the brief emergence of independent republics in the North Caucasus, the Volga Region and Siberia's Far East, history in these regions is on trajectory to repeating itself.

First, there is the role of the ethno-republic political leadership. Given their position within the structure of federal politics, they are of strategic importance to any mobilisation behind the separatist cause. As a consequence of *perestroika*, this elite became more indigenous in composition in the mid to late 1980s, but the personnel installed during the Gorbachev period has remained largely unchanged despite the Soviet Union's disintegration.[34] It is a political elite who have had to limit their career ambitions to provincial politics, in part due to a lack of opportunity to progress beyond the horizons of their own ethno-republics. If Russia is to take on more of the features of Western-style federations this may change, providing the possible opportunity structures necessary to ensure elite mobility, important also in preventing leadership disillusionment with federation. As Hanson notes, for the present 'because there is still no effective structure of political parties linking the careers of local politicians to positions at the national level, most local politicians . . . are not subject to any party discipline that would make them conform to Moscow's policies'.[35] Such elites therefore tend to look back on the republic, to engage in a rhetoric of federal politics which uses highly charged calls for 'sovereignty' and 'national self-determination' in order to maximise benefits from the federation but which, with the exception of Chechnia, has fallen short of calling for outright independent statehood.

Second, there is a lack of a shared collective sense of national self-determination within many ethno-republics where any understanding of an ethnic right to national self-determination does not necessarily coincide with a territorial meaning of the term. In some republics, notably in Dagestan and Kabardino-Balkaria, there exists a variety of indigenous ethnic groups with differing conceptions of the relationship between their understanding of ethnic and territorial self-determination. Indeed, in many respects, the existence of tensions at the local level between such ethnic groups vying for local political hegemony not only weakens the prospects of mobilisation behind the separatist cause but has also the potential to be used by an unscrupulous centre as part of a policy of divide and rule. The position of local Russians is also important given that they constitute a majority of the population in nine republics, in Adygeia, Buriatia, Gornyi-Altai, Karelia, Khakassia, Mordovia, Udmurtia, Komi, and Sakha, and a sizeable minority in all the others (Table 2.1). Although many Russians supported local autonomy, the sense of local identity among especially those immigrants who came into the republics in recent times, is poorly developed. Moreover, for reasons of self-interest, local Russians are more likely to continue to identify and support the territorial integrity of their territorial homeland, Russia, not least because separation from Russia would transform their status from being part of

---

34. *Rossiiskaia Gazeta*, 4 March 1992.
35. P. Hanson *op. cit.*, 1994, p. 23.

Table 2.1 **Composition of the Russian Federation's ethno-Republics**

	Population ('000s)	% Titular	% Russian
Central Russia			
Bashkortostan	3.9	22	39
Chuvashia	1.3	68	27
Karelia	0.8	10	74
Komi	1.3	23	58
Marii-El	0.8	43	47
Mordovia	0.6	32	61
Tatarstan	3.6	49	43
Udmurtia	1.6	31	59
North Caucasus			
Adygeia	0.4	22	68
Chechnia ⎫		58	⎧
Ingushetia ⎭	1.3	13	⎨ 23
Dagestan	1.8	80	⎩ 9
Kabardino-Balkaria	0.8	53	39
Kalmykia	0.3	45	38
Karachi-Cherkesia	0.4	31 (Karachis)	42
		10 (Cherkess)	
North Ossetia	0.6	53	30
Siberia			
Buriatia	1.0	24	70
Gornyi-Altai	0.2	31	60
Khakassia	0.6	11	79
Sakha	1.1	33	50
Tuva	0.3	64	32

Source: Based on data from the 1989 All-Union Soviet Census. *Natsional'nyi sostav naseleniia SSSR* (Moscow: Finansy i statistika, 1991)

the majority nation to that of a minority whose ethnic rights and status are more likely to be challenged. So given their sizeable if not majority status in a number of these republics, any local referenda on secession is likely to result in support for remaining part of the Russian federation.

Finally, although the ethno-republics do not possess an 'information set' regarding the likely economic implications of defederation, they nonetheless make judgements about its anticipated stream of costs and benefits. At one end of the spectrum are the poorer republics like Kalmykia and Tuva which are still heavily dependent on large economic subsidies from Moscow. The nature of this economic dependence and the tangible benefits of remaining part of a larger federal trading community may outweigh the greater and uncertain economic costs of nation-statehood. At the other end are the resource-endowed rich ethno-republics, such as Sakha which accounts for most of Russia's gold and diamond output, and oil-rich Tatarstan and Bashkortostan. Here it is unlikely that statehood would lead to them becoming 'Kuwaits of Northern Eurasia' overnight. The rhetorical strategy of secessionists, however, that international trade has benefits over the greater security of 'national' markets, can carry weight particularly given the chaos of resecuring market niches within the federal economy. If the ethno-republics are not willing to carry out the negative economic and social consequences that would necessarily follow in the short term from becoming sovereign members of an international trading community, the more acceptable and likely trade-off would be to continue to pursue a strategy of regionalism rather than of separatism.

Conclusion

For a post-totalitarian federation to survive, much will depend upon the ability of both the centre and the ethno-republics to develop democratic practices. On the one hand, this necessitates a federation whose institutions, conventions and procedures are rooted in democratic practices. On the other hand, without the development of a social basis to federalism it is unlikely that such a federation will flourish. Under conditions of economic crisis and structural change, this is unlikely to be easy. The temptation by the centre to continue down the path of a highly centralised form of federation in order to secure social stability and economic recovery may become too great.

Chapter 3

POLITICAL PARTIES AND THE PUBLIC

Stephen White and Matthew Wyman

For 70 years the USSR was dominated by 'the Party'. Although the law placed no restriction upon their number, only a single political organisation – the Communist Party of the Soviet Union (CPSU) – had a legitimate existence, and that party, under the 1977 Constitution, was the 'leading and guiding force of Soviet society and the nucleus of its political system, of all state and public organisations'. There had, in fact, been other parties in the early Soviet years: the first Soviet government, up to mid-1918, was a coalition with the Left Socialist Revolutionaries. But from this time forward political life came progressively under the control of a single party, and within that party under the control of a centralised and increasingly authoritarian leadership. When Mikhail Gorbachev came to power in 1985 he enjoyed more effective authority (as he put it himself) than any other world leader.[1] The party itself had enjoyed a monopoly of political initiative under the 1977 Constitution, and there did not appear to be much public pressure for a wider range of political choice. Even dissidents agreed that the party would win most of the votes if there were a genuinely contested election;[2] others, more cynical, responded, 'Two parties? Isn't one bad enough?'.

By the early 1990s the Soviet system had ended, and with it the predominance of a single party. The party had abandoned its leading role in 1990, allowing the constitution to be reformulated so as to permit 'other political parties, as well as trade union, youth and other public organisations' to 'take part in the elaboration of the policy of the Soviet state and in the running of state and public affairs'. A range of informal groups, and even parties, had come into existence on a national or republican basis. Competitive elections, from 1989 onwards, allowed them to compete for popular support; surveys found strong support for the principle of political diversity and choice.[3] The Russian Constitution, as amended in 1992,

1. *Izvestiia*, 6 April 1991, p. 1.
2. See for instance Boris Shragin, *Protivostoianie Dukha*, Overseas Publications Exchange, London, 1977.
3. Early Soviet surveys were ambiguous on this point: in 1989, for instance, 27.1 per cent of the 1583 respondents thought a multi-party system 'absolutely essential as a natural development of democracy', but 23.1 per cent had no opinion, 19.8 per cent thought the CPSU already represented a variety of opinions, and 18.8 per cent thought there would be little real benefit in such a change (*Obshchestvennoe mnenie v tsifrakh*, vyp. 1, September 1989, p. 7). Gibson and Duch, however, found 'fairly substantial majorities' opposed to a single party system (in Arthur H. Miller *et al.* (eds) *Public Opinion and Regime Change*, Westview, Boulder, Colorado, 1993, p. 82), and Jeffrey Hahn's respondents in Yaroslavl' were also favourable ('Continuity and change in Russian political culture', *British Journal of Political Science*, 21 (4), pp. 393–421).

committed the post-communist state to internationally recognised human rights, including freedoms of speech and movement, conscience and assembly (Chapter 5). The constitution that was adopted in December 1993 added a commitment to 'ideological diversity' and 'multi-partyism' (Article 13). And the first post-communist elections, conducted at the same time, saw a majority of the electorate choosing from what was initially a list of 130 parties and movements as well as from more than 3,700 individual candidates on a majoritarian and proportional basis.[4]

The process of democratic transition and consolidation, it was clear, would depend to a great extent upon the coherence and support of this new range of political actors. It is parties, in democracies, that structure the preferences of millions of electors, offering – at least in theory – a choice of coherent and distinctive programmes together with the leadership that is necessary to sustain them over a period of government.[5] In this chapter, using a Russia-wide survey conducted in December 1992, we examine these and other issues as they arise from the early experience of Russian post-communist politics. To what extent, first of all, did Russians conceive of their political preferences in terms of 'party'? And did they think there were parties through which their interests were represented? We ask, secondly, about the parties to which Russians, at this time, were prepared to give their support, and how that support was distributed within the society. Finally, more briefly, we examine party identities. To what extent, in these early post-communist years, did parties have distinctive identities in the perception of the electorate, and to what extent did their support constitute distinct attitudinal communities? Our answers to these questions reflect a particular period, in the immediate aftermath of communist rule; but they suggest at least preliminary conclusions about the role of parties during the crucial period between CPSU monopoly and democratic consolidation.

The emergence of party politics

Party formation, by the early 1990s, was still at a rudimentary level, with no clear association between the candidates' personal values, political programme and organisational affiliation and their subsequent behaviour in the legislature. By early 1991, nonetheless, just a few months after the adoption of a law that had given them the right of legal existence, there were at least 20 USSR-wide political parties with a membership ranging from a few dozen to tens of thousands. In addition, about 500 parties were active at the republican level.[6] Membership figures were difficult to establish: some of the parties kept no central register of members or regarded them as confidential, and almost all of them exaggerated their own numbers considerably. The new parties fell into two main types: 'vanguard parties' (which had adopted some of the organisational forms of the CPSU and were in some cases successors to it); and 'movement parties' (which were similar to the broadly based coalitions

---

4. *Izvestiia*, 23 October 1993, p. 2 (party numbers); *Rossiiskaia Gazeta*, 11 December 1993, p. 1 (candidates).
5. See for instance Geoffrey Pridham (ed.) *Securing Democracy: Political Parties and Democratic Consolidation in Southern Europe*, Routledge, London, 1990.
6. *Glasnost'*, 1991, 12, p. 2; *Pravda*, 28 February 1991, p. 2 (republican level).

that had been formed in Eastern Europe in the late 1980s). The Democratic Party, an example of the first of these, based itself on democratic centralism and exercised strict discipline over the activities of its members; the Democratic Union, which fell into the second category, did not impose the decisions of its leadership upon the mass membership and allowed the formation of organised factions (even of Communists) within its ranks.[7] All of these parties operated within the framework of the Law on Public Associations, approved in October 1990, which laid down the formal basis of a multi-party system.[8]

Association, the Law made clear, was an 'inalienable human and civil right'. The Law itself covered public associations of all kinds, including trade unions, women's and veterans' associations, sporting societies and creative unions as well as political parties. Associations could be created for a variety of purposes, including the 'exercise and protection of civil, political, economic, social and cultural rights and liberties', provided that their objectives did not extend to the 'overthrow of or violent change in the constitutional system or the forcible violation of the unity of the USSR, the union and autonomous republics or other autonomous formations; propaganda of war, violence or cruelty; the stirring up of social discord, including class as well as racial, national or religious discord; or the commission of other criminally punishable acts'. The creation of military formations was also prohibited, and associations whose activities were detrimental to the health, morality, rights or interests of other citizens were liable to prosecution. All associations had to operate within the framework of the Constitution and Soviet law.

At least 10 citizens were required to establish an association under the Law; they were then required to hold a founding congress or conference at which their statutes were adopted and executive bodies elected. An all-union party or trade union had to have a minimum of 5,000 members. The statutes of an association had to be registered at this point, with supporting documentation and a fee, with the USSR Ministry of Justice or its counterparts at other levels of government. Registration could be refused, if (for instance) the objectives of the association appeared to conflict with the law, but this decision could in turn be appealed against at the Supreme Court. Political parties, in particular, were supposed to have the basic goal of participation in bodies of state/power and administration; they had programmes, which were to be published for general information, and had the right to nominate candidates at elections, to campaign on their behalf and to form organised groups in the bodies to which they were elected. They were not, however, allowed to receive financial or other material assistance from foreign states or citizens, and they were legally liable for their actions up to their possible abolition. The registration of new

7.   This distinction is made in *Pravda*, 16 January 1991, p. 5.
8.   For the law see *Vedomosti S"ezda narodnykh deputatov SSSR i Verkhovnogo Soveta SSSR*, 1990, 42, item 840; also *Izvestiia*, 16 October 1990, pp. 1–2.

and existing parties, including the CPSU, began on this basis in the USSR Ministry of Justice at the end of 1990.[9]

There was certainly no shortage of parties, with or without the law that gave them a legal basis. A reference guide published in late 1991 listed over 200 of them, including nine anarchist parties, 17 different monarchical parties and no fewer than 53 'national-patriotic' ones.[10] Some restored the names of pre-revolutionary parties, like the Constitutional Democrats or Kadets; others took more obvious labels, such as the Liberal Democrats or Social Democratic Party; and others still were more inventive. There was a Humour Party, and an Idiots' Party of Russia which thought it was bound to do well in a 'land of fools';[11] by the end of 1993 there was a Beer Lovers' Party, with over four thousand members by the end of January 1994.[12] By the summer of that year there were 50 parties that were organised on a Russia-wide basis (some others refused to register with the authorities), with a further 300 'regional parties and organisations'.[13]

The parties that had come into existence by this time constituted a recognisable spectrum of interests (for a typology see Table 3.1). On the 'right', in the sense that they promoted the interests of capital and private ownership, were a number of business parties including the Conservative Party and the Party of Economic Freedom, headed by the wealthy financier Konstantin Borovoi.[14] There was a Bourgeois Democratic Party, a Conservative Party, an Order of Orthodox Monarchists and several Christian Democratic parties. More significant, among the new groupings, were the Liberal Democratic Party and a variety of parties or movements of a radical nationalist character, including *Paymat'* (Memory); the National-Republican Party of Russia, based in St Petersburg; the Russian National Sobor, founded in early 1992 as a coalition of communist and nationalist forces; the Russian People's Union, founded in late 1992 under the leadership of the prominent deputy Sergei Baburin; and the National Salvation Front, a coalition of communist and nationalist forces that was formed in October 1992 and was subject, for a time, to a presidential ban. It was

---

9.   Several useful listings of political parties are available, among them Vera Tolz, *The USSR's Emerging Multiparty System*, Praeger, London, 1991; Peter Lentini, *Political Parties and Movements in the Commonwealth of Independent States*, Lorton House, Manchester, 1992; M.A. Babkina (ed.) *New Political Parties and Movements in the Soviet Union*, Nova, Commack, New York, 1991; Vladimir Pribylovskii (ed.) *Dictionary of Political Parties and Organisations in Russia*, Postfactum, Moscow, 1992; V.N. Berezovsky *et al.* (eds) *Rossiia: Partii, assotsiatsii, soiuzy, kluby*, 10 vols, RAU Press, Moscow, 1992– [in progress]; V.G. Gel'bras (ed.) *Kto est' chto? Politicheskaia Moskva 1993*, Catallaxy, Moscow, 1993; and R. Medvedev (ed.) *Spravochnik: Politicheskie partii, dvizheniia i bloki sovremennoi Rossii*, Leta, Nizhnii Novgorod, 1993. Two useful short discussions are B. Slavin, 'U istokov mnogopartiinosti', *Sotsial'no-politicheskie nauki*, 1990, 8, pp. 33–44, and Slavin and V. Davydov, 'Stanovlenie mnogopartiinosti', *Partiinaia zhizn'*, 1991, 18, pp. 6–16.
10. See V.N. Berezovsky *et al.*, *Rossiia: Partii, assotsiatsii, soiuzy, kluby: Spravochnik*, Vol. 1, 2 parts, RAU Press, Moscow, 1991.
11. *Izvestiia*, 30 March 1991, p. 1, and 14 October 1991, p. 1.
12. *Ibid.*, 28 December 1993, p. 1; for its membership see *Novoe vremia*, 1994, 6, pp. 10–11.
13. *Vesti* (St Petersburgh), 26 July 1994, p. 2.
14. Any listing of this kind must be provisional and specific to the period in which it is conducted.

Table 3.1 **The Russian Political Spectrum, 1994**

'Oppositional' parties and movements			'Democratic' (pro-Yeltsin) parties and movements	
'Patriots'	'Communists'	'Centrists'	'Democratic Movements'	'Democratic Parties'
National-Republican Party of Russia (less than 1,000)	United Opposition (bloc)	Civic Union (bloc)	'Democratic Russia' (bloc; 200–300,000 'supporters')	Social Democratic Party (5,600)
Russian National *Sobor* (bloc)	All-Union Communist Party of Bolsheviks	Russian Social-Democratic People's Party (120,000)	Democratic Reform Movement (bloc)	Republican Party (7,000)
Russian All-National Union (bloc)	Labour Russia (bloc: up to 100,000 'supporters')	Al-Russian Union 'Renewal' (2,000) (*Obnovlenie*)		Free Democratic Party (2,000)
National Salvation Front (bloc; 40,000 'supporters')	Russian Party of Communists (10,000)	Democratic Party of Russia (40,000)		Constitutional Democratic Party (2,000 'supporters')
Liberal-Democratic Party (100,000, independent estimate 1,500)	Russian Communist Workers' Party (60,000)	Constitutional Democratic Party – Party of Popular Freedom (300)		Party of Economic Freedom (600)
	Union of Communists (10,000)	Agrarian Party		People's Patriotic Party (103,000)
	Socialist Workers' Party (50–80,000)			Peasant Party (14,000)
	Party of Labour			People's Party (*Gdlyan*) (10,000)
	Communist Party of the Russian Federation (500,000)			Christian-Democratic Union (5,000)
				Russian Christian Democratic Movement (7,000)
				Russia's Choice Party

Source: Adapted from *Spravochnik: politicheskie partii, dvizheniia i bloki sovremennoi Rossii* (Nizhnii Novgorod, 1993). Membership estimates in brackets are generally self-declared; some minor blocs or parliamentary fractions have been omitted; and the Liberal Democratic Party has been reclassified as 'patriotic'. The Russian Social Democratic People's Party was until 1994 the People's Party 'Free Russia'; Russia's Choice was founded as a party in 1994.

groupings of this kind that made up the 'irreconcilable opposition' to President Yeltsin in the mid-1990s.

The Liberal Democratic Party, formed in the summer of 1989, was formally committed to the idea of a state based on law and a market economy. In practice it became identified with the extravagant views of its leader, Vladimir Zhirinovskii, who came third in the Russian presidential elections of 1991 and was later a central figure in the post-communist parliament after his party had led all others in elections to the party-based section of the State Duma. Zhirinovskii called for the re-establishment of the Russian state within the boundaries of the USSR, or 'ideally' those of 1865, and his party supported the attempted coup of August 1991 and (later) military action against the Chechen republic.[15] On the 'right' but pro-government were 'Democratic Russia', founded in October 1990, a loosely structured coalition of political forces which was able to mobilise thousands in support of Boris Yeltsin during his campaign for the Russian presidency but declined in effectiveness thereafter;[16] and a Russia's Choice Party, led by Egor Gaidar, which emerged from Democratic Russia in June 1994 but was 'only beginning' the search for a mass membership some months later.[17]

About 20 different parties and movements represented the 'centre' of the political spectrum, including the Agrarian Party, the Constitutional-Democratic Party and the Democratic Party of Russia, led by former CPSU member Nikolai Travkin.[18] This, according to most estimates, was one of the largest of the new parties with about 40,000 members, although its numbers had fallen to about 15,000 in 1994 after a re-registration.[19] Founded in May 1990, the Democratic Party declared its aim to be the restoration of an independent Russian state within a voluntary union of republics. State power was to be decentralised, and a 'society of equal opportunities' was to be created on the basis of market relations and equality of all forms of property; science, culture and education were to be 'deideologised', and a pluralistic political system created.[20] Travkin, a USSR and Russian deputy, was the party's most prominent public spokesman; another, until his departure in early 1991, was the chess player Gari Kasparov.[21] The Agrarians, founded in early 1993, stemmed from a congress of collective farmers a year earlier and reflected the interests of state and cooperative rather than private forms of agriculture.[22]

---

15. *Izvestiia*, 12 February 1992, p. 3; and (for its support of the coup) A.S. Barsenkov *et al.*, *Politicheskaia Rossiia segodnia*, 2 vols., Moskovskii rabochii, Moscow, 1993, 1, p. 302. See also more generally *Sotsial'no-politicheskie nauki*, 1991, 1, pp. 97–9, and for its documents *Liberal'no-demokraticheskaya partiia. Dokumenty i materialy*, Politizdat, Moscow, 1991.
16. For a damaging split when three of its founding parties withdrew see *Kuranty*, 12 November 1991, p. 1.
17. *Rossiiskie vesti*, 15 June 1994, p. 1 (foundation); *Nezavisimaia Gazeta*, 30 September 1994, p. 5 (interview with Gaidar).
18. For a general discussion see *Sotsial'no-politicheskie nauki*, 1990, 11, pp. 66–74.
19. Medvedev, *Spravochnik*, p. 10. For the later membership figure see *Moskovskie novosti*, 1994, 36, p. 9.
20. *Izvestiia TsK KPSS*, 1990, 8, pp. 153–4. Reports of the founding congress appeared in *Sovetskaia kul'tura*, 2 June 1990, p. 2, and *Izvestiia*, 26 May 1990, p. 2. The Party's 'Declaration' is in *Voprosy ekonomiki*, 1990, 8, pp. 152–4.
21. *Izvestiia*, 26 April 1991, p. 4.
22. Medvedev, *Spravochnik*, p. 17.

Finally, there was a 'left' grouping based upon the Socialist and Social Democratic parties, the Greens and an anarcho-syndicalist confederation.[23] These groups were joined in November 1990 by the Republican Party of the Russian Federation, a 'left centrist party of the parliamentary type', which occupied an intermediate position between the CPSU and the Democratic Party and consisted largely of former members of the CPSU who had been members of its Democratic Platform before the 28th Congress.[24] Further to the left were the political groupings that claimed the political legacy – and often the property – of the CPSU, including the All-Union Communist Party of Bolsheviks, led by Nina Andreeva; the Russian Party of Communists, which was based on the former Marxist Platform within the CPSU; the Socialist Workers' Party, which included the historian Roy Medvedev; and a re-established Menshevik Party. The People's Party of Free Russia, from 1994 the Russian Social-Democratic People's Party, was led by former Vice-President Aleksandr Rutskoi; it was one of the largest of the new parties with a membership of over 112,000 in late 1992, though this had fallen to about 40,000 by the summer of 1994.[25] The Communist Party of the Russian Federation, revived in February 1993, claimed a still larger membership of 550,000 and was for some the 'only real political party, not an organised group of supporters of one or other politician'.[26] Many of these totals were clearly exaggerations and the number of activists of all parties taken together was estimated at just 30,000 in the early 1990s.[27]

Party supporters and party politics

The Political Parties of Russia Survey was carried out in December 1992 in 12 urban areas; the results are in practice representative of the Russian urban adult population.[28] There was certainly evidence of a rising level of political disillusion among our 1,509 respondents throughout the Federation. While 56 per cent had

---

23. On the Socialists and Social Democrats see *Sotsial'no-politicheskie nauki*, 1990, 12, pp. 88–95, and 1991, 5, pp. 97–105. On the Greens see *ibid*, 8, 1991, pp. 94–7, and on the anarchists, *ibid*, 10, 1991, pp. 84–91.
24. *Izvestiia TsK KPSS*, 1990, 12, p. 101 (the Party later gravitated towards the liberal right).
25. Gel'bras, *Kto est' chto*, p. 240; *Moskovskie novosti*, 1994, 42, p. 9. On the post-communist parties more generally see Peter Lentini 'Post-CPSU communist political formations', *Journal of Communist Studies*, 8 (4) (December 1992), pp. 280–92, and Ya.G. Ermakov *et al.*, 'Kommunisticheskoe dvizhenie v Rossii v period zapreta', *Kentavr*, 1993, 3, pp. 65–80.
26. *Nezavisimaia Gazeta*, 11 November 1994, pp. 1, 5.
27. *Izvestiia*, 20 April 1992, p. 2.
28. The Political Parties of Russia Survey was conducted by the Institute of Applied Politics in Moscow in December 1992. The survey was a random sample of 1,509 respondents aged 18 years or over resident in 12 urban centres: Moscow, Kursk, Ostrov, Saratov, Taganrog, Michurinsk, Sal'sk, Omsk, Izhevsk, Kopeisk, Ulan Ude, and Ussuriisk. For the purposes of the survey residence in Asian Russia is defined as living in Sal'sk, Omsk, Izhevsk, Kopeisk, Ulan Ude or Ussuriisk; the remainder are considered to be living in European Russia. For a fuller discussion of our survey and methodology see Ian McAllister and Stephen White, 'Democracy, political parties and party formation in postcommunist Russia', *Party Politics*, vol. 1, no. 1 (1995).

voted for Boris Yeltsin in the 1991 presidential elections, just 26 per cent said that they would do so again. A substantial proportion (37 per cent) saw the CPSU and its role in Soviet history in 'largely or entirely positive' terms, but a rather larger proportion (56 per cent) saw the party's contribution in 'largely or entirely negative' terms. There was also some unhappiness with democracy itself. Asked to choose between three statements, 26 per cent agreed that 'No normal society can exist without democracy, and the more democracy the better', but twice as many (51 per cent) opted for the more cautious view that 'In the final analysis it is impossible to manage without democracy, but there ought to be limits to it, since too much democracy is harmful to society'. The remainder, fully one in five, thought that 'Democracy does more harm than good; the main thing is that there is order and discipline in society'.

This disillusion was related to a feeling that Russia's leaders were no longer in control of events. Asked who or what ruled Russia, only 16 per cent suggested President Yeltsin and 4 per cent the Russian government; the largest single group, 23 per cent, thought 'the mafia' was in charge, closely followed by 'anarchy' or 'nobody' (13 per cent). A further 6 per cent thought former Party *apparatchiks* were still dominant, 4 per cent thought it was 'the rich', 3 per cent thought it was 'fools' or (the same proportion) Parliament, and 0.2 per cent respectively thought it was 'alcoholics', the KGB or 'enemies of the people'. Many were unable to answer the question at all, and almost no one (0.1 per cent) suggested that it was the people that ruled. Similarly, only 28 per cent felt that the governors appointed by President Yeltsin were in charge in their own local area, as compared with 24 per cent who thought the former Party apparatus was still in power, and 21 per cent who (again) thought it was 'the mafia'. Similar results have been obtained in other investigations, with either 'the mafia' or 'nobody at all' considered to be in power in the Russian Federation or in local areas;[29] across Russia as a whole, in early 1993, fully 50 per cent had no trust in any institutions of government whatsoever.[30]

How is this related to mass perceptions of the new political parties? Respondents, clearly, did not have a high opinion of them. Asked 'Are there any parties in Russia to which you are ideologically close, or which express the interests of people like you', just 22 per cent said there were, as compared with 78 per cent who were prepared to identify with no party at all. Asked whether they agreed or disagreed with a number of statements about the new parties, 12 per cent suggested they were the 'embryo of future democratic structures'; a further 15 per cent thought the new parties 'allowed everyone to participate in politics', and 10 per cent thought they would play a prominent role at some time in the future. Many more, however, thought the new parties played 'no significant role in political life' (20 per cent); 40 per cent thought their activities had 'no relevance to ordinary people'; and more than half (52 per cent) thought that 'All the new parties were founded by people who are greedy for power'. For a minority (11 per cent) the new activists were simply 'misfits with nothing better to do'. There was little trust in any political institution, in

29. See for instance *Ekonomicheskie i politicheskie peremeny: monitoring obshchestvennogo mneniia*, 1993, 5, p. 38.
30. *Izvestiia*, 6 April 1992, p. 2.

early post-communist Russia, but less in political parties than in any other institution mentioned in surveys including the army and police, television, the Supreme Soviet, trade unions, the state security service, local government or the courts.[31]

There was, accordingly, a widespread feeling that parties were playing a role of little significance in Russian politics, and there was a fairly general lack of interest in their activities. Thus, our survey revealed that a mere 4 per cent were 'rather strongly' or 'very strongly' interested in the activities of political parties, with another 19 per cent 'moderately interested'. Much larger proportions (34 per cent) were 'scarcely interested' or (39 per cent) 'not interested at all' in their activities. Asked which was the most influential party in their locality, 36 per cent had difficulty in responding; 21 per cent did not reply; 20 per cent thought there was no party of this kind; and 9 per cent had no interest in the question. Of the parties that were mentioned, only the Democratic Party of Russia and other reformist groupings were mentioned in any numbers (11 per cent altogether); in second place was the then-illegal CPSU, with 2 per cent. Fully 86 per cent, however, were unable to identify a party that was influential in the manner that was suggested by the question. Asked, similarly, which social forces were the most influential at that time, for the largest numbers of respondents there were no forces of this kind (23 per cent) or none that could readily be suggested (12 per cent).

This did not mean, however, that respondents were wholly unaware of the activities of the parties that were active in Russian politics at this time. Respondents, more specifically, were asked how they evaluated the political parties that were prominent at the time of our survey, and how they evaluated their leaders. Table 3.2 illustrates the results. At first glance, it appears that knowledge of parties is limited, with only the two communist successor parties evoking reactions – positive, neutral or negative – from more than half of our respondents (negative reactions, as for most of the other parties, greatly exceeded positive ones). This, again, is in line with the findings of other Russian surveys in the early post-communist period. As late as September 1993 only 24 per cent of a Russia-wide sample was able to identify even a single political party, movement or association;[32] in a related poll, Zhirinovskii's Liberal Democratic Party had the highest recognition factor (almost 30 per cent), but it was also the party that was most actively disliked.[33] A local study, conducted in 1991 in Nizhnii Novgorod (formerly Gorky), found that fewer than half of those who were asked had heard of the new parties;[34] in the Vladimir region, similarly, more than two-thirds of those who were asked had 'not the slightest idea' about any of the parties that were presented to them for consideration.[35]

A closer examination of the data, however, reveals a more complex picture. Just one in five had no views at all on any party. Only about a quarter were willing to express opinions about more than 10 of the parties under investigation, but the great

31. Richard Rose and Christian Haerpfer, *New Russia Barometer III: The Results*, Strathclyde Centre for the Study of Public Policy, SPP 228, University of Glasgow, 1994, pp. 31–3.
32. *Mir mnenii i mneniia o mire*, 1993, 3 (87).
33. *Argumenty i fakty*, 1993, 38, p. 1.
34. *Sotsiologicheskie issledovaniia*, 1992, 3, p. 11.
35. *Moskovskii komsomolets*, 2 February 1993, p. 2.

Table 3.2 **Attitudes towards political parties and leaders, December 1992**

	Positive	Neutral	Negative	Don't Know
All Union Communist Party (Bolshevik)	12	23	33	33
Nina Andreeva	*5*	*10*	*30*	*44*
Russian Communist Workers' Party	11	20	25	43
Viktor Anpilov	*4*	*8*	*24*	*64*
Democratic Party of Russia	18	19	10	53
Nikolai Travkin	*27*	*22*	*9*	*41*
Pamyat	5	11	31	54
Dmitrii Vasilev	*2*	*8*	*15*	*75*
Liberal Democratic Party	2	10	19	68
Vladimir Zhirinovskii	*6*	*11*	*50*	*33*
Movement for Democratic Reform	9	13	9	69
Gavriil Popov	*10*	*19*	*21*	*50*
Social Democratic Party of Russia	5	15	10	70
Oleg Rumiantsev	*5*	*12*	*7*	*76*
Party of Economic Freedom	7	12	7	73
Konstantin Borovoi	*10*	*17*	*10*	*62*
Russian Christian Democratic Movement	5	14	9	73
Viktor Aksiuchits	*3*	*8*	*13*	*76*
People's Party 'Free Russia'	3	16	8	73
Aleksandr Rutskoi	*43*	*19*	*7*	*30*
Constitutional Democratic Party	4	13	9	74
Mikhail Astafev	*4*	*11*	*14*	*72*
People's Party of Russia	5	14	6	76
Tel'man Gdlyan	*25*	*22*	*10*	*44*
Russian All-People's Union	3	9	8	80
Sergei Baburin	*12*	*13*	*22*	*53*

Source: Political Parties in Russia Survey, December 1992.

majority of respondents (79 per cent) had views about at least some of them. It would accordingly be a mistake to conclude that the new parties were operating in a political space that was entirely remote from the awareness and concerns of ordinary Russians. Still more important is the degree and forms of party support.

It is a familiar finding from Western survey research, for instance, that the proportion of party members is smaller than the proportion of party voters, which is in turn usually exceeded by the number who are favourably disposed towards a party or at least prefer it to any other.[36] Our data enable us to look at three of these dimensions in more detail: membership, voting intention, and feelings about political parties of a more diffuse kind.

Few Russians, clearly, have been motivated to become directly involved with the new parties. Our questionnaire asked respondents if they were members of any of the new political parties, and if so of which. Only 3 per cent, at the time of our survey, were members of any of the parties, and of these the overwhelming majority claimed to be members of the (still illegal) CPSU or of the parties that had succeeded it. The proportion of the population that was involved in party activity had fallen considerably since the collapse of communist rule: at that time a very much greater 23 per cent had been members of a party, which in this case meant the CPSU or its youth organisation, the Komsomol. There was also a clear distinction, in other surveys, between verbal support for a party and willingness to attend its meetings, to carry out party activities, or even to vote for the party with which one publicly identified (at the end of 1990, for instance, 60 per cent of Muscovites identified with Democratic Russia: but only 49 per cent were prepared to vote for its candidates, and no more than 14 per cent were likely to attend its meetings).[37]

When respondents were asked which political parties they would in fact be ready to vote for, as of December 1992, Nikolai Travkin's Democratic Party of Russia emerged as the most popular of the new groupings in our survey, with 17 per cent support, followed by two of the CPSU successor parties (the Communist Party of Bolsheviks and the Communist Workers' Party) with 8 and 7 per cent respectively. A rather larger proportion, however, were unable to say how they would vote (23 per cent), and 12 per cent did not intend to vote at all (these data raise some difficulties of interpretation in the absence at this time of any party that was closely aligned with the Russian President). Assessments of the new parties in more general terms, as Table 3.2 makes clear, were somewhat more positive, but even so the most popular party, Travkin's, was rated positively by just under one in five. No party, in fact, had been able to achieve a significant level of public acceptance by the time of our survey, which was more than two years after party politics had been fully legalised.

The Russian parties and their attitudinal constituencies

Political science has traditionally associated party identification not only with social class and status, but also with an individual's social attitudes and values. We

36. See for instance Roger Jowell *et al. British Social Attitudes: the 5th report*, Gower, Aldershot, 1988, p. 214.
37. *Sotsiologicheskie issledovaniia*, 1992, 2, p. 77.

Table 3.3 **Identification with parties and leaders by political views**

	Communist	Yeltsin supporter	Centrist	National Patriot	Identify with no party
All	19	26	23	23	48
Support private property	7	42	33	15	48
Oppose private property	45	6	12	35	40
Russia should be a great power	25	20	19	28	46
Russia should have no special role in the world	14	29	24	18	53
Positive view of communism	77	6	12	48	16
Negative view of communism	5	44	35	16	45
Positive view of democratic cause	9	48	44	19	36
Negative view of democratic cause	42	8	12	38	40
Positive view of national patriotic cause	31	13	23	46	38
Negative view of national patriotic cause	16	39	32	19	41

National Patriot here is taken to mean those who appraise positively at least one of Vladimir Zhirinovskii, Sergei Baburin or Albert Makashov.
Support private property = agrees that 'private property is necessary for economic development'.
Oppose private property = agrees that 'private property means the exploitation of man by man'.
Russia should be a great power indicates that the respondent chose the option 'Russia should be a great power respected by her friends and feared by her enemies'.
Russia should have no special role indicates that the respondent chose the option 'Russia should be a state without any pretensions to a special role in the world'.
Percentages in table do not sum to 100 as respondents were able to give multiple responses.
Source: Political Parties in Russia Survey, December 1992.

accordingly related support for the various political movements to opinions about some of the most important issues dividing Russian society (see Table 3.3). In each case we found a clear relationship between political attitudes and the likelihood of identifying with parties or with individuals that were representative of a particular current in the political spectrum of the time.

Communist identifiers, for instance, were much more likely to have views that were hostile to the market economy and to political democracy, while at the same time they were more likely than others to deplore the end of Russia's great power status and the break-up of the USSR. Thus, 19 per cent of the sample as a whole had positive views about one of the communist parties, but among those who thought that private property represented 'the exploitation of man by man', the proportion was 45 per cent. Among those who thought that the increasing gap between rich and poor was unacceptable, more than 38 per cent were communist identifiers; and among those who thought the 'new rich' should be jailed, 45 per cent were identifiers. Similarly, a third of those who were opposed to granting republics the right of self-determination, and 37 per cent of those who felt that democracy did more harm than good, aligned themselves with one or other of the communist parties. As well as being positive about the communist cause in general they also tended to be sympathetic to the national-patriotic movement, which stood for many of the same goals. Clearly, then, identifiers with the communist cause did to a considerable extent share the views of their leaders, people like Viktor Anpilov and Nina Andreeva, who both deplore marketisation and the increasing disorder that they perceive in Russian society.

The attitudes of those who intended to vote for Boris Yeltsin in a presidential election, and of those who took a positive view of one of the centrist parties, present a distinct contrast to those of communist identifiers. Fully 49 per cent of those who felt 'the more democracy, the better' were presidential supporters, compared with just a quarter of the sample as a whole. Similarly 42 per cent of those who believed that private property was necessary and 37 per cent of those who saw nothing bad in rising income differentials were Yeltsin supporters, compared with just 11 per cent among those who took the opposite view, and 6 per cent among respondents who believed that democracy did more harm than good. Prospective voters for Yeltsin also tended to be hostile to extremist movements of both right and left. Centrist supporters, as compared with Yeltsinites, had relatively similar characteristics in terms of attitudes, but tended to be slightly more lukewarm towards the market and slightly less positive about democracy.

The attitudes of those who identified themselves with nationalist politicians in our survey showed many similarities with those of communist identifiers in their hostility to democracy and to marketisation. Those who regretted the end of Russian great power status (28 per cent), opposed the idea of self-determination for other republics (31 per cent), felt that private property involved exploitation (35 per cent), that the new rich should be jailed (40 per cent) and that democracy did more harm than good (30 per cent) were significantly more likely to take a positive view of right-wing leaders such as Vladimir Zhirinovskii, Albert Makashov or Sergei Baburin than did the population as a whole. Nationalist identifiers also tended to be sympathetic to the communist cause in greater numbers. The closeness of views that exists at leadership level is accordingly reflected at the level of their supporters, and forms the basis for the so-called 'red-brown' or communist-nationalist alliance of opponents to the post-communist Russian government. There were also some differences: in particular, respondents who felt that all leading positions in the country should be occupied by Russians were more likely to identify themselves with the national patriots than with the organised left.

The political views of those who identified themselves with no party are also of interest, representing as they do the largest single group among our respondents. Were they hostile to the idea of party in itself, seeing it as a recipe for factionalism and chaos? Or did the size of the group reflect more the absence of any parties that supported the government at the time of our survey? The results, in fact, suggest a combination of these two factors. We found, for instance, that these respondents were significantly less interested in politics than party identifiers, and less likely to vote in any future presidential election. However, we also found that they were less likely to think that Russia should be a great power, more likely to support private ownership, twice as likely to be among those who admired the new rich than among those who thought they should be jailed, very much less likely to see private property as 'the exploitation of man by man', and less likely to feel that democracy did more harm than good. Non-identifiers, on the evidence of the survey, were accordingly not generally hostile to the market as such, nor to political democracy; and at least a section of this group would appear to represent a potential social base for pro-reform parties beyond that already identified in terms of their support for Boris Yeltsin.

We should not exaggerate the extent to which respondents, in these or other cases, were able to conceptualise their political beliefs in a clear and consistent manner. For example, when asked what social order had come into existence in early post-communist Russia, more than half (51.6 per cent) found the question impossible to answer; among the remainder responses ranged from 'capitalism' (10.5 per cent) to 'chaos and anarchy' (9.2 per cent) and on to 'feudalism' (7.9 per cent), 'socialism' (4.5 per cent) and even 'a slave-owning society' (0.3 per cent). It is equally a commonplace of Western political science that identification with a party or politician may be the basis on which views are adopted, rather than the result of a prior commitment to a given set of values. The fit, moreover, is never complete; theories of party identification and voting behaviour stress many factors other than social group and political views, including many short-term issues.[38] It is clear nonetheless on the evidence of our survey that there is a distinct social and attitudinal basis for the main currents of opinion and support that were characteristic of early post-communist Russia.

Conclusion: A party system without parties

The USSR, Gorbachev told a group of American senators in 1990, was the 'most politicised society in the contemporary world'.[39] And yet, in the early post-communist period, there was still little sign of the political parties that could channel those popular energies and bring the various preferences of citizens to bear upon the formation of public policy. The new parties, as we have seen, had limited memberships, and even these were subject to exaggeration (Zhirinovskii, it appeared, had included all those who attended its inaugural congress as members of the Liberal

---

38. 'The Pulse of Europe: A survey of political and social values and attitudes', Times-Mirror Center for the People and the Press, Washington DC, 1991, typescript, pp. 13–15. Similarly Vicki L. Hesli and Arthur H. Miller, 'The gender base of institutional support in Lithuania, Ukraine and Russia', *Europe–Asia Studies*, 45(3) (1993), pp. 505–32.
39. *Pravda*, 13 April 1990, p. 1.

Democratic Party and had added others without their knowledge; some reports suggested the party's entire membership was largely fictitious.[40] The parties split continually, usually on the basis of leadership intrigue rather than political principle. They failed to make common cause in the legislature (there were 'as many parties as deputies', remarked Anatolii Sobchak with some irritation);[41] and they moved very slowly to develop distinctive programmes and constituencies of support. How could the Democratic and the Social Democratic Party, for instance, be distinguished? Both of them, as *Literaturnaia Gazeta* pointed out, were in favour of social reform and the market, and both of them were opposed to what was then the CPSU; but the views of many of their members were reflected inside the CPSU, for many of whose membership their relationship with the party was 'like membership of the Anglican Church for the average Englishman'.[42] Of all the 1,500 parties that had been proclaimed to date, wrote a commentator in the paper *Nezavisimaia Gazeta*, 'not a single one is a significant political force'.[43]

In this chapter we have acknowledged the weak development of political parties in post-communist Russia, but found some evidence for a 'latent party system' based upon a clear structuring of the electorate in social and attitudinal terms. Some of the Russian parties, for instance, revived organisations that had their origins in the late tsarist years, when parties were legal and elections to the Duma could be contested (for example, the Mensheviks and Constitutional Democrats). In other cases parties were formed that had analogues elsewhere, particularly in Western Europe; there were Social Democrats and Christian Democrats, for instance, both of them enjoying the moral and material support of their counterparts in other countries. In our survey we found that the largest single group of respondents identified with none of the existing parties or movements. But communists, nationalists, centrists and Yeltsin supporters did attract distinctive groups of supporters. Moreover, their supporters were often in agreement on central issues of public policy. A clustering of values, demographic characteristics and party identities was also apparent in the December 1993 elections, with high levels of support for Yeltsin among supporters of 'Russia's Choice', and a greater degree of support for the continuation of economic reforms (communist supporters were strongly opposed, by 58 per cent as compared with 14 per cent), but 'Russia's Choice' supporters came out even more strongly in support, by 87 per cent as compared with only 7 per cent that were against them.[44]

There were still formidable obstacles to the development of a more coherent party system that could engage a wider section of the Russian public. One of these, certainly, was a well-developed antipathy to the concept of party after 70 years in which it had stood for political monopoly and sometimes repression. As K. Lozovskii, a teacher from Vitebsk, wrote to *Izvestiia*, 'wouldn't it be better without parties altogether?' What was a party anyway but 'always and everywhere a struggle for

---

40. See for instance Radio Free Europe/Radio Liberty *Research Report*, 1(4) (26 January 1992), p. 3.
41. Anatolii Sobchak, *Khozhdenie vo vlast'* Novosti, Moscow, 1991, p. 163.
42. *Literaturnaia Gazeta*, 20 February 1991, pp. 1, 3.
43. *Nezavisimaia Gazeta*, 14 July 1993, p. 3.
44. *Izvestiia*, 1 December 1993, p. 4.

posts and positions', fed by a lust for power that was 'more powerful than any narcotic'? Better, surely, to let the 'demagogues and hypocrites, power-lovers and careerists, flatterers and opportunists' fight it out while ordinary people tried to encourage the spiritual qualities that had always sustained them in the past.[45] Or as a 45-year-old woman, formerly in the CPSU, told *Argumenty i fakty*, 'I don't believe in any of the parties any more. . . . All the ones we have at the moment are only interested in getting into power, and no one is concerned about ordinary people. Not even the communists.'[46] Civil society, moreover, was still weakly developed, with few of the autonomous business and labour associations that supported parties in other countries; and there were practical difficulties of many kinds in circumstances of high inflation, falling newspaper circulations and a television service dominated by the President and his administration.

There were obstacles, finally, in the system of presidential government itself.[47] Yeltsin had resigned his CPSU membership in 1990, but joined no other party. As President, he claimed to stand above party and to represent all citizens. In the December 1993 elections he ostentatiously refrained from endorsing any of the contending parties or blocs. And under the constitution that was approved at the same time, the new Parliament had relatively little influence over the choice of government. The outcome was to focus political division, once again, upon a president (representing, in this case, 'reform') and a parliament (which was generally taken to represent 'conservatism'). This was a constitutional issue, not a political cleavage between the blocs that had competed in the elections. Parliamentary majorities, as a result, had little meaning, and the struggle for influence was very often diverted into local power struggles and the assertion of regional autonomy in relation to the federal government. The executive presidency had been devised to give the country firm leadership, free of the constraints of Parliament or even the courts, and able to respond effectively to short-term crises. Political parties, it appeared, were much more likely to be encouraged when Parliament was the locus of authority, when a greater degree of attention was given to consensus and coalition building rather than executive action, and when the composition and conduct of government directly reflected the outcome of parliamentary elections.[48]

45. *Ibid*, 10 January 1992, p. 3 (slightly adapted).
46. *Argumenty i fakty*, 1993, 7, p. 2 (slightly adapted).
47. As Scott Mainwaring has noted, the combination of a multi-party system and presidentialism is 'especially inimical to stable democracy' *Comparative Political Studies*, 26 (2) (July 1993), pp. 198–228. Further contributions to this discussion are in Arend Lijphart (ed.) *Parliamentary versus Presidential Government* Oxford University Press, Oxford, 1992; Matthew Shugart and John M. Carey, *Presidents and Assemblies: Constitutional Design and Electoral Dynamics* Cambridge University Press, Cambridge, 1992; and Juan J. Linz and Arturo Valenzuela (eds) *The Failure of Presidential Democracy: vol. 1, Comparative Perspectives*, Johns Hopkins University Press, Baltimore, Maryland, 1994.
48. The authors of Chapter 3 are glad to acknowledge the assistance of Professor McAllister in the preparation and presentation of their data on the Political Parties of Russia Survey, and of Olga Kryshtanovskaya of the Institute of Sociology, Russian Academy of Sciences, in making the data available.

Chapter 4

THE CHANGING COMPOSITION AND STRUCTURE OF THE POLITICAL ELITES

David Lane and Cameron Ross

The collapse of the USSR government and the declarations of sovereignty by the previous republics of the USSR pose important questions concerning the role of political elites in political change. Three questions may be addressed here. First, who were the counter-elites leading the forces of radical political reform which brought down the previous Soviet governments? Second, to what extent do the new incumbents in the formal political apparatus of power replace the previous holders? Third, do the new political leaders represent new social or class forces and do they form a unitary or a divided elite? To answer these questions, we consider the leadership of the Russian Parliament clustered around Yeltsin which effectively seized power, and the consistency and circulation of members of the state bureaucracy – now constituted as the Russian government under the presidency of Yeltsin.

The elite of the Supreme Soviet of the Russian Federation 1990–93

The role played by the leaders of the Russian Parliament was crucial in the collapse of the USSR and the evolution of the Russian state. Who were these leaders? What was their background? And to what extent were they linked to the Soviet regime?

Defining the political elite of any institution is an extremely difficult process. In this research we have adopted a 'positional' methodology. We have assumed that office holders of positions (defined below) in the Supreme Soviet constitute its elite, and have identified an elite of 245 members in the period March 1990 to October 1993. These were the crucial years in the formation of the Russian Federation and its breakaway from the USSR.

This was a period of considerable turnover of the leading cadres in the Parliament. It should be remembered that due to the requirement of membership rotation many positions were subject to considerable change in personnel and our research may not have included all office holders. However, we are confident that our study includes by far the overwhelming majority. Our data base includes the holders of the following positions:

1   The Chair, First Deputy Chair and Deputy Chairs of the Supreme Soviet;
2   The Chair and Members of the Presidium of the Supreme Soviet and the Chair of the Supreme Economic Council of the Presidium;
3   The Chairs of the Standing Committees and Commissions of the Supreme Soviet;

4 Deputy Chairs, Secretaries and a sample of ordinary members of key commissions of the Supreme Soviet (Budget, Legislation, Defence and Security, and members of the Constitutional Commission).[1]

5 Finally are included most of the chairs (or coordinators) of political factions and groups and of major political parties in the Congress and Supreme Soviet.

It must be borne in mind that many of these positions overlap. For instance, a member of the Presidium might be a chair of a standing committee.[2] The total number of people occupying these different positions came to 245. We were unable to find sufficient information on seven and these were deleted from the survey, leaving a total sample of 236.[3] Here we consider their socio-economic backgrounds compared to the members of the Congress.

Social background of the members of the Congress and Supreme Soviet and its elite

Before Gorbachev's reforms, the legislative bodies were not freely elected; the deputies were carefully selected on the basis of social criteria. The guiding principle of the selection of deputies was that those elected would reflect the occupational, national, and gender composition of the population: hence there was a quota of workers, women and other relevant groups to secure such representation. With contested elections, however, these criteria no longer applied. The social background of the members of the Congress and the elite we have defined above was as follows.

Education

The educational background of the deputies was significantly different from the population as a whole. Less than 10 per cent of those elected had only primary or secondary education. Of the deputies elected in 1990, 92.7 per cent had completed higher education and among these 40 per cent had degrees in engineering, 9.2 per cent in medicine, 7.6 per cent in law, 6.9 per cent in education and 4.4 per cent in economics. There was one full member and two corresponding members of the USSR Academy of Sciences, 65 held doctorates and 150 were candidates of science.[4]

This pattern continued among the members of the Supreme Soviet elite. Of the 204 persons on whom we have information, only six did not have higher education,

---

1. The elite were chosen from the committees as follows:
   Commissions of the Soviet of the Republic (27)
   Commissions of the Soviet of Nationalities (20)
   Committees of the Supreme Soviet (105).
2. For the composition and membership of the committees and commissions of the Supreme Soviet in May 1992 see V. Pribylovskii, *Politicheskie Fraktsii i Deputatskie Gruppy Rossii-skoga Parlamenta* (Informatsionno-Ekspertnaia Gruppa 'Panorama', Moscow, May 1992).
3. In the final section below concerned with voting data, we were only able to locate the biographical histories of 212 deputies which is the total sample there.
4. *Parlamentskaia Nedelia*, 16 May 1990–1 October 1991, p. 11.

by far the majority (49) were engineers, a significant proportion had been educated at 'party schools' (27) (here we include the higher educational institutions of the Komsomol and the KGB and Ministry of Internal Affairs; only one other had a social science background). We also considered the place of higher education: here, of the 181 people for whom we were able to locate information, 57 were educated in Moscow, 25 in Leningrad, and the remaining 99 outside those towns.

Gender and age

Fifty-seven members of the Congress were women (5.3 per cent) and in the Supreme Soviet this rose to 7.6 per cent; in our Supreme Soviet elite 19 (8.0 per cent) were women. As in the Congress of People's Deputies of the USSR, this represented a significant decline in the proportion of women elected compared to the earlier pre-Gorbachev period.

Of the total number of deputies, four-fifths were in the age group 36 to 55 and 16 were over 60 years of age.[5] Of the elite, the majority were in middle age: 57.6 per cent were between 36 and 50 years old; another 25.8 per cent were between 51 and 60, a fair number, 15.2 per cent, were under 35 and few (only 1.2 per cent) were over 60 years of age.

Nationality and Regional Affiliation

The national composition of the Congress was predominantly Russian. Of the 47 nationalities represented in the Congress, Russians made up the largest group with 828 deputies (See Table 4.1).[6] The leadership reflected quite accurately the composition of the Congress: all the minority groups had some position of authority.

The place of birth is an important social variable in developing countries and particularly so in Russia. By far the majority of the elite were born in the provinces: of the 167 leaders for whom we were able to find the place of birth, 143 were born in provincial areas. Only 18 were born in Moscow (another three were from the Moscow area), and three were born in Leningrad.

Occupation/Social Status

First, we consider all the delegates who were members of the Congress and then consider its elite, as defined above.

Of all the delegates, only 5.7 per cent were self-defined as being workers, 4.5 per cent were collective farmers, 4.3 per cent were military, 19.5 per cent were from the scientific and creative intelligentsia; 24.8 per cent were from Party,

---

5. *Ibid.*
6. Deputies came predominantly from the following areas: Moscow – 54, Moscow Oblast – 48, St Petersburg – 32, Krasnodar Krai – 28, Sverdlovsk – 32, Nizhegorodskaia Oblast – 27, Cheliabinsk Oblast – 24, Bashkortostan Republic – 27, Tatarstan Republic – 24, Udmurt Republic – 13, Chuvash Republic – 12, Dagestan Republic – 12, Komi Republic – 11.

Table 4.1 **Ethnic composition of the Congress of People's Deputies and its elite**

Nationality	N	Congress Per Cent	Supreme Soviet Elite Per Cent
Russian	828	(78.3)	75.9
Ukrainians	46	(4.4)	3.6
Tatars	27	(6.2)	2.2
Jews	16	(1.5)	1.8
Mordovians	11	(1.0)	1.8
Chuvash	9	(0.9)	0.9
Buriats	8	(0.8)	0.9
Chechen	8	(0.8)	1.3
Germans	8	(0.8)	1.3
Ossetians	6	(0.6)	0.5
Kalmyks	5	(0.5)	0.5
Tuvinians	5	(0.5)	0.9
Iakuts	5	(0.5)	0.9
Armenians		n.a.	1.3
Other minorities		n.a.	6.3

Soviet and public organisations and 5.6 per cent from legal and security; 23.2 per cent worked in industry, construction, transport and communications and 12.0 per cent in agriculture.[7]

Research by A.A. Sobianin[8] has claimed that most of the deputies were from management. In 1990, he claims, 78 per cent of the deputies worked in management and of these, 228 (22 per cent) were from higher managerial positions in the top ranks of the CPSU, or were senior ministerial officials or chairs of higher level soviets; 386 (36 per cent) were middle-level officials, local party secretaries, leaders of local soviets, military commanders, KGB officials, factory and farm directors; 213 (21 per cent) came from the lowest managerial tier involved in local management – section heads of research institutes, secretaries of factory party committees.

The social background of the deputies, therefore, was predominantly weighted toward the professional and managerial strata. This even increased over the life of the Congress as a number of the members began to work full-time in the Supreme Soviet and in government at the local levels. In October 1991, 531 of the deputies worked in Soviet Organs and of these 320 worked full-time in the RSFSR Supreme Soviet.[9]

7. The data are taken from the Supreme Soviet's official publication, Piatyi (Vneocherednoi) S″ezd Narodnykh Deputatov RSFSR.–Parlamentskomu Korrespondentu, prilozhenie k informatsionnomu biulleteniu, *Parlamentskaia Nedelia*, 16 May 1990–1 October 1991, pp. 1–287, p. 11.
8. Cited by Richard Sakwa in *Russian Politics and Society*, Routledge, London, 1993, p. 57. From A.A. Sobianin (ed.) *VI S″ezd Narodnykh Deputatov Rossii; Politicheskie Itogi i Perspektivy*, Organisational Department of the Presidium of the Supreme Soviet of the Russian Federation, 1992, Moscow, pp. 14, 21–22.
9. *Parlamentskaia Nedelia*, 16 May 1990–1 October 1991, p. 11.

These data, of course, refer to their occupational status when elected and tell us nothing about their origin or background. For the Supreme Soviet elite we were able to work out the social background directly from data collected on their biographies. We found information on the life history of 212 deputies. Each position was coded according to the type of work or activity. We then calculated the number of different posts held in each group and worked out the total length of time each position was held. By totalling all the entries under each group, we were able to show in which occupational areas the elite members were concentrated during their careers.

Consider the career origins of the Russian Supreme Soviet elite. Those entries related to the occupations begun between the ages of 17 and 25 were aggregated. Table 4.2 shows the composite data. For instance, examination of the table shows 227 different positions of 'student' – obviously, some of the elite members had been students at more than one institution – and there were only five positions of agricultural worker. The third column shows the total time the elite members were in each status group. Time spent at study, for instance, was 1029.36 years – this includes time which continued in jobs which lasted into and after the age of 25. In the final column, the various groupings are expressed as a percentage calculated on the basis of the time in that status divided by the time in all positions held between the ages of 17 and 25.

Table 4.2   **Supreme Soviet Elite: occupational statuses between the ages of 17 and 25**

Status	Positions (Years)	Total time in position	Total time as % all time
Student	227	1029.36	23.65
Industrial worker	80	309.27	7.1
Industrial executive	40	187.37	4.3
Professional/research	37	223.5	5.14
Non-manual	36	2232.6	51.3
Military service	29	69.04	1.58
Military (career)	21	138.26	3.17
Party executives*	15	76.13	1.75
Government executive	7	23.0	0.52
Agricultural executive	6	41.1	0.94
Agricultural worker	5	12.0	0.27
Trade union/voluntary	2	10.0	0.22

*includes Komsomol executives and Party professionals

These data show the overwhelmingly middle-class occupational origins of the Supreme Soviet elite. Other non-manual occupations were predominant, taking up 51.3 per cent of the total time, followed by higher education. Industrial and agricultural manual work accounted for the next largest number of occupational positions (80 and 5), but relatively little time was spent in them – 7.1 per cent and 0.27 per cent respectively.

These then were the occupations in which the elite started out. But what happened later in their lives before they rose to elite position? We considered the positions held in the period between 1 January 1985 and 1 March 1990 (i.e. prior to the elections of 4 March 1990 which returned the Parliament which brought down the Soviet Union). Immediately prior to election to the Congress of People's deputies, by far the majority of the elite were employed in professional and research jobs (33.1 per cent), next came positions in the government and Party apparatuses (21.6 per cent). Very few were manual workers (5.8 per cent) or from trade unions (2.8 per cent). The elite was fundamentally non-manual and professional by class position.

Continuity with previous government and party elites

In an earlier study of the Supreme Soviet of the USSR, we showed that its elite was dominated by people who also had positions in the elites of government and Party.[10] We shall show that this was not true of the Supreme Soviet of the Russian Federation.

Prior to the elections of 4 March 1990, of the 236 members of the Supreme Soviet elite, only 55 had had *any* previous position in the Soviet government at an all-union or republican level. None had been major figures in the USSR government. Only one, Yeltsin, had been a government minister – he had been a first chair of the USSR State Building Committee; another, E. Basin (Chair of the Parliament's Commission for Construction), had been Deputy USSR Minister for Transport Construction from 1986 to 1988. Twenty-three had occupied posts of First Deputy Minister in the government of the Russian Republic (RSFSR): for instance, A. Kamenev (Chair of Commission for Social Development of Rural Areas) had been First Deputy Chair of Gosplan RSFSR.[11]

It was at the middle levels of administration in the provinces that a significant representation of the government apparatus was present. Thirty-four people had leading *oblast* posts, such as chair or deputy chair or head of department (including Deputy Chairs of the Supreme Soviet, V. Agafonov and Iu. Iarov). At the local levels there were relatively few people: four held posts at city level, such as Iu. Kirpichnikov (member of the Commission on the Work of Soviets), who had been the Chair of the Executive Committee of the Sosnovoborsk Soviet of People's Deputies. Four held posts at the *raion* (district) level and three had held middle-ranking positions in the KGB and MVD. Another six had lower administrative positions in the administration.

Thus there were very few people elected to the Supreme Soviet of the Russian Republic who could be said to have had very high status in the government apparatus of the RSFSR or the USSR. These were largely men of middle-ranking officialdom.

10. David Lane and Cameron Ross, 'The social background and political allegiance of the political elite of the Supreme Soviet of the USSR: The terminal stage, 1984–1991', *Europe–Asia Studies*, 46 (3), 1994, pp. 437–63.
11. Data here refer to the last or highest post and thus each person is counted only once. Of course the total number of posts in the government exceeds the number of individuals because of mobility between posts.

The other major institution of Soviet power was the Party organisation. Of the 45 people with a position in the Party apparatus, there was only one who had reached the rank of All-Union Secretary of the CPSU. This was again the fallen figure of Yeltsin, who had held the position briefly under Gorbachev. There were no heads or deputy heads of the All-Union Central Committee *apparat*. Only four persons, R. Abdulatipov (Chair of Council of Nationalities), V. Bokov (Chair Sub-Committee of the Commission for International Relations), G. Saenko (Co-Chair of National Salvation Front), V. Syrovatko (Deputy Chair Council of Nationalities), had held the minor posts of 'instructor' in the Central Committee *apparat*. Again it was the provincial party apparatus where a significant number had had positions of power. There were 13 people who had been First or Second *obkom* secretaries – such as S. Osminin (Chair Sub-Committee of Commission for Social Development of Rural Areas) from Kirovsk *obkom* and V. Syrovatko from Krasnodar. There were another seven departmental or deputy heads at *obkom* level, and seven held middle positions such as 'instructor'. At the city level there were five *gorkom* secretaries and another nine with positions at lower levels of administration.

Here again the picture is one of people with middle-ranking Party status, having roots in the provinces. None of the established Party leaders ran for office in the Russian Republic, believing that its government was a minor source of power. We make two conclusions from this analysis. First, the members of the RSFSR Supreme Soviet elite had only a minor stake in the major institutions of Soviet power in the USSR. Second, it can hardly be argued that the Supreme Soviet replicated the traditional form of Soviet power: the leaders of Party and Soviet state were largely absent.

Voting and political alignment

One of the most important attributes of elites is the extent of their consensus and division. It is widely held that one of the major determinants of political stability is consensus among leaders. We noted earlier (see Chapter 1) the ways in which divisions in the Congress of People's Deputies became more important after the collapse of the USSR, and conflict became endemic between President and Russian Parliament. Here we consider first, the extent to which these divisions were paralleled among the elite of the Supreme Soviet and second, whether there were any significant groupings of interests among the leaders.

Many commentators have asserted that the factional or political alignment of the deputies in the Russian Parliament are not good indicators of political preference. Richard Sakwa, for example, in discussing the voting at the Sixth Congress in April 1992, has remarked that 'Factors other than allegiance to a bloc have to be found to explain actual voting behaviour. The key factor in voting patterns was the social and occupational structure of the Congress.'[12] The notion here is that parties lacked an ideological basis and were shifting associations of individuals clustered around leading figures.

12. Richard Sakwa, *Russian Politics and Society*, Routledge, London, 1993, p. 61.

In order to explore these topics, we considered the voting records of the Congress between December 1990 and March 1993. Issues were selected on the basis of their importance and whether there had been division of votes. In order to test the hypothesis that voting was linked to occupation and social background, we analysed the voting of the elite of the Supreme Soviet in three social categories and then considered the factional alignment.

As to the social categories, first we considered those who had held senior government or Party posts during the period from 1 January 1985 to 1 March 1990 (this included persons in post or taking up a post during this time); 77 out of a total of 212 on whom we could find adequate biographies came into this category. Of the 77, 22 had posts in both the Party and the government executive. The objective here was to discover the voting pattern of members of the Soviet elite with experience in the *apparat* in the Soviet Union. This, we believe, is a better way of understanding the social class of the deputies than considering their last or present occupation which is given in the records of the Congress and is usually utilised by most commentators.

Second, we considered elite members who were from the 'intelligentsia' in the sense of deputies having professional positions (senior researchers, journalists, academics, doctors) between the period from 1 January 1985 to the end of 1993. This gave a total of 82 people.

Third, we analysed elite members by age; here we divided the elite into those under and over 40 years on 1 March 1990 when they were elected to the Congress.

The detailed voting is shown in Table 4.3. The 'Total Vote' refers to the Congress voting given in the Protocols. The 'Vote Pref.' column defines the number of the issue (discussed below) and the aggregate voting results. We searched the voting records for each of our elite members and the aggregate for each group is shown in the Gov/Pty column (votes by the Party government elite), Prof (professionals) and Under 40. (Source of voting: Indem data base, Moscow).

The first issue considered was the vote on Silaev's report of the Council of Ministers with respect to the government's policy of economic stabilisation and conversion to a market economy. Here there appeared to be general accord between the members of the Supreme Soviet elite and the deputies in the Congress. Those with a professional background were particularly enthusiastic – 83 per cent voting in favour. The ex-members of the Party-government elite were also overwhelmingly in favour of the motion, though 22 per cent did not vote.

The second vote was a resolution on the introduction of private property, which aimed to insert into the Constitution the principle of 'sanctity and inviolability of private property'. This was a divisive issue and was rejected by the Congress, 61 per cent voting against and 26 per cent for. Here we see some division among the Soviet's elite: 36 per cent of its younger members voted in favour, as did nearly half (49 per cent) of the professionals; however, 69 per cent of the previous government and Party leadership were against. A similar distribution of votes occurred with respect to the private ownership of land for agricultural production, the Party-government executives voting somewhat more strongly against than the other elite members.

The fourth vote gave to the government bodies of the RSFSR greater powers to carry out measures to deal with the economic and political crisis; to vote in favour was

Table 4.3 **Voting at Supreme Soviet of RSFSR 1990–93 (selected issues) by total vote and occupational background**

Motion	Date Vote (m/d/yr)	Result	Vote Pref*	Total Vote†	Total Vote %	Gov/Pty N	Gov/Pty %	Prof N	Prof %	Under-40 N	Under-40 %
Silaev Reforms	12/07/1990	Adopted	1.<+>	835	77.9	55	71.4	68	82.9	51	72.8
			1.<->	41	3.8	2	2.5	2	2.4	3	4.2
			1.<=>	32	3	3	4	0	0	2	2.8
			1.<?>	164	15.3	17	22	12	14.6	14	20
For institution of private property	12/12/1990	Rejected	2.<+>	283	26.4	17	22	40	48.7	25	35.7
			2.<->	650	60.6	53	68.8	31	37.8	36	51.4
			2.<=>	59	5.5	3	3.9	5	6.1	6	8.5
			2.<?>	80	7.5	4	5.2	6	7.3	3	4.2
For private ownership of land	12/12/1990	Rejected	3.<+>	379	35.4	21	27.2	18	21.9	21	30
			3.<->	552	52.5	48	62.3	44	53.6	35	50
			3.<=>	36	3.4	3	3.9	4	4.8	3	4.2
			3.<?>	105	9.8	5	6.5	16	19.5	11	15.7
For presidential power to perform anti-crisis measures	4/05/1991	Adopted	4.<+>	491	45.8	31	40.2	57	69.5	42	60
			4.<->	383	35.7	39	50.6	12	14.6	17	24.2
			4.<=>	50	4.7	1	1.3	3	3.6	0	0
			4.<?>	148	13.8	6	7.8	10	12.2	11	15.7
For adoption of Draft Union Treaty	5/22/1991	Adopted	5.<+>	635	59.2	45	58.4	41	50	36	51.4
			5.<->	76	7.1	7	9	10	12.2	7	10
			5.<=>	36	3.4	3	3.9	2	2.4	3	4.2
			5.<?>	325	30.3	22	28.5	29	35.3	24	34.2
To give Yeltsin right to rule by decree	11/01/1991	Adopted	6.<+>	575	53.6	46	59.7	44	53.6	36	51.4
			6.<->	266	24.8	16	20.7	19	23.1	18	25.7
			6.<=>	58	5.4	5	6.5	4	4.8	6	8.5
			6.<?>	173	16.1	10	13	15	18.3	10	14.2

Table 4.3 continued

Motion	Date Vote (m/d/yr)	Result	Vote Pref*	Total Vote†	Total Vote %	Gov/Pty N	Gov/Pty %	Prof N	Prof %	Under-40 N	Under-40 %
Impeachment of the President	12/01/1992	Rejected	7.<+>	352	32.8	22	28	14	17.0	21	30
			7.<->	428	39.9	33	42.8	44	53.6	26	37.1
			7.<=>	77	7.2	7	9	6	7.3	3	4.2
			7.<?>	215	20.1	15	19.4	18	21.9	20	28.5
Confidence in the government	12/01/1992	Rejected	8.<+>	423	39.5	29	37.6	21	25.6	26	37.1
			8.<->	357	33.3	25	32.4	33	40.2	25	35.7
			8.<=>	54	5	6	7.8	3	3.6	1	1.4
			8.<?>	238	22.2	17	22	25	30.4	18	25.7
For pre-term elections of President and Supreme Soviet	3/12/1993	Adopted	9.<+>	532	49.6	38	49.3	47	57.3	42	60
			9.<->	222	30.7	12	15.5	8	9.7	7	10
			9.<=>	42	3.9	2	2.6	2	2.4	2	2.8
			9.<?>	276	25.7	25	32.4	25	30.4	19	27.1
Sets out referendum questions (against Yeltsin)	3/27/1993	Adopted	10.<+>	621	57.9	48	62.3	37	45.1	33	47.1
			10.<->	223	20.8	14	18.1	24	29.2	14	20
			10.<=>	36	3.4	4	5.2	2	2.4	7	10
			10.<?>	192	17.9	11	14.2	19	23.1	16	22.8

Key
* Voting Preferences:
+ For
− Against
= Abstained
? Did not vote
†Total vote refers to total of members of Congress of People's Deputies of Russian Parliament

to support the Yeltsin leadership. Here there were important differences between the members of the Supreme Soviet's elite: a majority of the one-time executives voted against, whereas 70 per cent of the professionals were in favour. The sixth vote was also concerned with strengthening the powers of the executive branch in the period of radical economic reform. Here the Soviet executive and the Congress had similar levels of voting, though the ex-Party and government executives were rather more in favour (i.e. 60 per cent had a positive vote). The vote on the Union Treaty (vote 5) was passed with relatively little dissention, though over a third of the deputies did not vote.

When one considers the impeachment of the President (vote 7), divisions in the Congress as a whole were replicated among its elite: notable here, however, is the firm backing given to Yeltsin by the professionals – this was the only category in which more than 50 per cent voted in his support. They also voted rather more positively against a resolution to put on the agenda a motion of no confidence in the government.

By March 1993, Yeltsin's support had waned in the Congress and also among the elite of the Supreme Soviet. Motions which called for the elections of President and Supreme Soviet before the end of the constitutional period and the questions in the Referendum of spring 1993 (Votes 9 and 10) were all adopted. The final vote which defined the questions in the Referendum – including one of confidence in the President and the number of votes cast – had considerable support from the ex-Party-government officials (62 per cent) and rather less so (45 per cent) from the professionals.

In Table 4.4, we have calculated how the voting of these three social constituences compared with all the other members of the elite. Hence in the Gov/Pty elite column, we calculated the chi-square for the difference between how the government-Party elite voted and the other members of the elite. The table shows that age was not a significant variable. This is rather interesting, as it is often asserted that generational differences are a major determinant of political orientation. Only on three issues did social background have any significant effect. Those with a professional background voted in favour of private property and strongly supported Yeltsin and his policies, whereas the previous government-Party executive members voted consistently the other way on these key issues. Overall, however, study of the voting patterns in the Congress of the Parliament shows that the elite reflected the divisions of the Congress. There were significant divisions *within* these social categories though previous occupational background correlated with left–right issues. Hence one could agree with Sakwa that on some issues there was a relationship between occupational position and political preference, but this was not always the case.

Our second task was to analyse the voting of the Supreme Soviet elite by factional allegiance. Table 4.5 shows the voting records of 203 members of the elite divided by four major political blocs: the Coalition for Reform (CR) (N=50), the Democratic Centre (DC) (N=57), Creative Strength (CS) (N=41) and Russian Unity (RU) (N=55) (for the remainder of our defined elite, we either had no data or they belonged to no faction). (For descriptions of these factions see Chapter 1.)

The voting preferences by faction would suggest that political allegiance indicated a significant political division. The most consistent voting patterns are to be found

Table 4.4 **Significance of elite voting preference by previous government-party position, professional background and age**

Voting Prefer Issue	Gov/Ptg Elite	Prof	Age*
1.	no	no	no
2.	yes	yes	no
3.	no	no	no
4.	yes	yes	no
5.	no	no	no
6.	no	no	no
7.	no	yes	trend
8.	no	trend	no
9.	no	no	no
10.	trend	trend	no

Statistic calculated on basis of for (+) and against (–) votes only.
*Calculation based on voting members under and over 40 years of age.
Yes, No: Significant at 0.05 level
Trend: Level of significance between 0.05 and 0.1

among the members of Russian Unity. Examination of the data in the final but one column indicates the high level of consistent voting in this group: only on giving rights to the President to carry out anti-crisis activity was there any significant division and even here 60 per cent were against. It is clear that the major conflict was between Russian Unity and the Coalition for Reform: votes here were completely asymmetrical. Solely within the Democratic Centre and Creative Strength was there any ideological division, but on many issues there was consensus between the members. With the exception of the issue setting out the referendum questions (not in support of the President) the Democratic Centre displayed a very similar set of preferences to the Coalition for Reform. This bloc was almost equally divided over the issue of ownership of property and land.

The voting data indicate the formation of ideological blocs most clearly distinguished by the voting of the coalition for Reform and Russian Unity. The results of a chi-square test shown in the final column indicate that on seven of the ten issues there was a significant difference in the pattern of voting of the elite members of the factions. Clearly, the elite of the Supreme Soviet was fundamentally divided along political and ideological lines. Not only on left–right matters but also on political issues in the Supreme Soviet, party allegiance defined political choice.

The governing elite under Yeltsin 1991–93

While seizing political power and deposing the formal leaders of a regime is one important aspect of political revolution, an even more significant question is the

Table 4.5 **Voting at Supreme Soviet of RSFSR 1990–93 (selected issues) by factional allegiance of elite**

Motion	Vote Pref	Total Vote	Total Vote %	CR N	CR %	DC N	DC %	CS N	CS %	RU N	RU %	Sig at .05
Silaev Reforms	1.<+>	835	77	39	78	45	78	31	75	41	74	no
	1.<->	41	3	1	2	0	0	3	7	2	3	
	1.<=>	32	3	0	0	0	0	2	4	3	5	
	1.<?>	164	15	10	20	12	21	5	12	9	16	
For institution of private property	2.<+>	283	26	34	68	22	38	13	31	5	9	yes
	2.<->	650	60	7	14	26	45	22	53	45	81	
	2.<=>	59	5	7	14	5	8	3	7	0	0	
	2.<?>	80	7	2	4	4	7	3	7	5	9	
For private ownership of land	3.<+>	379	35	16	32	24	42	14	34	7	12	yes
	3.<->	552	52	24	48	23	40	22	53	41	74	
	3.<=>	36	3	2	4	3	5	0	0	2	3	
	3.<?>	105	9	8	16	7	12	5	12	5	9	
For presidential power to perform anti-crisis measures	4.<+>	491	45	42	84	38	66	23	56	15	27	yes
	4.<->	383	35	4	8	11	19	10	24	33	60	
	4.<=>	50	4	0	0	2	3	1	2	2	3	
	4.<?>	148	13	4	8	6	10	7	17	5	9	
For adoption of Draft Union Treaty	5.<+>	635	59	21	42	38	66	23	56	37	67	yes
	5.<->	76	7	13	26	2	3	3	7	4	7	
	5.<=>	36	3	4	8	2	3	0	0	1	1	
	5.<?>	325	30	12	24	15	26	15	36	13	23	
To give Yeltsin right to rule by decree	6.<+>	575	53	31	62	30	52	24	58	36	65	no
	6.<->	266	24	10	20	18	31	9	21	9	16	
	6.<=>	58	5	3	6	4	7	3	7	1	1	
	6.<?>	173	16	6	12	5	8	5	12	9	16	

Table 4.5 continued

Motion	Vote Pref	Total Vote	Total Vote %	CR N	CR %	DC N	DC %	CS N	CS %	RU N	RU %	Sig at .05
Impeachment of the President	7.<+>	352	32	4	8	6	10	10	24	32	58	yes
(Rejected)	7.<->	428	39	37	74	35	61	14	34	8	14	
	7.<=>	77	7	4	8	2	3	2	4	6	10	
	7.<?>	215	20	5	10	14	24	15	36	9	16	
Confidence in the government	8.<+>	423	39	5	10	10	17	15	36	40	72	yes
(Rejected)	8.<->	357	33	33	66	25	43	11	26	2	3	
	8.<=>	238	22	12	24	17	29	12	29	10	18	
	8.<?>	238	22	12	24	17	29	12	29	10	18	
For pre-term elections of President	9.<+>	532	49	22	44	30	52	25	60	33	60	no
and Supreme Soviet	9.<->	222	20	5	10	9	15	8	19	2	3	
	9.<=>	42	3	2	4	3	5	2	4	1	1	
	9.<?>	276	25	21	42	15	26	6	14	19	34	
Sets out referendum questions	10.<+>	621	57	10	20	33	57	25	60	39	70	yes
(against Yeltsin)	10.<->	223	20	29	57	11	19	4	9	5	9	
	10.<=>	36	3	0	0	2	3	5	12	1	1	
	10.<?>	192	17	11	22	11	19	7	17	10	18	

Key
CR Coalition for Reform
DC Democratic Centre
CS Creative Strength
RU Russian Unity
Final column indicates chi-square significant (or not) at .05 level (calculation based on for (+) and against (−) vote only.

extent to which the previous governing elite may be removed and replaced with another one.

The institutions of politics in countries under communist rule had a much greater influence over the distribution of political and economic power that in Western societies where the economy is privately owned and controlled. The personnel of the government apparatus had legitimate control not only of the coordination of the economy but also of economic production and exchange. Seizure of the communist apparatus of government therefore is potentially of greater immediate consequence than in capitalist-type societies.

Following the collapse of the Communist regime under Gorbachev and the assumption of power by Yeltsin, new political institutions have been created and a new political elite has been installed. However, the extent to which the post-Soviet political leadership represents new class and social forces is a matter of controversy. It is sometimes asserted that the former *nomenklatura* continues under a different form of legitimation.[13] Yeltsin himself, for instance, has occupied major positions in the former USSR: Secretary of the Central Committee of the Communist Party, member of the Politburo and a ministerial status in the government under Gorbachev. Others, particularly the new incumbents of power, plead that they represent a different social formation. To examine these propositions we consider the extent to which the holders of top political positions under Yeltsin had origins in the previous Soviet political elites.

We studied the backgrounds of all 145 government leaders[14] in post under Yeltsin between June 1991 and October 1993: this included the leaders in four administrations headed by Prime Ministers Silaev, Gaidar, Yeltsin and Chernomyrdin.[15] This group we define as the Russian governing elite. To establish continuity or renewal, we trace the origins of this group in the previous Soviet administrative, Party and Supreme Soviet elites.

13. Bob Deacon, 'Social change, social problems and social policy', in Stephen White *et al.* (eds) *Developments in East European Politics*, Macmillan, 1993, p. 226. Here Deacon refers to Central and Eastern Europe.
14. During this period of turmoil the ministerial elite was subject to considerable change and there is no single source which records all the appointments. The data collected here may therefore not include every person, but we are confident that most are defined in our database and certainly the major positions are included.
15. Silaev was elected Chair of the Council of Ministers of the RSFSR in June 1990 and he remained in this post until the end of September 1991. We believe it is important, however, to distinguish between the Silaev leadership in the period before the coup of 18–21 August and the post-coup Silaev leadership when Yeltsin and the Russian government were dominant.
    Yeltsin was elected RSFSR President in June 1991 and he took on the additional post of Russian Prime Minister in November 1991. On 15 June, under pressure from the Parliament, Yeltsin gave up his post as Prime Minister and appointed Egor Gaidar in his place. Gaidar in turn was replaced by Chernomyrdin on 22 December 1992, and Chernomyrdin was still in power at the end date of our study in June 1993.

Overlap with the Gorbachev governing elite

Between April 1984 and August 1991, there were 230 persons who had the status of minister of the USSR government.[16] Of the people with USSR ministerial status in post before 21 August 1991, only nine were absorbed into the Russian government under Yeltsin. Three of these, however, had been appointed during the last few months of Gorbachev's administration: S. Anisimov (appointed 13.07.91), N. Ermakov (11.07.91) and O. Soskovets (8.03.91). The remainder, with the exception of I. Silaev, were all appointed to their first ministerial post under Gorbachev: V. Gerashchenko (1989), V. Iakovlev (1989), V. Chernomyrdin (1985), B. Yeltsin (1987), and A. Sterligov (1990). I. Silaev was appointed a USSR minister in 1977 and promoted to the Presidium of the USSR Council of Ministers under Gorbachev in 1985.[17]

In addition to the USSR government, which controlled the major institutions of Soviet power on an all-union level, were the governments of the republics, which also had their own ministerial apparatus. Yeltsin, it will be recalled, was elected Chair of the RSFSR (the Russian Federation) Supreme Soviet in May 1990 and President of the RSFSR in June 1991. In June 1990, Yeltsin was able to form a new RSFSR government under the leadership of Ivan Silaev which was to replace the jurisdiction of the USSR government after the unsuccessful coup of August 1991. Of those who were appointed to Russian government posts over the period 1990 to August 1991, 33 ministers and three members of the Presidium – I. Silaev (RSFSR Prime Minister 1990), Iu. Skokov (1990), and O. Lobov (1991) – continued into the post-August 1991 governments of the Russian Republic. Only four members of the post-August 1991 RSFSR governments had been appointed in the period 1985–89 (P. Guzhvin, G. Kulik, O. Lobov and A. Shubin) and none in the period before 1985. Eleven members of the post-August 1991 presidential administration were also appointed in the period 1990–91.

These men (there were no women)[19] provided important continuity with the previous Soviet government. Many of the new governing elite were 'in place' under Yeltsin before the collapse of the USSR. This suggests that even if the attempted coup of August 1991 (which consequently was used to legitimate Yeltsin's own

---

16. For an analysis see D. Lane and C. Ross 'Limitations of Party control: the government bureaucracy in the USSR', *Communist and Post-Communist Studies*, 27 (1) (1994), pp. 19–38.

17. These individuals held the following principal posts in the Russian government and presidency: Anisimov (Minister of Trade), Ermakov (Chair of Presidential Commission on Economics), Soskovets (First Deputy Chair of Russian Government), Silaev (Russian Prime Minister), Gerashchenko (Chair of State Bank), Iakovlev (Chair Presidential Commission for Rehabilitation of Victims of Political Repression), Yeltsin (President and Prime Minister), Sterligov (Administer of Affairs). See the biographical appendix for further information about individuals cited in this chapter.

18. These held the following principal posts in the Russian Government and Presidency: Skokov (Secretary of the Security Council), Lobov (First Deputy Chair RSFSR Government and Secretary of Security Council), Guzhvin (Chair RSFSR Statistics Committee), Kulik (Deputy Chair of RSFSR Government and Minister of Agriculture), Shubin (RSFSR Minister of Forestry).

19. There were only eight women in total out of the 145 members of the political elite.

coup) had not taken place, an alternative governing elite was waiting to take power. However, it is important to qualify the above analysis in two ways: first, Yeltsin inherited Gorbachev appointees to the administration of the USSR and the RSFSR and second, many of these leaders did not stay permanently in the political elite.

We shall argue that there was relatively little overlap between the Gorbachev and Yeltsin political elites and we shall show that the Russian governing elite was constituted from two groups: first, new people who had entered government from positions outside the state administration and were placed in position by Yeltsin and second, a significant number of the Yeltsin elite were appointed to the government of the Russian republic before the significant events of the Autumn of 1991.

Posts held under the Soviet regime

Our first task is to consider the origins of the new ruling elite. We noted above that relatively few had been in the USSR governing elite. It is possible, however, that they may have held, if not the very top posts in the Soviet regime, ones of influence in lower positions in the administration or in the Party network. In order to examine these propositions, we analysed the careers of the Yeltsin government elite in previous government and Communist Party posts. We created a government saturation index (GOVSAT) in which we measured the number of years in Soviet government executive posts weighted by their rank.[20]

It should be noted that only previous executive positions in the state apparatus (ministers and lower-level executives) are included here; representative and elected positions (such as deputy status in the Supreme Soviet or local soviets) are ignored. While our data are based on published biographical data and cannot be considered to include every position held by every member, they certainly contain all the major figures and their chief posts.

20. Thus each government post was classified according to the following ranks; the weights used in calculations are given in brackets.

G1   Members of USSR Presidium (50)
G2   Administrative Posts within the USSR Council of Ministers (25)
G3   USSR Ministers and Chairs of State Committees (50)
G4   USSR First Deputy Ministers and First Deputy Chairs of USSR State Committees (40)
G5   USSR Deputy Ministers and USSR Deputy Chairs of State Committees (40)
G6   Administrative Posts within USSR Ministries and State Committees (i.e., heads of main administrations) (20)
G7   Members of Presidiums of Republic Councils of Ministers (30)
G8   Ministers, First Deputy and Deputy Ministers and Chairs, First Deputy and Deputy Chairmen of Republic Governments (30)
G9   Republic level administrative posts within ministries and state committees (20)
G10 *Oblast* (regional level) and *Sovnarkhoz* (Regional Economic Council) posts (10)
G11 City level posts (10)
G12 *Raion* (district level) posts (10)

Hence, a person having had ministerial status for one year would have an index of 50 (1 × 50), and a minister in a republican government for three years would have an index of 90 (3 × 30).

Did the government apparatus 'renew itself' in a new guise under Yeltsin? We studied the positions held by the elite members of the four different Russian government administrations (Silaev, Yeltsin, Gaidar, Chernomyrdin) and the President's apparatus to determine what positions they occupied in government and Party before 21 August 1991; after that date Yeltsin and his supporters strongly influenced appointments to the USSR government even when Gorbachev was nominally in power.

The average government participation of the 145 executives as measured by our index was only 152 (we included here all posts up to and including those held on 21 August 1991). This included 34 people who had had no participation at all in the government apparatus. By way of comparison, the 212 government ministers in post under Brezhnev and Gorbachev had an index average of 693 (including all their posts).[21]

On closer examination of the careers of the 145 making up the Yeltsin ruling elite we were able to distinguish three types of executive:

1   Those with a saturation of over 200: 35 people whom we have defined as 'career officials'. This group was headed by people such as Guzhvin, Silaev, Vorontsov, A. Iakovlev, Lazarev, Chernomyrdin and Gerashchenko.[22]

2   Those with indexes of 40 to 200: 64 leaders we have called 'intermediates'. This group includes people who had recently joined the state bureaucracy, such as Yeltsin, O. Lobov, S. Anisimov, Iu. Skokov. (Yeltsin, of course, also had experience in the Party administration.)

3   Those with scores under 40, including the majority (34) who had no government experience at all. This group of 46 we have termed 'new men'. In terms of elite circulation, this group is the most important to study as its members have entered state service from the outside and may represent new class interests. Only by a careful analysis of their background can one establish whether they are in fact a 'new class' or whether they had links with the previous institutions of Soviet power. They include people such as: Egor Gaidar, Georgii Khizha, Vladimir Shumeiko. (For occupational histories, see biographies in Appendix.)

We have made the cut-off points rather severe to bring out the differences between the top group of established officials and the 'new men'. Remember that here, in order to establish the continuity of the political elites, we are measuring their time in government and (presidential) executive posts begun before 21 August 1991.

The occupational background of the Yeltsin political elite

In order to generalise about the extent to which the new political elite represented a new political stratum or class, we have to analyse their previous occupational background as a major indicator of their class position (we use class in a Weberian sense). Here we appraised the work backgrounds of the governing elite in the period

---

21.   Data based on analysis of biographies.
22.   Lazarev (RSFSR Minister of Finance), Vorontsov (Adviser to Yeltsin on Foreign Policy), Iakovlev (Chair of Russian Supreme Arbitration Court).

before Gorbachev lost power in August 1991. Each activity was coded as shown and an index was constructed on the basis of time in each category. (No weights were used in this strategy.)

Figure 4.1 summarises the occupational backgrounds of the three groups of executives: Career officials, intermediaries and new men. The data here refer to the complete life history of the elite executives before 21 August 1991. Clearly, our first group had spent nearly all their working lives in government and significantly more had had experience in the Communist Party as executives (PE) – we shall consider this later.

Moreover, a further qualification is necessary. As some of the political elite owed their promotion to Gorbachev himself (notably, Yeltsin) they could not be considered to have been part of the 'traditional' Soviet administration. Therefore, we examined the background of every member of the Yeltsin elite from January 1960 to March 1985. We also excluded periods of employment of under three continuous years duration on the grounds that their occupational status would be determined by fairly long periods of service.

Figure 4.2 summarises the years of service in various activities of the career officials and the new men. The former had already begun a career in government service and had overlap with spells in the Party executive and agricultural and industrial supervisory work. The new men were overwhelmingly of intelligentsia background, having had positions in the professions (law, journalism, university teaching) or research (particularly in the Academy of Sciences); a significant number had also spent a considerable time in study (much of which was at post-graduate level) and a small number, unlike under Gorbachev, had had a military background.

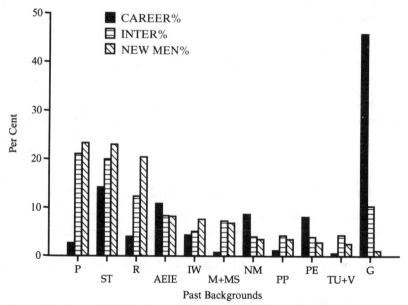

Figure 4.1 **Graph 1: Yeltsin Ruling Elite Career Government Officials and New Men**
(See Key on page 75)

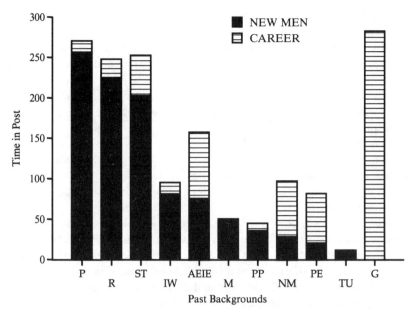

Figure 4.2 **Graph 2: Yeltsin Ruling Elite Backgrounds: 1960–85**
(See Key on page 75)

Links with the previous Communist Party elite

Membership and participation in the Communist Party is obviously an important determining characteristic of the previous Soviet elite. Of the total Yeltsin governing elite, 69 (or 47 per cent) of the 145 governing elite claimed to have been members of the Party, though here one must bear in mind a possible tendency on the part of the respondents not to make public previous involvement (we have searched for biographical information in both the Soviet and post-Soviet periods; most of our information is derived from the latter). Only 40 people had had any position in the party apparatus or in one of its institutions: here we include what we have defined as 'Party professionals' (PP) who may have been working on Party journals or in its educational institutions (such as higher Party schools or academies); only one of the new governing elite had had any significant position in the Komsomol. A caveat here is necessary: for many people Party membership may have been something of a ritual, a necessary condition of certain jobs or an important agency for socialisation and the making of contacts. An analogy may be made with Church membership in the later middle ages: all citizens were members, though not all believers. Non-membership, however, may be important in a negative way by indicating those who had not been part of the previous system and therefore could not in any way be said to be exercising 'inherited' party privilege.

What is important from the point of view of the replication of previous status is the overlap of people with top executive and political posts. Only three people (Primakov, Chair of Russian State Committee on Foreign Intelligence, Yeltsin and

A. Iakovlev) had been Politburo members. A total of 12 had been members of the Party's Central Committee, which might be taken as the political elite of the Soviet Union. Twenty-seven had been full-time members of the Party bureaucracy in some capacity; seven had work experience of 10 years[23] or more and another seven had five to ten years experience.

Party professionals are intellectuals whose role it is ideologically to legitimate the system of communist power. They are people who worked on the leading Communist Party journals and newspapers and also provided the intellectual cadres of the Party's leading higher schools and academies, which awarded their own degrees and diplomas. There were only seven men who had served in such capacities and three had over 25 years service (Kostikov, Press Secretary to Yeltsin; Poltoranin, Russian Deputy Prime Minister and Minister of Mass Information and Media; and Primakov, noted above).

It might be objected, however, that our weighting of the very top jobs obscures many other influential persons in the Party and especially its apparatus. We therefore calculated the participation of the three groups of executives in all statuses in the party: Party professionals, Party executives (including Komsomol executives), membership of the Central Committees and Politburos. The results are shown in Table 4.6[24] and confirm the findings above.

Table 4.6 **Yeltsin elite, by time in previous party posts (years)**

Party position	Career officials	Intermediate	New Men
Executive	93.1	67.2	35.2
Central committees	71.4	18.4	0
Party professional	9.0	77.0	43.0
Politburos	3.0	2.8	0
Komsomal executive	0	9.0	0
No/Tot	11/35	19/64	10/46

Overall, apart from a few senior politicians, such as Yeltsin himself, the background of the Russian ruling elite contained relatively few people with a Party career or background, by far the majority have come from careers outside the previous power structure. However, though the numbers of ex-Party office holders are relatively small (from 17 per cent to 22.8 per cent), the new governing elite did absorb, even at its highest levels, a significant number of people with established positions under Gorbachev which may be the basis of division under Yeltsin. Such a hypothesis would be consistent with our findings with respect to the voting of the ex-government and Party executives in the Supreme Soviet discussed above. But the evidence does not suggest that the traditional Soviet Party elite reconstituted itself as a political elite under Yeltsin.

23. Iakovlev, Petrov, Yeltsin, Bychkov, Tkachenko, Chernomyrdin and Iliushin.
24. The data in the table refer to the (unweighted) time in each category of party affiliation.

Links with the soviets

As we have already emphasised, among the most important agents of change in the transition from Soviet rule to capitalism were the congresses of people's deputies and elected soviets which were important institutions for the legitimation of change both under Gorbachev and Yeltsin. These bodies became springboards, as it were, for aspiring politicians. How far then did persons with a position here make it to the new ruling elite? Among the 145 members of the governing elite relatively few had been major figures in the soviets: nine had been chairs of standing committees from the USSR Parliament and 11 from the Russian Parliament. Primakov had previously held the post of Chairman of the Council of the Union in the USSR Supreme Soviet. Yeltsin had chaired a committee in the USSR Supreme Soviet (on architecture and construction) and was chair of the RSFSR Supreme Soviet. S. Filatov (Head of the Presidential Administration) was a First Deputy Chair, and Iu. Iarov (Deputy Chair of Russian Government) and V. Shumeiko (First Deputy Chair of Russian Government) held Deputy Chairs in the RSFSR Supreme Soviet. D. Volkogonov (Adviser to Yeltsin on Defence Policy) was a Deputy Chair of the Council of Nationalities in the Russian Parliament. Others, such as G. Khizha (Deputy Chair of Russian Government) and A. Chubais (Deputy Chair of Russian Government in charge of privatisation) made their names in local politics in Leningrad. S. Stankevich (State Councillor on Political Affairs and Adviser to Yeltsin) gained great popularity in the USSR Congress and later as First Deputy Mayor of Moscow. Important as these men were, however, the Congresses and Soviets did not provide a major avenue of political promotion.

Presidential and government apparatus

The ruling elite which came to power under Yeltsin was made up of two different institutions: the government and the presidential apparatus. It is sometimes suggested that these institutions replicate the former division between Party Politburo and government – the Council of Ministers.[25] To examine this thesis we compare the Russian government ministers with members of Yeltsin's presidential apparatus.

Figure 4.3 shows the past background of all 145 members of the governing elite divided by their position in the government and the presidential apparatus. In order to see if there are any particular political differences linked to the old regime we have included here previous Communist party membership (PT) and membership of its ruling bodies (Politburo and Central Committee).

The major difference in the backgrounds of members is that the members of the government had had a greater participation in government work and more experience in agricultural and industrial executive positions. The members of the Presidential apparatus had rather stronger links with the previous Communist Party – a higher rate of membership both in the Party (PT) and in its apparatus (PE). Yeltsin had brought into his presidential administration a number of former colleagues in the Sverdlovsk

---

25. R. Minasov 'Nomenklatura prepares to take revenge', *Rossiiskaia Gazeta*, 4 March 1992, p. 2. Reprinted in *CDPSP* XLIV (9), 1992, pp. 22–3.

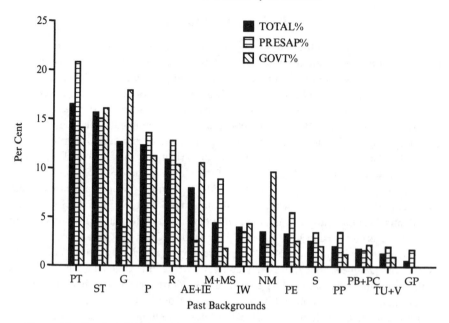

Figure 4.3 **Graph 3: Yeltsin Ruling Elite Presidential Apparatus and Government Posts**
(See Key on page 75)

Regional Party Committee (such as Iliushin, First Assistant to Yeltsin; O. Lobov, Head of Group of Experts; Petrov, Head of Administration; V. Semenchenko, Head of Chancellery). The Presidential apparatus also had slightly more people from a research, professional and military background.

Taking all these facts into account, the results here do not show very much difference between the members of the government and the presidential apparatus. There is insufficient evidence to suggest that they represent significant political blocs analogous to the Politburo and Council of Ministers under the old Soviet system.

Conclusion

In August 1991, Yeltsin and his supporters effectively destroyed the power of the USSR government. The Russian government then began to take over in its territory the institutions previously controlled by the USSR government. Such actions were legitimated by the Parliament of the then Russian Federation, and at first its members were generally in accord with a policy of sovereignty for Russia. This body had no previously high-ranking political personalities. It was composed overwhelmingly of people with a non-manual, higher education background with roots in the provinces. However, after gaining power, divisions appeared in the Supreme Soviet elite. Socially, the President's power was most firmly supported by those people having a professional background and more strongly opposed by its members coming from the middle ranks of the previous Party and government hierarchy. Such social division was greatest on left–right issues; on others, personal allegiances and preferences appear to be the most significant forms of division. There are significant and consistent differences, reflected in their voting behaviour, between members of the elite, determined by their allegiance to political factions and groups. Our research shows that Russian politics is developing along lines in which political factions are highly correlated with ideological stances on a left–right axis. The parliamentary elite is internally divided.

By January 1992 Yeltsin had created a new 'reform government' and, under the guidance of Egor Gaidar, Russia embarked on a programme of price liberalisation and radical economic reforms. Our study has shown that the reform government contained very few members of the previous ruling elite – either of the USSR or the Russian Republic – in post before 1989 (only one, Silaev was in post before 1985). Very few of the previous Party elite continued into the Yeltsin period: Yeltsin himself is most exceptional. The basis of continuity is formed by people appointed to the Russian government and in place in the 1990–91 period. We may hypothesise that Yeltsin, under his authority as President of the RSFSR, had already formed the core of a counter-elite to that incumbent under Gorbachev. At least half of the elite in power under Yeltsin were people new to government. Our study shows that a significant renewal of the ruling elite had taken place: the 'new men' did not occupy even lowly positions in the apparatus of Party or government. They were recruited largely from academic institutions, particularly research institutes. While the congresses of people's deputies provided a focus for and legitimation of the reform programme, our study shows that relatively few of its members were subsequently recruited into the ruling elite. As far as the ruling elite is concerned, the revolution in Russia cannot simply be regarded as the same wine in different bottles – the old *nomenklatura* has not reproduced itself. Rather, some middle-ranking officials from the old apparatus have been promoted and these have provided continuity. More important, moreover, is the influx of new men who have formed an important part of the policy-making, cultural and social apparatus. A circulation of elites would seem to have taken place.[26]

Abbreviations used in Figs. 4.1–3

AE	Agricultural Executive	**PB**	Politburo
AW	Agricultural Worker	**PC**	Party Committee
G	Government exec. post	**PE**	Party Executive
GP	Russian Presidential exec. post	**PP**	Party Professional
IE	Industrial Executive	**PT**	Member of CPSU
IW	Industrial Worker	**R**	Research
M	Military (career)	**S**	Legislative post
MS	Military Service (conscript)	**ST**	Student
NM	Non Manual	**TU**	Trade Union
P	Professional	**V**	Voluntary

26. The authors acknowledge the support of the British ESRC East–West Initiative in carrying out this work and the research assistance of Julie Hemment.

Chapter 5

'WOMEN OF RUSSIA' AND WOMEN'S REPRESENTATION IN RUSSIAN POLITICS

Wendy Slater

The transition in Russia from state socialism to a market economy, and from a one-party state to a form of democracy, has had a particular impact on women. Although women in the Soviet Union were disadvantaged in a number of areas, the economic and political reforms, which began under Mikhail Gorbachev in the late 1980s and accelerated in the 1990s under Boris Yeltsin, threatened further to erode women's position. Economic pressures and political reforms began to push women back into the domestic arena, and their participation in political decision-making bodies declined dramatically. And yet in mid-December 1993, a women-only political movement proposed a list of candidates for the elections to the new State Duma, and won 24 seats. This group, which called itself 'Women of Russia', represents a unique experiment in attempting to overcome women's low political status in Russia. This chapter aims to examine 'Women of Russia' in the context of the transition and to assess the validity of a women-only political movement.

Discrimination against women in the Soviet Union has been well documented. Their concentration in low-paid, low-status jobs, and their poor participation in political decision-making bodies, have been linked to their almost exclusive responsibility for the heavy burdens of domestic tasks and child care, which were exacerbated by the shortage of consumer goods and services.[1] In the Soviet period, and particularly since 1956, policy towards women rested upon what Russian feminists have termed: 'the construct Mother-Woman'.[2] In the socialist state, the infamous 'double burden' was, admittedly, alleviated by the social provision of child care facilities, which were intended to enable women to combine production and reproduction. Nevertheless, Marxism–Leninism, as it developed in the Soviet Union, failed to tackle patriarchal attitudes, perpetuating women's traditional domestic role whilst declaring their equality with men in all other spheres.[3] Tat'iana Mamonova, a Russian feminist

1. See, for example, Gail Warshofsky Lapidus *Women in Soviet Society: Equality, Development, and Social Change*, University of California Press, Berkeley, 1978; Dorothy Atkinson, Alexander Dallin, Gail Warshofsky Lapidus (eds) *Women in Russia*, Harvester Press, Brighton, Sussex, 1978; chapters by Buckley, Attwood, Peers, Allot, and Browning in Barbara Holland (ed.) *Soviet Sisterhood*, Indiana University Press, Bloomington, 1985.
2. Anastasia Posadskaya 'Changes in gender discourses and policies in the Former Soviet Union' in Valentine M. Moghadam (ed.) *Democratic Reform and the Position of Women in Transnational Economies*, Clarendon Press, Oxford, 1993, p. 166.
3. Joan B. Landes 'Marxism and the "woman question"' in Sonia Kruks, Rayna Rapp, Marilyn B. Young (eds) *Promissory Notes*, Monthly Review Press, New York, 1989; Mary Buckley 'The "woman question" in the contemporary Soviet Union', *ibid*, pp. 269–73. For details of the benefits available for women see 'Zhenshchiny i deti v SSSR' *Vestnik statistiki* 1, 1989, pp. 41–65.

dissident, has written: 'Ideally, a woman is expected to have children, be an outstanding worker, take responsibility for the home, and, despite everything, still be beautiful.'[4]

The structure of Soviet benefits and labour legislation treated women as a specific demographic group which needed special protection in order to be able to combine the demands of work and motherhood. As a 1991 article on the women's movement remarked: 'It has long been the case that [woman] is a sort of "social minor": it is no coincidence that, in all official documents, she is listed together with children, the elderly, and invalids – that is, with those who need help because of infancy, old age, or sickness.'[5]

With the shift from a socialist to a market economy, however, these benefits for women could no longer be maintained. The treatment of women in labour legislation as an abnormal group needing special provisions also meant that the economic constraints imposed by market relations have made it more economical for enterprises to employ men than women. Women are thus not only the social group most affected by unemployment in present-day Russia but, when women do find work, it is, presumably, far harder for them to combine it with domestic duties and motherhood.[6]

The encroachment of the market on areas formerly the responsibility of the state – for example, child care or the health service – is a phenomenon common to all urban industrialised countries since the rise of neo-liberalism in the late 1970s in the West, and its adoption after the collapse of communism in the East. The debate pitting the benefits of the market against those of the (welfare) state usually fails to include women in the equation. Danish political scientist Drude Dahlerup has concluded that the combined effect of free-market and patriarchal systems means that: 'the consequences of privatisation may very well be that unpaid women should take care of the same tasks in private which today are performed by the public, giving paid work to female employees.'[7]

It has been suggested that Russian women might welcome the chance to return to 'their purely womanly mission', as Gorbachev termed it.[8] The Russian Deputy Labour Minister, Valerii Ianvarev, for example, claimed at a conference in September 1994 that two-thirds of unemployed women were unconcerned by their situation. Women's groups reject this, and are trying to improve women's chances of employment.[9] The

4. Tat'iana Mamonova 'Introduction: the feminist movement in the Soviet Union' in Mamonova (ed.) *Women and Russia*, Blackwell, Oxford, 1984, p. xx.
5. E. Shcherbanenko 'Feminizm v otechestvennykh tonakh', *Pravda*, 8 May 1991.
6. Liudmila Zavadskaia 'Raznye liki diskriminatsii', *Literaturnaia gazeta*, 13 October 1993; Ruth Pearson 'Questioning *Perestroika*: a socialist–feminist interrogation', *Feminist Review* 39, Winter 1991; Grigorii Gendler and Marina Gildingersh 'A socioeconomic portrait of the unemployed in Russia', *ibid* 3, 21 January 1994.
7. Drude Dahlerup 'Learning to live with the state. State, market, and civil society: women's need for state intervention in East and West', *Women's Studies International Forum* 17(2–3), 1994, p. 122.
8. Mikhail Gorbachev, *Perestroika*, Collins, London, 1987, p. 117.
9. Radio Maiak; Ostankino Television, 21 September 1994.

retreat to the domestic sphere has, however, been seen as a conscious rejection of the old system, for domesticity was viewed as a refuge from pervasive state influence and a forum for individual realisation; it was even idealised as an island of matriarchy in a society dominated by men. Russian feminists have therefore expressed concern that, by rejecting a purely domestic role, they risk being perceived as favouring the old political system and the 'double burden'.[10]

Russian feminists have also complained that women unwittingly made common cause with the system by accepting their role in it. They note, for example, that legislative amendments which might have challenged the 'double burden', such as extending the provisions of maternity leave to other family members, including fathers, were ahead of public opinion.[11] Rather like Western women before the development of feminism in the 1960s, Russian women appear to have accepted a socially imposed definition of gender which perpetuates inequality based upon the 'double burden'.[12] Moreover, the language available to Russian women to discuss the problems of gender inequality is severely restricted. The ideas of feminism, and the terms it used such as 'solidarity' or 'emancipation', have been discredited in Russia by their identification with the language of the Soviet period, particularly that used to describe state policy on women's affairs.[13]

Among the ideas rushing to fill the vacuum left in Russia by the retreat of communism are conservative and nationalist ideologies which define women's role narrowly as that of wife and mother. These ideologies are often imbued with the traditions of Russian Orthodox Christianity, and draw heavily on the portrayal in Russian literature of women as the embodiment of moral perfection and the spirit of the nation.[14] Reacting against Soviet proclamations of sexual equality, they insist that female emancipation had a harmful effect on women's 'natural femininity', and was responsible for social problems such as marital breakdown, and health problems which complicated women's reproductive role. In addition, they blame the relaxation of cultural restrictions under *glasnost'* for sullying the purity of Russian women and, consequently, for the rise in problems such as prostitution or single motherhood which they class as moral issues, but which may more usefully be considered as the result

10. Barbara Einhorn 'Democratisation and women's movements in Central and Eastern Europe: concepts of women's rights', in Moghadam (ed.) *Democratic Reform*, pp. 58–63; interview with Anastasia Posadskaya, *Feminist Review*, 39, Winter 1991, p. 139.
11. Valentina Konstantinova 'The women's movement in the USSR: A myth or a real challenge', in Shirin Rai, Hilary Pilkington, Annie Phizacklea (eds) *Women in the Face of Change: The Soviet Union, Eastern Europe and China*, Routledge, London, 1992, p. 207; Natalia Rimashevskaia 'Perestroika and the status of women in the Soviet Union', *ibid*, p. 17; Alla Sariban 'The Soviet woman: support and mainstay of the regime', in Mamonova (ed.) *Women and Russia*, pp. 205–312.
12. Barbara Evans Clements 'Later developments: trends in Soviet women's history, 1930 to the present' in Barbara Evans Clements, Barbara Alpern Engel, Christine D. Worobec (eds) *Russia's Women: Accommodation, Resistance, Transformation*, University of California Press, Berkeley, 1992, p. 277.
13. Barbara Einhorn 'Democratisation and women's movements in Central and Eastern Europe', pp. 70–71. Anastasia Posadskaya interview, *Feminist Review, op. cit.*, pp. 133–140.
14. On this subject, see Barbara Heldt *Terrible Perfection – Women and Russian Literature*, Indiana University Press, Bloomington, 1987.

Table 5.1 **Percentage of women in Eastern European parliaments, 1988 and 1990–91 (single chamber or lower chamber)**

Country	1988	1990–91
Albania	28.8	6.2
Bulgaria	21.0	8.5
Czechoslovakia	29.5	6.0
GDR	32.2	20.5
Hungary	20.9	7.0
Poland	20.2	13.3
Romania	34.4	3.5
USSR	34.5	15.6
Average	27.7	10.1

Source: United Nations Office at Vienna. Centre for Social Development and Humanitarian Affairs, *Women in Politics and Decision-Making in the Late Twentieth Century*, Martinus Nijhoff Publishers, Dordrecht, 1992, p. 16.

of social and economic factors.[15] Concern about Russia's declining population in 1992 and 1993 has fed these conservative attitudes. High abortion and divorce rates, and the large number of childless women, worry nationalists and demographers.[16] Feminists, realising that the demographic lobby poses a threat to women's rights, have attempted to counter its influence in the legislative bodies.[17]

In political terms, the effect of the transitional period and the reforms in Russia has been further to exclude women from the decision-making process. Indeed, the sharp drop in the proportion of women in national legislatures since the abolition of a one-party state is a phenomenon common to all countries of Eastern Europe, as Table 5.1 shows. The reasons for this are twofold: first, and most obviously, the abolition of a system of quotas, or reserved seats, for women as well as for other social groups cut their numbers in national legislative bodies. But the abolition of quotas was part of a more fundamental shift towards giving legislatures more genuine power and making elections more democratic. Whilst less representative of society in terms of its class and gender composition, Russian parliaments since 1989 have better reflected the true distribution of power in society. In this sense, rather than representing a victory for women's rights, the old quota system had served to disguise the true nature of their access to power. With the abolition of quotas, however, tokenism was overtaken

15. For examples of conservative attitudes to women, see Aleksandr Solzhenitsyn 'Kak nam obustroit' Rossiiu?', *Komsomol'skaia pravda, Literaturnaia gazeta*, 18 September 1990; Valentin Rasputin 'Cherchez la femme', *Nash sovremennik*, 3, 1990, pp. 168–72; Tat'iana Okulova 'Nam dobrye zheny i dobrye materi nuzhny', *ibid*, pp. 173–87.
16. Vadim Pervyshin, *Rossiiskaia gazeta*, 10 July 1993. Pervyshin has used the same data to support allegations of a deliberate policy to annihilate Russians: 'Istreblenie', *Molodaia gvardiia*, 8, 1993.
17. Anastasia Posadskaya 'Self-portrait of a Russian feminist', *New Left Review*, 195, 1992, p. 15.

by the problem of other constraints on women entering politics. These included women's limited access to resources and expertise, widespread prejudice against female politicians, and women's disinclination to undertake political activity in the face of the mounting struggle to cope with domestic problems.[18]

Given the economic pressures to return to a domestic role, the strengthening traditional ideologies, and women's 'false consciousness', it is fair to comment, with economist Lynn Turgeon, that: 'the model for women in former command economies is one that also applied to women in capitalist economies before the Cold War and women's liberation.'[19]

The Women's Movement

The activists who formed 'Women of Russia' to fight the December 1993 elections had concluded that a radical strategy of forming an all-women electoral bloc was the only way to increase the number of women in parliament, given the evident unwillingness of other parties to field women candidates.[20] Their success was remarkable. Defying predictions, 'Women of Russia' managed to collect more than the 100,000 signatures required to stand.[21] In the elections themselves on 12 December, they took 8.1 per cent of the vote for party lists in the State Duma (which translated into 21 seats), and also gained three seats from contests in the single-mandate districts. Without the efforts of 'Women of Russia', only 5 per cent of deputies elected to the State Duma in December 1993 would have been women: this projected figure equals the proportion of women in the RSFSR Congress of People's Deputies elected in March 1990.

The experience of the 'Women of Russia' electoral bloc in Russia's 1993 elections was, therefore, crucially important in demonstrating how female activists in post-Communist societies can increase their influence in the national legislatures and thereby defend threatened women's rights. The problems of the 'double burden' and women's periodic exclusion from the labour market can be resolved successfully only in societies where implicit patriarchal assumptions that women bear sole responsibility for domestic tasks and child care are challenged. This challenge can be facilitated by state intervention, and one mechanism enabling this is to increase women's representation in national legislatures. But strategies to raise the number of women in Parliament do not, necessarily, culminate in a challenge to patriarchal systems. The aims and policies of 'Women of Russia' demonstrate, paradoxically, that

18. Galina Sillaste 'Glavnaia pobeda dlia zhenshchin – ne dat' sebia pobedit',' *Novaia ezhednevnaia gazeta*, 2 July 1993; Iraida Stekol'shchikova 'Pora razbit' stekliannyi potolok', *Cheboksarskie novosti*, 6 November 1993.
19. Lynn Turgeon, 'Afterword' in Moghadam (ed.) *Democratic Reform*, p. 357.
20. New political formations throughout Eastern Europe have been accused of treating women's rights as 'at best of secondary importance, at worst a luxury or a non-necessity' Barbara Einhorn, *ibid*, p. 56.
21. In a survey of parties, *Izvestiia*, 28 October 1993, predicted that 'Women of Russia' would not manage to gather sufficient signatures to qualify, citing the low level of organisation and political activity among its members. The group in fact collected 130,000 signatures (*Nezavisimaia Gazeta*, 9 November 1993).

women who gain political power can actually risk reinforcing the stereotypes about women's role.

The development of both the unofficial, and the official, women's movements in Russia suggests the context from which the 'Women of Russia' movement emerged. The first attempt to question the nature of Soviet women's emancipation was made in the 1970s in a *samizdat* journal entitled *Zhenshchiny i Rossiia: al'manakh zhenshchinam o zhenshchinakh* (Women and Russia: an almanac for women about women). Like feminists in the United States a decade earlier, its editors emerged from dissident (civil rights) circles, disillusioned by the prevailing patriarchal attitudes they had experienced there. Unlike United States feminists, four of the editors were deported, and the *al'manakh* itself was suppressed.[22]

Subsequently, under Gorbachev, a relaxation in ideological and cultural controls allowed similar independent women's groups to form. The regime's awareness that it had to address the issues of female employment, marital breakdown and the possible connection between them, allowed Russian feminist academics their first opportunity to voice fundamental criticisms of the system. They drew attention to the existing stereotyped roles for women, and for men. In the article '*Kak my reshaem zhenskii vopros*' ('How we resolve the woman question'), published in 1989 in *Kommunist*, radical criticisms previously made only by dissident groups, such as the editors of the *al'manakh*, were heard in official organs for the first time.[23] The views of these academics were solicited by the Soviet government in 1989, leading, the following year, to the establishment of a new research institute, the Centre for Gender Studies, under the aegis of the USSR Academy of Sciences' Institute of Socio-economic Studies of the Population.[24]

Among informal women's groups which emerged to question the Soviet system from a feminist perspective were the Independent Women's Democratic Initiative (known by its acronym *NeZhDI*, which means 'Don't Wait!'), founded in 1990, whose slogan was 'Democracy without women is no democracy!'; and the Independent Women's Forum of the Soviet Union, which held its first meeting in 1991, and established a permanent structure in December 1992.[25] In addition to these groups pursuing a feminist agenda, other informal women's organisations emerged, such as professional associations, or conservative groups urging women to adopt a more traditional role.[26]

22. Issue 1 of the *al'manakh* was published in English as *Women and Russia: First Feminist Samizdat*, Sheba Feminist Publishers, London, 1980. Mamonova *Women and Russia op. cit.* is a collection of essays by Russian feminists, many involved in the *al'manakh*.
23. N. Zakharova, A. Posadskaia, N. Rimashevskaia, 'Kak my reshaem zhenskii vopros', *Kommunist*, 4 March 1989, pp. 56–65.
24. Posadskaya 'Self-portrait of a Russian feminist', *op. cit.*, pp. 10–11.
25. The founding documents of *NeZhDI* and the Women's Independent Forum were published in *Feminist Review*, 39, Winter 1991, pp. 127–32 and 146–48; on the Forum, see also the articles by Ruth Steele in *The Guardian*, 4 April 1991, 14 December 1992, 1 November 1993.
26. Mary Buckley 'Political reform' in Buckley (ed.) *Perestroika and Soviet Women*, Cambridge University Press, Cambridge, 1992; Ol'ga Lipovskaia, 'New women's organisations', *ibid*; Gail Warshofsky Lapidus, 'Gender and restructuring', *op. cit.*, p. 154.

The Soviet state consistently denied that there was a need for a women's movement to encourage female emancipation, for that problem was held to have been solved by the end of economic exploitation. At various times during the Soviet period, however, women's movements were established, or abolished, at the behest of the Communist Party in order to mobilise women in support of the state and encourage them to meet its need for women as workers, or women as mothers. The first such movement was the *Zhenotdel* (women's section), founded in 1919, which aimed to encourage women's political activity in the new Soviet institutions. The *Zhenotdel* was abolished in the 1930s as Stalinism took hold. In 1941, however, the Anti-Fascist Soviet Women's Committee was established to increase support for the war effort. This body continued to function after the war, largely in a foreign public relations capacity, and was renamed the Soviet Women's Committee (SWC) in 1956. A second type of officially sanctioned women's organisation, the *Zhensovety* (women's councils), had existed at a local level since before the war. Under Khrushchev, and again under Gorbachev, these bodies were revived as part of the general trend towards democratising the system. In 1986, they were placed under the aegis of the SWC, thereby attaining national status. In the 1989 elections to the USSR Congress of People's Deputies, the SWC proposed 75 women, nominated by the *Zhensovety*, to fill their quota of the 750 seats reserved for social organisations.[27]

Because these official organisations had been founded in support of the state, they excited suspicion amongst the feminist groups emerging under *perestroika*. They accused the *Zhensovety* and the SWC of being 'anti-democratic', of harbouring the *nomenklatura* and of failing to challenge women's role as subjects, but not agents, of political change.[28] By the late *perestroika* period, these accusations against the state-sponsored women's movements were unjustified. By 1991, for example, the SWC, under its new leader, Alevtina Fedulova, was threatening to go into 'constructive opposition' if its legislative initiatives on women's and children's issues were not discussed. The SWC also began working to prepare women for political office in an attempt to counter the precipitous decline in the number of women in politics since reforms began, and it called for the reintroduction of quotas for women in parliament.[29] Finally, it was the SWC, renamed the Union of Women of Russia in February 1992, which formed the basis of the 'Women of Russia' electoral bloc in the December 1993 elections.

The December 1993 elections

These elections, and the constitutional referendum held simultaneously with them, formally legitimised a new Russian legislature and constitution, which replaced the

---

27. Alena Heitlinger *Women and State Socialism*, Macmillan, London, 1979, pp. 56–64; Genia Browning, 'The Zhensovety revisited' in Buckley (ed.) *Perestroika and Soviet Women, op. cit.*, 1992, pp. 97–117.
28. Konstantinova, 'The women's movement in the USSR', *op. cit.*, pp. 205–6; Posadskaya, 'Changes in gender discourses and policies in the former Soviet Union', *op. cit.*, p. 167; Posadskaya interview, *Feminist Review, op. cit.*, p. 136.
29. Fedulova interviewed in *Izvestiia*, 6 August 1991; Buckley, 'Political reform', *op. cit.*, p. 67.

old Soviet era institutions. They also marked the imposition, by force, of a functioning form of democracy to replace the stalemate between presidency and Supreme Soviet which had lasted most of 1993 and had culminated in the seige and shelling of the old legislature. The results of the 1993 elections demonstrated a prevailing disillusion with conventional politics and politicians. Nostalgia for the certainties of the pre-reform period, and a preference for simplistic, extremist policies influenced the election victories of the new Communist Party of the Russian Federation and of Vladimir Zhirinovskii's Liberal Democratic Party. The success of the 'Women of Russia' electoral bloc may also be explained in terms of a rejection of conventional politics. It is significant that the pre-election campaign of this non-traditional political movement focused on the private sphere and the family, rather than on wider political issues.

'Women of Russia' was formed specifically to fight the elections, with the aim of increasing the number of women in Parliament to make it more representative of the electorate and encourage the consideration of issues affecting women.[30] The impetus behind the decision to found 'Women of Russia' had been provided by the abysmal response to a campaign by women's activists to persuade parties to field women candidates and represent women's issues in the election. Their suspicion that these other parties would not represent women was quite justified. Women constituted only 8.8 per cent of all candidates on the lists of parties or blocs other than 'Women of Russia', which stood in the elections, and they rarely occupied high positions on those lists, further reducing their chances of election. Table 5.2 shows the role of women in the major parties (other than 'Women of Russia') standing for election. For only two of these parties did women constitute more than 10 per cent of the list: the Communist Party (10.6 per cent) and the Iabloko (Iavlinskii, Boldyrev, Lukin) bloc (13.4 per cent). For most parties, particularly those representing sectors traditionally dominated by men, such as agriculture or manufacturing industry (the Agrarian Party, Civic Union), women represented a negligible proportion of candidates. There was a relatively high number of women on the Iabloko list because the bloc included the Social Democratic Party which had promised representation to 15 women from the Independent Women's Forum.[31]

The 'Women of Russia' electoral bloc, which also registered itself as a political movement, united three major national women's organisations: the Union of Women of Russia; the Union of Women in the Navy; and the Association of Businesswomen of Russia. These organisations retained their independence after the formation of 'Women of Russia' and are active at a local level in their specific fields. They also consult regularly with their representatives in the Duma. Other women's groups, such as the Women's Independent Forum, refused formally to join Women of Russia, despite repeated invitations.[32] The Forum did, however, cooperate with candidates from 'Women of Russia' at a local level as part of its campaign to improve the chances of all women from any party standing for election.[33]

30. Interview with Alevtina Fedulova, *Solidarnost'*, 10, 1994; interview with Ekaterina Lakhova, Ostankino Television, 20 July 1994.
31. Ruth Steele, *The Guardian*, 1 November 1993.
32. Author's interview with Ekaterina Lakhova, 17 November 1994.
33. Ruth Steele, *The Guardian*, 1 November 1993.

Table 5.2 **Women on lists from other parties standing in December 1993 elections**

Party	% Women on party list	Highest position of woman on list	Total elected to Duma from party list	Number of women
Agrarian Party	4.8	70	20	0
Iabloko*	13.4	8	20	2
Civic Union	3.3	5	0	0
Communist Party of the Russian Federation	10.6	4	31	3
Democratic Party of Russia	6.6	9	14	1
Russian Movement for Democratic Reforms	7.8	20	0	0
Liberal Democratic Party	6.1	31	60	5
Party of Russian Unity and Concord	3.6	60	18	0
Russia's Choice	7.1	3	41	2

*The Iabloko bloc included the Social Democratic Party, which was the chosen vehicle for the political ambitions of fifteen women from the Independent Women's Forum. Ruth Steele, *The Guardian*, 1 November 1993.
Source: Calculations from *Rossiiskaia Gazeta*, 12 November 1993.

Alevtina Fedulova attributed the remarkable success of 'Women of Russia' to local women's networks and grass-roots activism: 'We relied on women's groups all over the country, and they waged a powerful word-of-mouth campaign. Women told women, families told families, and people were convinced. Politics will never be the same here again.'[34]

The result of the poor representation of women in other parties was that, whilst 'Women of Russia' achieved 21 of the 225 seats in the State Duma contested by proportional representation from party lists (9.3 per cent), a mere 13 women from other parties also won seats on that basis (5.8 per cent). Of the remaining 225 seats in the Duma, contested in single-mandate districts, 26 (11.9 per cent) of the 219 seats elected went to women, three of whom belonged to 'Women of Russia'. Overall, therefore, women took 60 seats in the State Duma, or 13.5 per cent. This figure

34. Alevtina Fedulova, quoted in *The Chicago Tribune*, 17 December 1993.

Table 5.3 **Percentage of women in Soviet/Russian parliaments 1984–94**

Body	Date of election	Percentage of women
USSR Supreme Soviet	March 1984	31.9
(i) Soviet of the Union		30.0
(ii) Soviet of Nationalities		33.2
USSR Congress of People's Deputies	March 1989	15.7
USSR Supreme Soviet		18.5
(i) Soviet of the Union		16.2
(ii) Soviet of Nationalities		20.7
RSFSR Congress of People's Deputies	March 1990	5.4
RSFSR Supreme Soviet		7.5
(i) Soviet of the Republic		8.7
(ii) Soviet of Nationalities		6.4
Russian Federation Federal Assembly	Dec. 1993	11.2
(i) State Duma		13.5
(ii) Federation Council		5.2

Sources: Mary Buckley, 'Political Reform' in Buckley (ed.) *Perestroika and Soviet Women.* Cambridge University Press, Cambridge, 1992, p. 57; calculations from lists in BBC Monitoring Service, *Composition of the USSR Supreme Soviet, 1984 Convocation.* BBC Data Publishers, 1984; *Rossiiskaia Gazeta*, 28 December 1993.

was only slightly below the proportion of women in the 1989 USSR Congress of People's Deputies, in which seats had been reserved for women's organisations. The proportion of women in the Duma was also well above that in the RSFSR Congress of People's Deputies, elected in 1990, in which no seats were reserved for women, or any other group. Nine women (or 5.2 per cent of the total) were elected to the upper house of the new Russian parliament, the Federation Council, which consisted of two representatives from each of Russia's 89 republics and regions. This figure reflects the low number of women occupying top local executive or legislative posts, from which the new deputies to the Federation Council were generally drawn.[35] The fluctuations in women's representation in Soviet and Russian legislatures since 1984 are summarised in Table 5.3. This demonstrates the dramatic fall in the number of women in Parliament with the partial, and then total, abolition of quotas in 1989 and 1990, and the rise in women's representation in 1993, largely due to the efforts of 'Women of Russia'.

35. Author's calculations from lists of newly elected deputies published in *Rossiiskaia Gazeta*, 28 December 1993.

Women's underrepresentation in national legislatures is a global phenomenon, reflecting the structural and situational barriers limiting women's access to political power.[36] The Inter-Parliamentary Union has calculated that, as of June 1993, only 10.3 per cent of the world's parliamentarians in lower chambers or single-chamber legislatures were women. Various strategies have been devised in some countries to increase the number of women in the national legislature, such as reserving parliamentary seats for women, setting quotas within political parties, or creating women's sections in parties to assist women who wish to stand for election. Advocates of such measures suggest that they provide a way of encouraging women to enter politics; opponents counter that they encourage tokenism and avoid the underlying issues of why women are underrepresented.

In Russia, the reintroduction of a system of reserved seats for women in the legislature is a topic of debate amongst women's organisations and has, in the past, been advocated by some of the current members of 'Women of Russia'.[37] This policy has not been adopted by the movement, however. Informally, its leaders say they aim to see women occupy one-third of posts in decision-making bodies, taking the Scandinavian countries as their model. Ekaterina Lakhova, chairperson of the 'Women of Russia' faction in the Duma, suggested that the movement would welcome the introduction of quotas for women in political parties – another measure which has been successful in Scandinavia. She pointed out that in Europe it took decades to form strong women's sections within political parties, and claimed that in Russia in December 1993, a women-only party was the only possible way to reverse the precipitous decline in women's representation in the legislature, given that the established political parties did not feel it imperative to encourage women's representation.[38]

The issue of quotas is a delicate one in Russia, for it is argued that, under the Soviet system they actually worked against women by discrediting those in Parliament as unelected 'puppet women' or formidable 'iron ladies', obedient to the interests of the state rather than concerned with women's issues.[39] Women wishing to enter politics in Russia today confront ingrained prejudices against perceiving them as competent politicians. These prejudices are manifested, for example, in the claim that women deputies were 'decorative' rather than effective in the old legislature; the idea that women's 'feminine qualities' might exert a 'softening' and civilising influence on the tough, amoral business of politics; or the claim that women are by nature incapable of separating their personal emotions from their professional activity.[40] Fedulova pointed out the principal flaw in this argument, which is that

---

36. United Nations Office at Vienna Centre for Social Development and Humanitarian Affairs, *Women in Politics and Decision-Making in the Late Twentieth Century*, Martinus Nijhoff Publishers, Dordrecht, 1992, pp. 34–40.

37. Galina Sillaste, '*Kuda dvizhetsia zhenskoe dvizhenie?*' *Izvestiia*, 30 October 1990; report on the Tenth Russian–German Mulheim Conference in *Literaturnaia gazeta*, 13 October 1993; Fedulova quoted in Reuters, 22 October 1993.

38. Author's interview with Lakhova.

39. Programme of *NeZhDI*, *Feminist Review* 39, Winter 1991, p. 129.

40. *Segodnia*, 5 October 1993; *Komsomol'skaia pravda*, 11 November 1993; *Pravda*, 16 December 1993.

the entire legislative body under the Soviet system played a largely symbolic role, for 'in the former Supreme Soviet it was not just women who were a decoration but men too.'[41]

The new parliamentary deputies from 'Women of Russia' recognised that, in this context, their activity would either 'discredit the women's movement or strengthen it.'[42] Lakhova has described 'Women of Russia's' greatest achievement as 'the fact that we have been accepted', and declared that the parliamentary deputies have proved that 'women in parliament have the strength to work as well as, or perhaps even better than, men.'[43] This is not to say that they are immune from the occasional sexual innuendo. In September 1994, 'Women of Russia' was reported to have won a court case against the weekly journal, *Sobesednik*, which had claimed that members of the parliamentary faction had decided to 'withhold their conjugal obligations' in order to exert pressure on the parliamentary resolution of social issues.[44]

The candidates

The composition of the 'Women of Russia' electoral list offers a clearer picture of the sort of women who constitute the parliamentary faction. Candidates were listed together with their date of birth, profession and geographical area, allowing them to be categorised as follows: professional politicians (at a local or federal level); business women (running either state, newly privatised, or private businesses); women engaged in charity or social organisations; academics; women in the arts; and women employed in the medical profession. All had attained top positions in their chosen fields. In 1993, the average age of the women on the list was 45.5 years. Around half of them (47 per cent) came from Moscow, or the Moscow oblast.

The breakdown of the list by occupation, as shown in Table 5.4, implies that women in Russia are most likely to attain political power at a national level if they

Table 5.4 **Distribution of candidates from 'Women of Russia', according to occupation**

'Women of Russia' candidates occupation	Number	Percentage
Politicians	11	30
Business women	11	30
Heads of charity/social organisations	5	13
Academics	4	11
Women in the arts	3	8
Medical professionals	3	8
Total	37	100

Source: Calculations from *Rossiiskaia Gazeta*, 12 November 1993.

41. *Rossiiskie vesti*, 3 December 1993.
42. Interview with Fedulova, *ITAR–TASS* 10 December 1993.
43. Author's interview with Lakhova.
44. Radio Rossii, 27 September 1994.

have already achieved prominence in other fields. Positions which allowed women to wield economic power, such as business management, or political power, such as local government, were most likely to provide them with a means of entering federal-level politics. Other fields from which women came included the nurturing or creative professions in which they are well-represented, such as medicine, the arts, or charity organisations. Only two of 'Women of Russia's' candidates had served in the former Russian federal parliament. Lakhova, a Supreme Soviet deputy, and Fanuza Arslanova, elected to represent the Iamalo-Nenetsk Republic in the Congress of People's Deputies.

'Women of Russia' selected its best-known candidates – Fedulova, Lakhova and Natalia Gundareva – to head its party list. The first three names on party lists were included on the actual ballot paper, and were therefore most important in attracting voters. Fedulova had led the Young Pioneers organisation and the *Komsomol* from 1971 to 1984, before being elevated from the position of deputy to head the Committee of Soviet Women in February 1991. She had served on the Central Committee of the CPSU in 1990 and 1991. Lakhova, also a member of the CPSU, trained as a doctor; had been elected to the Russian Supreme Soviet from Sverdlovsk in 1990, where she had been part of Yeltsin's team; and was Advisor to Yeltsin on Women, Families and Children. Gundareva was a well-known cinema and theatre actress.

As can be seen from this brief biographical information, the two leading members of 'Women of Russia' have wide political experience. In 1992, Lakhova was described as 'very hostile' to the Union of Women of Russia; she has also been termed Fedulova's 'opponent'.[45] It could be argued, however, that both have emerged from that section of the Soviet establishment which supported reforms. When asked about discord within the Duma faction, Lakhova denied that there were any internal conflicts, whilst admitting that complete harmony was unlikely within any group of successful women.[46] It appears that the principal aim of the group – to raise the profile of women in Russian politics – still overrides disagreements about, for example, tactics or economic policy. Existing as they do in a hostile environment, the members of the 'Women of Russia' faction cannot afford to squander their energies or damage their reputation by infighting. In this sense, the organisation recalls the dynamic of the democratic movement in the *perestroika* period in its struggle to wrest power from the CPSU.

Women in leadership

Having gained admission to the legislature, how successful were women in rising to positions of influence there? One measurement of this is the leadership of parliamentary committees. Women were elected to be committee chairpersons, or deputy chairpersons, roughly in proportion to their representation in the Duma as a

---

45. Posadskaya 'Self-portrait of a Russian feminist', *op. cit.*, p. 11; Ella Shcherbanenko 'Budut li u nas "zhelezhye ledi"?', *Pravda*, 16 December 1993.
46. Author's interview with Lakhova.

whole. Three of the 23 committees were chaired by women; and 11 of the 70 available positions of committee deputy chairperson were allocated to women (15.7 per cent). In addition, the aim of 'Women of Russia' to see a woman occupy one of the three posts of Duma deputy chairperson was realised in the person of Fedulova.[47] Thus 14.8 per cent of top-level posts in the Duma went to women (compared with 13.5 per cent of women in the Duma as a whole).

The posts which women occupy are, however, concentrated in the sphere of female responsibilities, as defined by the ethos of the Soviet era: social affairs, the family, youth, education and health. Women chair the committees of Health Protection (Bela Denisenko from 'Russia's Choice'); Education, Culture and Science (Liubov' Rozhkova from 'New Regional Policy' – a non-party faction); and Women's Affairs, Family and Youth (Galina Klimantova from 'Women of Russia'). Two of the three deputy chairpersons on each of the committees for Labour and Social Protection; Health Protection; and Women's Affairs, Family and Youth are women. (The remaining five female deputy chairpersons serve on the Committees for Ecology, International Affairs, Natural Resources, Security, and Social and Religious Organisations.) This pattern is repeated in the Federation Council, where the Social Policy Committee is chaired by Galina Karelova. In the executive, too, women are found almost exclusively in the social sphere. The only female government minister is the Minister for Social Protection (this 'female' post was first occupied by Aleksandra Kollontai). In May 1994, Liudmila Bezlepkina was appointed to head the ministry; her predecessor, Ella Pamfilova, became Chair of the Council for Social Policy under the President after resigning from the Ministry for Social Protection. Ekaterina Lakhova chairs the Commission for Questions of Women, Families and Demography attached to the President's Office. Finally, Tat'iana Regent is the head of the Federal Migration Service: an agency concerned primarily with the welfare of refugees. The pattern which emerges is depressingly similar to that of women's standard political roles in the West.

Evidently, in Russia, women in positions of leadership are concentrated over-whelmingly in social policy, which is perceived as the natural sphere for their contribution to public life, and indeed constitutes a virtual ghetto for women in the elite. In July 1994, for example, at a conference of women's organisations, Vladimir Shumeiko, chairman of the Federation Council, encouraged women's organisations and women in political bodies to be more active in influencing social policy.[48] However, it is in social policy that changes are essential before women can participate equally with men in other areas. It is therefore important to examine how 'Women of Russia' approaches issues of social policy and what significance they have for the faction.

In their pre-election broadcasts and subsequent interviews, spokeswomen from 'Women of Russia' explained that the movement aimed to influence state policy on 'women's issues', which were neglected by the other parties where women were poorly represented.[49] During the election campaign, 'Women of Russia' proposed

---

47. *Rossiiskie vesti*, 10 January 1994. The list of committee chairpersons and deputy chairpersons was carried in *Rossiiskaia gazeta*, 26 January 1994.
48. Radio Rossii, 7 July 1994.
49. Ostankino Television 17 and 20 July 1994; *Solidarnost*, 10, 1994.

that social provisions, including housing and consumer goods, should be made a government priority. The movement's economic programme included fixing prices for essential goods, including baby food; lowering taxes on basic goods; and reducing wage differentials.[50] In their election campaign broadcasts, however, 'Women of Russia' also stated that they did not advocate privileges for women, and did not 'acknowledge female or male policy'.[51]

During the first six-month session of the State Duma, the 'Women of Russia' parliamentary faction claims to have adhered to this policy of tackling social issues in general rather than those relating specifically to women, such as female unemployment. Lakhova stated that the faction aims, rather, to tackle current psychological patterns and patriarchal attitudes 'through the family, since 90 per cent of people live in families'. When asked to identify policies which 'Women of Russia' had pursued in the Duma, she emphasised their 'categorical opposition to the privatisation of the social sector', for, whilst in favour of private property, the faction believes that state control is essential in spheres such as education and the health service. Its members opposed the first reading of the budget because of insufficient social provisions, and successfully lobbied for an amendment to Article 43 of the Constitution, reinstituting the Soviet guarantee of full, free secondary education. Other initiatives singled out by Lakhova included 'Women of Russia's' advocacy of an amnesty for both political and criminal prisoners, in order to avoid causing potentially damaging rifts between the Duma and the President, and its support for the presidential 'Treaty on National Accord'.[52]

Conclusion

'Women of Russia' thus does not pursue women-centred policies or fight for an exclusive platform of female electors. Its deputies are gradually changing ingrained perceptions about women in politics, working hard to be taken seriously. When compared with women's traditional political roles, however, their policies are revealed as conforming to the stereotype by emphasising social issues and advocating conciliatory tactics. The establishment of a women-only party, which has been successful in gaining parliamentary seats through fighting a democratic election, rather than filling reserved seats, appears to be a unique experiment in the global women's movement. Separatist politics tend to have a poor record in established democracies and the unexpected success of 'Women of Russia' demonstrates the fluidity of political structures and parties in Russia, and the general disillusion with traditional politics. 'Women of Russia' was careful to avoid addressing itself exclusively to women or appearing in any way segregationist in its election campaign. Instead, it tackled the quotidian concerns of the electors, particularly about social provision and the availability of basic consumer goods. The paradox of 'Women of Russia' is that, whilst its members have begun to challenge the negative expectations of women in politics, their concentration on social issues risks strengthening the perception of women as primarily responsible for this area, in both the private and public spheres.

50. Ostankino Television, 1 and 3 December 1993; interview with Irina Vyborovna, *Delovoi mir*, 7 December 1993.
51. Fedulova, quoted in *ITAR-TASS*, 10 December 1993.
52. Author's interview with Lakhova. These issues related to the aftermath of the violent confrontation between presidency and former Parliament in October 1993.

Chapter 6

SOCIAL RESPONSES TO REFORM IN RUSSIA

Stephen Whitefield

Since the beginning of *perestroika* in 1985, and especially after the failed conservative coup of 1991, Russians have been grappling with reforms which have transformed the environment in which they now work, raise families, save and consume, participate in and relate to the governing authorities, and regard the rest of the world. Six dimensions of change have been of particular importance. First, market mechanisms were introduced which entailed liberalisation of commodity prices as well as the diminution of state control of the economy, raising the attendant possibilities of unemployment and bankruptcy. Second, privatisation has been pursued with the stated aim of creating owners with a stake in their property and society: however, the policy in practice has frequently been attacked for leading to corruption, insider dealing, and growing inequalities of wealth. Third, the political system has been transformed from one-party authoritarian rule to an emerging system of multi-party and multi-candidate competition for control over political institutions which were designed on the model of liberal democracies. Fourth, alongside this, individuals and social organisations have been afforded the opportunity to speak out in defence of their own views and, often, against those of the authorities and prevalent opinion. Fifth, the last 10 years have witnessed a massive opening to the West, involving not only greater economic, political and security cooperation but also the import of a new set of market liberal democratic norms to legitimate private and public relationships. Finally, at the same time, the former Soviet Union disintegrated and Russia has emerged as an independent state.

Much of the academic research into the transformation in the former Soviet Union has focused on elite behaviour and conflict.[1] Without wishing to deny the importance of this approach, this chapter concentrates on the subjective responses of the citizens of Russia to these transformations. As such, it adds to a growing body of work which has emerged since it became politically possible for former Soviet and Western

---

1. See, for example, G. Gill 'The sources of political reform in the Soviet Union', *Studies in Comparative Communism*, 24, 1991, pp. 235–58; P. Roeder *Red Sunset: The Failure of Soviet Politics*, Princeton University Press, Princeton, 1993; R. Bova 'Political dynamics of the post-communist transition: a comparative perspective', *World Politics* 44 1991, pp. 113–38; D. Lane and C. Ross, 'The social background and political allegiance of the political elite of the Supreme Soviet of the USSR: the terminal stage, 1984 to 1991', *Europe–Asia Studies*, 46, 1994, pp. 437–63.

researchers to collect data about individual reactions of ordinary citizens to change.[2] Most of the literature on mass attitudes, however, has so far tended to focus on the structure of beliefs and not on the social factors which underpin them; and even where respondents' backgrounds have been taken into account, only a few variables – mainly age, education and income – have been considered. In what follows, much greater attention is given than before to the breadth of social distinctions among Russians which might influence their attitudes towards reform.

Elite and popular-based studies do not, and should not, comprise mutually exclusive approaches to the study of transition. It is important to study mass attitudes because, especially in conditions of the market and democracy, classes, strata and mass organisations can act as independent economic and political players. Even if the interests of elites remain dominant in setting the agenda for change, absolute levels of support among the public for policies can constitute a limit to how far elites can push. The results of the December 1993 elections afford a perfect example of this, when quite contrary to the expectations of radical groups then dominating policy-making in Russia, the electorate opted for parties supporting more gradual or even negative approaches to economic reform.

The aim of this chapter is to provide a view of how Russians are responding to the various kinds of reforms outlined above. It is not to be expected that each era of change is taken up with equal enthusiasm (or lack of it) or that the pattern of support for change among different elements in society is uniform across reform dimensions. Support for democracy, for example, might be weakly or evenly inversely correlated with support for the market or with freedom of speech. Entrepreneurs may be highly supportive of privatisation but workers may be the most (or least) nationalist). Moreover, it is important to bear in mind all of the inter-relationships and overlapping affiliations and identities of individuals before drawing conclusions about real associations between their position in society and their attitude towards change. Women, for example, are widely perceived to have been disproportionately affected by the negative effects of change. How far is this true, particularly when all

---

2. See William M. Reisinger, Arthur Miller, Vicki L. Hesli and Kristen Hill Mayer 'Political values in Russia, Ukraine and Lithuania; sources and implications for democracy', *British Journal of Political Science* 24, 1994, pp. 183–223; Raymond Duch 'Tolerating economic reform: popular support for transition to a free market in the former Soviet Union', *American Political Science Review* 88, 1994, pp. 590–608; Arthur Miller, Vicki L. Hesli and William M. Reisinger 'Reassessing mass support for political and economic change in the former USSR', *American Political Science Review* 88, 1994, pp. 399–411; A. Miller, W. Reisinger, and V. Hesli (eds) *Public Opinion and Regime Change: The New Politics of Post-Soviet Societies*, Westview Press, Boulder, Colorado, 1993; R. Dobson and S. Grant 'Public opinion and the transformation of the Soviet Union', *International Journal of Public Opinion Research* 4, 1992, pp. 302–20; J. Gibson, R. Duch and K. Tedin 'Democratic values and the transformation of the Soviet Union'. *The Journal of Politics* 54, 1992, pp. 329–71; J. Gibson and R. Duch 'Anti-semitic attitudes of the mass public: estimates and explanations based on a survey of the Moscow Oblast', *Public Opinion Quarterly* 5, 1992, pp. 1–28; J. Gibson and R. Duch, 'Political intolerance in the USSR: the distribution and etiology of mass opinion', *Comparative Political Studies* 26, 1993, pp. 286–329; J. Hahn 'Continuity and change in Russian political culture', *British Journal of Political Science* 21, 1991, pp. 393–421.

of the things other than gender – such as levels of education and income – which vary among individuals, are controlled for?

The data for this analysis of social responses to reform in Russia is drawn from a national random probability study of adult Russians conducted in the summer of 1993.[3] Names of potential respondents were selected from the list of privatisation vouchers and sampling was stratified first into 10 regions and then into 56 regional settlements. Three call-backs were allowed for each potential respondent. The overall response rate was 85 per cent. The number of respondents included in this analysis is 1,883. The rest of the chapter is divided into three main sections. First, the various dimensions of reform are operationalised from items in the questionnaire and consideration given both to the absolute levels of support for change of the types outlined above and to the relationships among reform dimensions. In addition, a distinction is drawn between *normative* and *evaluative* ways of measuring attitudes. As the analysis shows, absolute levels of support and the pattern of relationships among the reform dimensions vary considerably depending on whether norms or evaluations are under consideration.

Second, each category of reform is then related to the social and other characteristics of respondents. At a theoretical level, commentators investigating the ways in which reform may be impacting on Russian society have singled out attributes such as organisational affiliation, class identity or sectoral location, religion, ethnicity, region and age – in addition to education, income and gender mentioned earlier – as significant predictors of how an individual may be responding to change. Much of the empirical work so far, however, has dealt with only a relatively narrow range of social factors, many of which prove only weakly related to responses to change. Moreover, other analyses have shown social factors to be insignificant once the respondent's other ideological commitments are included in the model. This latter conclusion is not surprising. Attitudes towards the market are almost certain to be closely associated both with attitudes to democracy and, say, the income of the respondent, and if included in a model predicting views of democracy these attitudes are likely to remove income effects. However, it would be wrong to conclude on this basis that income has no effect on views of democracy; rather, the effects of income and other social characteristics of respondents on their ideological commitments can only be reliably estimated when other attitudes are excluded from the model. The section on 'Social responses to reform' provides the most thorough and rigorous examination to date of the impact of social factors and suggests some surprising conclusions, particularly with regard to the importance of regionalism in shaping responses to change.

Finally, consideration is given to the political impact of attitudes to reform and the social characteristics of respondents. Again, the little empirical work published so far on this subject tends to deal with the ideological bases of voting and with only a very

3. The survey was commissioned as part of an Economic and Social Research Council grant (no. Y 309 25 3025) to study 'Emerging forms of political representation and participation in Eastern Europe' awarded to G. Evans, S. Whitefield, A. Heath and C. Payne. The fieldwork in Russia was directed by Professor Vladimir Iadov, director of the Institute of Sociology of the Russian Academy of Sciences with the assistance of Elena Danilova and Sergei Kukterin.

narrow range of social bases to political allegiance.[4] Clearly, the voting intentions of Russians are likely to be in a state of even greater flux than their responses to reform itself. However, the pattern of support for reform and anti-reform figures in the summer of 1993 which emerges does presage the results of the December 1993 elections and illustrates the political difficulties which have been experienced by reformers in Russia.

Dimensions of reform in Russia

Six areas of reform have been highlighted above: democratisation, political liberalisation, marketisation, privatisation, opening to the West, and nation-building. To investigate the responses of Russians to change, questions included in the survey relating to each of these areas are used as the basis for analysis. In order to be sure that underlying attitudes towards a *dimension* of reform were being measured rather than (possibly deviant) responses to single issues, where possible a number of items have been combined to form scales ranging in most cases from strong opposition (1) to 'in between' (3) to highest form of support (5) for the reform in question. These scales were then tested for reliability – in other words, to ensure by measuring the internal consistency of the questions combined that a single underlying concept was being measured. (Details of the questions and reliabilities can be found in Appendix A (p. 112).)

At the same time, a distinction was made between normative and evaluative responses to change. The former relates to how an individual might view an ideal society; the latter, however, concerns how someone might respond to change in practice. It is possible that those with high normative commitment to democracy might feel very frustrated with how their commitments are being translated into practice in Russia. Conversely, those with low normative commitments might evaluate slow progress in implementation of things they do not strongly support in a comparatively positive light. For these reasons, separate normative and evaluative scales have been formed for democracy, political liberalisation, the market and privatisation. The scale for nationalism is essentially normative while the measure of attitudes toward Western involvement is evaluative.[5]

Table 6.1 shows the strength of the correlations between any two of these reform dimensions. What is immediately noticeable is that in almost every case the relationship is both positive and statistically significant. In this sense, Russia differs from some other former communist societies where much weaker associations are evident.[6] A number of factors may account for this strength of association but

4. See Stephen Whitefield and Geoffrey A. Evans 'The Russia election of December 1993: public opinion and the transition experience', *Post-Soviet Affairs*, 10, 1994, pp. 38–60; S. White, I. McAllister and O. Kryshtanovskaya 'El'tsin and his voters: popular support in the 1991 Russian presidential elections and after', *Europe–Asia Studies*, 46, 1994, pp. 285–303; J. Hough 'The Russian election of 1993: public attitudes toward economic reform and democratisation', *Post-Soviet Affairs*, 10, 1994, pp. 1–37.

5. Unfortunately, the questionnaire does not contain items which would allow for this distinction to be drawn with respect to Western involvement, which is measured using a single evaluative question, or nationalism which is measured in a mainly normative manner.

6. See S. Whitefield and G. Evans 'Mass responses to reform in Eastern Europe', Paper presented at the ESRC Conference on Change in Eastern Europe, London 1994.

Table 6.1 **Correlations among dimensions of reform**

	Democratic norms	Democratic evaluation	Liberal norms	Liberal evaluation	Market norms	Market evaluation	Privatise norms	Privatise evaluation	Western influence	Nationalism
Democratic norms	1.00	0.38	0.22	0.21	0.49	0.37	0.33	0.25	0.16	0.17
Democratic evaluation	0.38	1.00	0.08	0.35	0.36	0.54	0.30	0.49	0.28	0.20
Liberal norms	0.22	0.08	1.00	0.07	0.32	0.09	0.27	0.00	0.06	0.15
Liberal evaluation	0.21	0.35	0.07	1.00	0.18	0.20	0.16	0.17	0.13	0.11
Market norms	0.49	0.36	0.32	0.18	1.00	0.48	0.57	0.30	0.27	0.42
Market evaluation	0.37	0.54	0.09	0.20	0.48	1.00	0.40	0.58	0.31	0.28
Privatise norms	0.33	0.30	0.27	0.16	0.57	0.40	1.00	0.28	0.23	0.29
Privatise evaluation	0.25	0.49	0.00	0.17	0.30	0.58	0.28	1.00	0.27	0.18
Western influence	0.16	0.28	0.06	0.13	0.27	0.31	0.23	0.27	1.00	0.37
Nationalism	0.17	0.20	0.15	0.11	0.42	0.28	0.28	0.18	0.37	1.00

the comparative literature suggests that it may be a function of the stage of the transition from communism; when the battle against the old order is still fresh in people's minds or incomplete, one area of reform is more likely to be related to another. The importance of the stage of reform will be further evident below.

Some relationships, however, are particularly strong for survey research where high levels of 'noise' in the answers of respondents is to be expected. This is particularly the case when normative attitudes on one dimension are compared with those on another – and, in the same way, when evaluations are compared across dimensions. For example, democratic norms correlate with market norms at 0.49; democratic evaluation correlates with market evaluation at 0.54; market norms correlate with privatisation norms at 0.57; market evaluation correlates with privatisation evaluation at 0.58; and democratic evaluation correlates with privatisation evaluation at 0.49.

Besides these, other associations are comparatively weak. Democratic norms are only related to nationalism at 0.17 and to attitudes towards Western involvement at 0.16. For those committed to democracy, therefore, these latter areas of reform are clearly less core than some others. The most strikingly weak relationships, however, exist between the two political liberalisation dimensions and the others. Democratic and liberal norms, for example, correlate at only 0.22, while liberal norms and democratic evaluation are related at 0.08. Again, liberal norms and attitudes towards Western influence and nationalism are correlated at only 0.06 and 0.15 respectively. Similarly, liberal evaluation is weakly related to market norms (0.18), privatisation norms (0.16) and privatisation evaluation (0.17).

It is also evident that there is a weaker relationship between normative and evaluative aspects of the same reforms than that which obtains between normative or evaluative dimensions across reforms mentioned above. For example, compared with the figures mentioned above, market norms correlate with market evaluation at 0.48, democratic norms correlate with democratic evaluation at 0.38, liberal norms with liberal evaluation at only 0.07, and privatisation norms with privatisation evaluation at 0.28. Again, the tentative conclusion to be drawn is that different factors are at work underpinning normative commitment from those which explain how Russians respond to change in practice. The next section investigates what these various factors might be.

Social responses to reform

There are numerous theories and hypotheses about the relationship between social position, affiliation and identity and attitudes towards reform in post-communist societies. The most simple might account for the discrepancy just noted between norms and evaluations. The association evident among norms may be the result of certain features of social development which work to support *commitment* to reform. In particular, factors working more or less uniformly across society such as rising education, social participation and secularism, as well as generational replacement, may give rise to far greater openness and receptivity to change as an *ideal*. However, much more precise effects on individuals and specific groups may be more likely to explain how change is evaluated in practice. Here, specifically socially located factors such as income, class identity or sector, region, ethnic group or gender may explain *judgements*. In other words, general factors associated with modernisation in society may account for the ideals of Russians, but diverse actual experience in a job or part of the country may account for their evaluations.

Table 6.2 allows for an initial investigation of the relationship between social position and attitude towards reform. Again using data obtained from the questionnaire, social categories have been constructed. 'Organisation', for example, refers to membership of at least one independent social organisation. Other, separate, organisational variables include trade union membership, membership in the CPSU before its dissolution in 1991, and church attendance over and above religious identities. These categories are included in order to test propositions associated with 'civic society' models of reform which highlight the importance of participation in autonomous groups to the willingness of individuals to support change. Communist Party or trade union membership, of course, might have opposite effects from participation in other kinds of organisation. Following this, there are four occupation-related variables: respondents declared their class identity from a list including working class, entrepreneurs, managers and administrators, peasants and any other category. Sectoral location is comprised of private, which might be expected to be pro-reform; cooperative (including those in coops and collective farms) which might be ambivalent; and state (including those in state industry, state farms and any other state organisation). Those who are dependent on state benefits – students, the unemployed, pensioners and the disabled – are distinguished in these times of high inflation and budgetary difficulties from those on incomes; and household income itself is included as a separate variable. Finally, region, religion, ethnicity and gender allow a range of social positions and identities to be considered. Full details of the coding of these (and other) variables can be found in Appendix B (p. 115).

The first row of Table 6.2 gives information about the mean score for each reform dimension for the population as a whole. While it is important to take care in comparing absolute scores derived from multi-item scales, it is perhaps notable – as well as encouraging from the point of view of the success of the transition – that the means for three of the normative items are above the mid-point of 3 (strong support = 5, support = 4). There is clearly broad support (mean = 3.76) for the values of freedom of speech and of organisation. Levels of commitment to democratic norms are also more than middling at 3.21. Normative support for the market is comparatively lower at 3.19, whilst there is rather more opposition than support for privatisation as an ideal. The rather higher score for democracy, however, ought not to give rise to too much satisfaction among democrats. It seems much easier to argue that there could be a real scale on economic questions, where a score of 3 would indicate commitment to a mixed economy. Democracy, by contrast, is a much more categorical phenomenon, admitting of far fewer degrees. In this sense, the relatively high level of support for democracy may be much more normatively fragile in reality.

The only other dimension for which there is even mild support concerns attitudes towards nationalism (a high score indicates an anti-nationalist position). Opposition to nationalism, it should be noted, does not translate into support for Western involvement. The most notable negative scores, however, are for the evaluative

Table 6.2 Mean scores of independent variables by dependent variable (lowest over highest scores)

	Democratic norms = 3.21	Democratic evaluation = 2.30	Liberal norms = 3.76	Liberal evaluation = 2.95	Market norms = 3.19	Market evaluation = 2.28	Privatise norms = 2.59	Private evaluation = 1.72	Western influence = 2.68	Nationalism = 3.38
Organisation	N = 3.18 Y = 3.56	N = 2.28 Y = 2.40	–	–	N = 3.17 Y = 3.31	N = 2.26 Y = 2.39	N = 2.56 Y = 2.75	N = 2.56 Y = 1.81	–	N = 3.36 Y = 3.51
Trade union	–	–	–	–	–	–	–	–	–	N = 3.34 Y = 3.43
Communist	–	–	–	–	–	–	Y = 2.43 N = 2.63	–	Y = 2.32 N = 2.67	Y = 3.27 N = 3.40
Social group	Peas = 3.06 Entr = 3.48	Peas = 2.15 Entr = 2.55	Peas = 3.56 Entr = 3.97	–	Peas = 2.99 Entr = 3.62	Wor = 2.22 Entr = 2.71	Peas = 2.42 Ent = 3.18	–	–	Peas = 3.18 Entr = 3.51
Sector	–	Oth = 2.56 Priv = 2.78	–	S = 2.89 Oth = 3.22	S = 3.13 Priv = 3.41	Oth = 2.21 Priv = 2.54	Oth = 2.50 Priv = 2.95	–	–	C = 3.31 Priv = 3.52
Benefit	Y = 3.12 N = 3.24	–	Y = 2.97 N = 3.07	–	Y = 3.01 N = 3.25	–	Y = 2.45 N = 2.65	–	Y = 2.46 N = 2.67	Y = 3.26 N = 3.43
Region	Nov = 3.08 Cau = 3.58	Volg = 2.19 Ural = 2.47	Eart = 3.56 Cau = 4.09	SibE = 2.52 Cau = 3.26	Nov = 3.04 Cau = 3.35	Nov = 2.12 SibE = 2.51	E/N = 2.29 Cau = 3.10	Cau = 1.54 SibE = 1.92	Nov = 2.16 SibE = 3.04	Cau = 3.03 SibE = 3.59
Religion	–	–	Orth = 3.67 Ath = 3.87	–	Orth = 3.14 Ath = 3.26	Orth = 2.24 Ath = 2.32	Orth = 2.53 Ath = 2.65	–	–	–
Ethnic	–	–	–	–	–	–	–	–	R = 2.58 NR = 2.86	–
Gender	F = 3.17 M = 3.26	F = 2.24 M = 2.36	F = 3.71 M = 3.81	–	F = 3.14 M = 3.24	F = 2.25 M = 2.33	F = 2.54 M = 2.66	–	–	–

Reported scores are significant at p > .01.

dimensions. The practice of democracy and markets are both judged negatively in practice, as is the availability in reality of political freedoms, and the score for the implementation of privatisation is especially low. Clearly, whatever encouragement to these reforms may be derived from the commitments of Russians, the evaluation of the transition so far is largely negative.

Table 6.2 also provides some preliminary evidence concerning the differential impact of change on society and on the validity of the theories and hypotheses mentioned above. It is worth looking briefly at each social category in turn, bearing in mind that no firm conclusions can be drawn on the basis of the bivariate relations (multivariate regressions are presented later).

First, those respondents with an organisational affiliation do appear to be more likely to show support for a variety of reforms at both the normative and evaluative levels. Being in a group seems to mean either that the individual was already more committed on joining or that participation has the effect of raising the respondent's normative support for reform. And the experience of change of those with such affiliations seems generally to be more positive. Moreover, those in an organisation appear less nationalist than those who are not. It is notable, however, that there appears to be no effect of group affiliation on attitudes towards political liberalism. At the same time, while membership in trade unions produces the same effect with respect to nationalism, in other respects it appears to have no impact. By contrast, having been a member of the Communist Party does appear likely to give rise to greater nationalism and anti-Western sentiment. Interestingly, the only other area of reform in which it appears to matter is with respect to privatisation norms, suggesting that it was not Party rule or the market *per se* but state property which was the core element of communist ideology.

There is a distinctive pattern which emerges from the data on class identity. On most dimensions of reform, peasants show the least, and entrepreneurs the most, support for change. This is probably what one would expect, but it does not apply across the board and, thus, cannot be simply attributed to how peasants in particular might be inclined to answer a questionnaire. Note that there are no significant differences among groups with respect to their evaluation of privatisation – *everyone* seems to think it has proceeded badly – or with respect to Western influence[7] and the evaluation of political liberalisation. Sectoral differences appear on all dimensions except commitment to democracy; again, as expected, those in the private sector are notably pro-reform. The influence of source of income on attitudes seems to be quite distinctive: for each of the first four areas of reform, those on benefits appear to be less normatively committed, though this is not evident

---

7. Although not quite statistically significant, perhaps the most interesting suggestion from these bivariate relations, which again may be seen in other post-communist societies, is the division between the relatively negative view of managers and administrators, on the one hand, and positive entrepreneurs, on the other, with respect to attitudes towards Western involvement. Measurement of this issue is strongly evaluative and the difference between the two groups who are often close together on other issues, may reflect similar expectations but very different experiences of the West in practice. See S. Whitefield, 'Comparing social responses to reforms: Russia, Ukraine, Estonia, and Lithuania', work in progress.

when evaluations are considered. Moreover, those on state benefits seem to be more nationalist and anti-West.

Striking differences also appear on a regional level. High levels of support for reforms are found consistently in the Caucasus, particularly on normative issues, and in Eastern Siberia. These two regions diverge markedly, however, in their assessment of the impact of privatisation in practice and in their views of the importance of national integrity. At the other extreme, the Nizhnii–Novgorod region is frequently the low marker; it has the lowest levels of normative commitment to democracy, the market and private property, and evaluates the market and Western influence comparatively most negatively. Although, again, nothing can be concluded on the basis of these bivariate relationships, three hypotheses suggest themselves which may play some part in an explanation of regional diversity in attitudes. First, that there is something about the specific regional political cultures, their inherited normative identities, which may account for some of these associations. Second, that peculiar local labour market and economic conditions – rates of employment, regional inflation figures – may be at least part of the explanation. Third, and most appealing on the basis of the evidence presented here, is that the pattern is the result of the transition stage in each region. It is a general feature of post-communist societies that norms are high and evaluation low when the transition has yet to begin or is at an early stage.[8] Once reforms have been introduced, the level of normative and evaluative support tends to move in one of two ways; either the reforms work, in which case norms typically fall marginally as people experience the reality but evaluations rise; or reforms fail, in which case *both* norms and evaluation fall steeply. An initial response to the data here, therefore, which fits the evidence about the transition process in the three regions which most clearly emerge in Table 6.2 is that: reform has yet to begin properly in the Caucasus and so is valued as an ideal but criticised in practice; reform has begun in Eastern Siberia and is thought to be working comparatively well; and reform has proceeded without much success in Nizhnii-Novgorod. Given the degree of attention the West has heaped on the last region, it is perhaps surprising and discouraging that it is the area which appears most critical of Western involvement.

The impact of religion, ethnicity and gender seem relatively straightforward. On most dimensions, Orthodoxy appears comparatively less supportive of reform than lack of religious belief. By contrast, only with respect to nationalism, where it is perhaps to be expected, do non-Russians appear to differ from Russians. Finally, there is at least *prima facie* support for the thesis that women and men are likely to have different responses to many reforms, with women showing notably less enthusiasm on the question of democracy and the economic reform in both normative and evaluative ways.

However, as has been indicated already, these bivariate relationships do not provide a conclusive basis on which to assert the existence of significant differences among these social categories. The level of correlation between each of the social categories is not especially high – with the exception of intellectuals and level of education. For this reason, it is not possible to conclude that the apparent differences

---

8.   See G. Evans and S. Whitefield, 'The politics and economics of democratic commitment', *British Journal of Political Science*, forthcoming 1995.

between men and women will remain once differences in their level of education, rates of participation, or social class identity are taken into account. In other words, it may be class differences which account for the variance in support for democracy and not gender at all. Similarly, the regional differences which are evident in Table 6.2 may be the result of the greater presence of peasants or of old people in Nizhnii-Novgorod over the Volga and before the two can be confidently distinguished, these differences must be controlled for.

This is the aim of the regression models presented in Tables 6.3–6.5. These models allow for the *net* impact of any social factor on the reform dimensions to be estimated. The multivariate regression technique allows for a fuller explanation of the reform dimensions, since it is unlikely that attitudes are structured in response to a single cause. Moreover, the effect of any given variable on levels of support is made more certain because the technique removes the distorting effects of other variables.[9] Three statistics are of importance in each of the models presented: a *beta* coefficient is given for each social factor, which provides a standardised estimate of the change in the dependent variable which results from a unit change in the social factor, net of other factors; an estimate of the statistical significance of each of the *beta* coefficients; and an estimate of the amount of the total variance in the dependent variable which is explained by the independent variables in the model – r^2.

Moreover, for each of the reform dimensions in Tables 6.3–6.5, two models are presented. The first estimates the explanatory power of just the organisational, occupational, regional and identity factors; the second adds gender, age, secularism, and education. The purpose in this is to assess whether the latter group of factors, which are less socially located and more connected with modernisation and generational replacement – does indeed have relatively more impact on the r^2 when normative issues are considered, and the former more explanatory power over evaluations.

One feature of all of the models presented below, however, should be noted at the outset. In none of them is there a high r^2 or proportion of variance explained. There is no simple explanation for this. In some cases, the concept of reform may be measured inadequately by the questions in the survey. This is almost certainly the case with those models which are most weakly predictive – democratic norms and liberal evaluation. The likelihood is that the importance of some of the factors which are currently near or achieve significance in the models for each of these dimensions would increase if the measurement problem were overcome. On the other hand, low levels of predictiveness may not simply be wholly an artefact of measurement. While there may be regular differences in the way in which social groups respond to change which can be identified, social factors as a whole may not *in reality* account for much of the individual-level variation in responses. The post-communist world is likely to be highly complex and individuals must form their positions on new issues without great experience or education. Russia may be facing even greater confusion in transition than other post-communist countries, and finds itself at a relatively unadvanced stage in the achievement of reform. In this context, it is interesting to note that the level of

9.   For a more detailed explanation, see M. Lewis-Beck, *Applied Regression: An Introduction*, Sage, Beverly Hills, 1980.

variance in reform dimensions explained by social factors in those countries in which the transition has gone further is greater.[10]

Table 6.3 presents models for the normative aspects of democracy, political liberalism, the market and privatisation. It provides some initial evidence in favour of the view that on normative issues factors associated with modernisation – generational replacement, education, and secularism – are more highly predictive than those of experience in a particular region, part of the social structure or organisation. Gender is included with the first group of variables because it is relatively evenly distributed. For each of the reform dimensions, the addition of the former variables in Model 2 substantially increases the r^2. This is most clear in the case of market and privatisation norms, where r^2 goes from 0.11 to 0.14 and 0.09 to 0.12 respectively; however, again, the underlying concepts are more adequately measured in these cases, so the impact of the addition of the second set of variables on democratic and liberal norms, though evident, may well be underestimated.

Considerable research has already been undertaken in both East and West on the effects of education on support for democratic and market reform, at least at the normative level.[11] Not surprisingly, therefore, each of the full models for the reform dimensions in Table 6.3 shows that education has a strong positive association. (Note that when education is included in the models, the effects of identification with the intelligentsia are removed.) The importance of the finding is nonetheless worth emphasising again. First, the connection of education with support for reform indicates the relative weakness of formal pro-communist official socialisation. Second, though educational levels in the former Soviet Union have been rising over time, the effects of education are net of the effects of age and not just a proxy for it. Third, educational attainment might be considered to be simply an indication of income; however, again the effect of more education is evident even once income levels are controlled for. This is not to say that age and income are unimportant factors in their own right in predicting support for reform. As the table shows, age is of great importance in explaining support for the market and private property – though, interestingly, not democracy or political liberalism – suggesting that the young are much more likely than the old to be able to orient themselves in new economic

10. S. Whitefield 'Comparing social responses to reforms: Russia, Ukraine, Estonia, and Lithuania', work in progress.
11. For Western cross-national evidence, see F.D. Weil 'The variable effects of education on liberal attitudes: a comparative-historical analysis of anti-Semitism using public opinion survey data', *American Sociological Review* 50, 1985, pp. 458–74 and A.F. Heath, B.J. Taylor and G. Toka 'Religion, morality and politics', in R. Jowell, L. Brook and L. Dowds (eds) *International Social Attitudes: the 10th BSA report*, Dartmouth, Aldershot, 1993. For Eastern European findings, see J. Gibson, R. Duch and K. Tedin 'Democratic values and the transformation of the Soviet Union', *The Journal of Politics*, 54, 1992, pp. 329–71; J. Gibson and R. Duch, 'Political intolerance in the USSR: the distribution and etiology of mass opinion', *Comparative Political Studies* 26, 1993, pp. 286–329; A. Miller, V. Hesli and W.M. Reisinger, 'Reassessing mass support for political and economic change in the former USSR', *American Political Science Review* 88, 1994, pp. 399–411; W.M. Reisinger, A. Miller, V. Hesli and K. Hill Mayer, 'Political values in Russia, Ukraine and Lithuania: sources and implications for democracy', *British Journal of Political Science* 24, 1994, pp. 183–223.

Table 6.3 **Predictors of reform norms**

	Democratic Norms		Liberal Norms		Market Norms		Privatistion Norms	
	Model 1	Model 2	Model 1	Model 2	Model 1	Model 2	Model 1	Model 2
Organisation	.01	.01	−.04	−.04	.01	.00	.05	04
Trade Union	.02	.01	−.01	−.01	.03	−.04	−.04	−04
Communist	.04	.03	.00	.02	−.03	−.02	−.07*	−06
Churchgoing	.04	.07*	−.01	.01	.01	.05	.00	02
Entrepreneur	.03	.00	.02	−.02	.05	.01	.06	.03
Intelligentsia	.12**	.06	.14**	.04	.11**	.06	.06	.02
Manager	.01	−.02	.03	−.03	.05	.03	.01	−.01
Peasant	.05	.05	.03	.04	.03	.03	.01	.02
No class	.07	.04	.11**	.06	.11**	.07	.06	.01
Coop	.02	.01	−.01	−.02	.00	−.01	.05	.03
Private	.02	.01	.03	.03	.06	.05	.10**	.09**
Other	.03	.03	.03	.04	−.01	−.02	−.02	.02
Benefit	.00	.04	−.06	−.02	−.09**	−.02	−.08*	.00
Income	.10**	.07	.10**	.07	.22**	.16**	.10**	.03
Ethnic	.05	.04	.05	.04	.10**	.08**	.05	.03
Earth	−.04	−.04	−.02	.01	.03	.04	−.02	−.01
Novgorod	−.03	−.05	−.02	−.03	−.02	−.04	−.03	−.05
East Siberia	.02	.00	.01	−.01	.09*	.08*	.04	.04
West Siberia	.00	.00	−.04	−.04	.00	−.02	.02	.02
Volga	−.03	−.03	.06	.06	−.01	−.01	.09*	.09*
Caucasus	.11**	.11**	.16**	.16**	.06	.05	.16**	.16**
Urals	−.04	−.03	.03	.05	.01	.01	.06	.07*
St Petersburg	−.04	−.04	.07	08*	−.05	−.05	.03	.03
education		.11**		.18**		.10*		.09*
atheist		.07		.07*		.09**		.03
age		.07		.05		.15**		.20*
gender		−.03		−.02		−.05		−.03
Adjusted r^2	.03	.05	.05	.08	.11	.14	.09	.12

*significant at p > .05
**significant at p > .01.

circumstances. Income also turns out to be the most significant factor of all in predicting whether an individual supports the market. Similarly, there are significant effects from atheism in the expected direction on two dimensions. Non-believers are more likely to be politically liberal and market-oriented.

Alongside this evidence for the importance of modernising factors on norms are also indications of the impact of a range of more specific and socially located

Table 6.4 **Predictors of reform evaluation**

	Democratic evaluation		Liberal evaluation		Market evaluation		Privatisation evaluation	
	Model 1	Model 2	Model 1	Model 2	Model 1	Model 2	Model 1	Model 2
Organisation	.04	.04	−.05	−.05	.06	.06	.06*	.06
Trade Union	.07*	.07*	.08*	.08*	.03	.02	.01	.01
Communist	.00	−.01	−.02	−.04	−.07*	−.05	−.07*	−.06
Churchgoing	−.01	.01	.02	.03	.02	.05	.04*	.08*
Entrepreneur	.06	.06	−.03	−.03	.11**	.09*	.05	.04
Intelligentsia	.03	.02	−.01	−.01	.02	.01	.00	.00
Manager	.06	.05	−.04	−.04	.01	.01	.04	.05
Peasant	−.02	−.02	.00	−.01	.02	.02	−.03	−.03
No class	.04	.03	.01	.01	.04	.01	.07*	.05
Coop	−.01	.00	.05	.07	.04	.03	.03	.02
Private	.06	.06	.04	.04	.11**	.09**	.03	.02
Other	.01	.00	.11**	.10**	.01	.00	.03	.02
Benefit	.02	.03	.05	.03	.02	.07	.03	.07
Income	.11**	.08*	.02	.01	.10**	.05	.13**	.10**
Ethnic	.02	.00	.07*	.07*	.08*	.06	.03	.01
Earth	.01	.02	.01	.01	−.03	−.03	−.04	−.04
Novgorod	−.07	−.08*	.00	.01	−.07*	−.09*	−.05	−.07*
East Siberia	.02	.01	−10**	−.10*	.13**	.13**	.07*	.06
West Siberia	.04	.05	−.05	−.04	.00	.00	.02	.02
Volga	−.09*	−.09*	−.06	−.06	−.08*	−.08*	−.12**	−.13**
Caucasus	−.09*	−.09*	−.04	−.04	−.09**	−.10**	−13**	−.14**
Urals	.02	.03	.04	.06	.04	.04	.01	.00
St Petersburg	−.07	−.07*	−.09**	−.08*	−.07	−.08*	−.06	−.07*
education		.05		.01		.02		.01
atheist		.05		.01		.08*		.08**
age		.00		−.04		.13**		.10**
gender		−.07*		−.04		−.03		−.04
Adjusted r^2	.05	.05	.03	.03	.10	.11	.07	.08

*significant at p > .05
**significant at p > .01

characteristics of respondents. As already noted, income is highly significant on most dimensions as a source of support for reform. The impact of membership in 'civic society', however, is notably weak. There is nearly a statistically significant effect for former membership in the Communist Party on attitudes towards privatisation. And the regularity of attendance at church appears as a predictor of positive support for democracy only once the differences between believers and non-believers have been controlled for; atheists are more democratic than believers, but regular believers appear more democratic than irregular ones.

Occupational differences are notably and surprisingly weak. The appearance of effects for intelligentsia and for those without class self-identities is removed in the full models.[12] This also applies in the case of those receiving state benefits. The only exception concerns attitudes towards private property, where those in the private sector show significantly higher levels of support. Entrepreneurs and managers, however, are no more likely than other groups to support the market or private property.

The only other socially located factors which prove significant in discriminating the norms of Russians are ethnicity and region. In the former case, the distinction appears to be limited to attitudes towards the market where non-Russians are more supportive. As suggested by the bivariate relationships above, regional differences are clearly visible in Eastern Siberia – which appears more supportive of the market – and in the Caucasus, which shows very high levels of support for democracy, liberalism and privatisation. Whether the higher levels of support in these regions is the result of the success or absence of reform needs to be considered next in the context of evaluation of change.

The claim that norms are more related to general 'modernising' factors and evaluations to specific experiences receives further support from the data in Table 6.4. As the r^2 for the two models in each dimension indicates, the addition of the general variables adds very little to the amount of variance explained.[13] How respondents relate to change in practice appears to be the product of their concrete experience rather than their orientation. Nonetheless, non-believers do appear more likely to support the market and private property in practice, as do the young; the attitudes of the latter group may be more easily explained by their greater flexibility in adapting to changing labour market conditions. It is also notable that women are less supportive than men of democracy as it has been practised in Russia. However, women do not appear more likely to oppose the market in practice, contrary to many expectations to the contrary based on the assumption that women have fared worse under market conditions than men.

The main differences on the evaluative dimensions are socially specific. While 'civic society' variables proved to be weak in explaining norms – again contrary to some theories – they are more adequate in accounting for some of the variation in experience. Surprisingly, the effects of trade union membership are not evident in the economy, where they may have little effect; but trade unionists are more likely to evaluate positively the practice of democracy and freedom of speech and organistion where their organisations have traditionally had little opportunity to act independently. Regular churchgoers, somewhat oddly, appear to be more supportive of the practice of privatisation than non-attenders, perhaps because privatisation has given them the opportunity to rebuild neglected churches. In the full models, the

12. The absence of class identity effects may be a function of the weakness of self-reported class identity as a measure of class position. More reliable indicators of class based on detailed job descriptions are currently under preparation.
13. This picture is further confirmed by models not presented for sake of space which include only education, atheism, age and gender.

effects of membership in the former Communist Party are just removed; however, the negative direction of their response to the market and private property is as expected.

Again, there are no class identity effects on evaluation. Income remains important to responses to democracy and privatisation, though the effects are weaker than for the normative dimensions, but not for liberalism in practice or, more surprisingly, for judgements of the market in practice. And those in the private sector are clearly more supportive of the market than others.[14] Non-Russians also appear more positive in their evaluation of the presence of political liberties; and they are likely to see their high market norms supported in practice via their evaluation of the market.

The main evaluative differences, however, are regional. While the Volga region in southern Russia, unlike its Caucasus neighbour, was not notably more normatively committed to reform, the two regions share a profound and general negative evaluation of reform in practice. The operation of democracy, the market, and privatisation are all poorly regarded in these regions. We find some confirmation in these places, therefore, for the picture which has emerged in other post-communist countries, that reform is widely supported because it has been so poorly implemented. We should note, conversely, that Novgorod and St Petersburg regions are also regularly negative in their assessment of reform in practice. The explanation here is unlikely to be the same, given the high profile the regions' leaders have had in support of reform, which has been backed up to some degree particularly in the practice of privatisation. There is some evidence in the generally negative direction of the coefficients for the normative dimensions for these regions that negative evaluation is a function of a more advanced stage of change. Poor implementation has resulted in low norms and significantly lower evaluation of reform.[15] The final example is that of Eastern Siberia, which despite showing a negative evaluation of political liberalism in practice, is even more positive in its evaluation of the market than it was in its normative commitment to it. Normative commitment there, in other words, appears to be sustained by a perception of the effectiveness of markets in practice.

The final issues to be addressed in this section concern the social bases of attitudes toward nationalism and Western involvement. In the context of the previous discussion, it will be remembered that the former was measured normatively and the latter evaluatively, and the r^2 for the models in Table 6.5 provides further evidence for the importance of general factors to commitments and specific ones for judgements. With respect to both issues, however, the biggest effects are provided by age, with the young again less nationalist and welcoming of Western involvement. Women, notably, are also less nationalist.

14. There is also a positive effect on liberal evaluations for those claiming to be in employment other than the state, private, or cooperative sectors. Further work needs to be done in order to discover the occupational characteristics of those respondents which might lead to them holding such pro-liberal judgements.
15. The exception to this picture is the relationship between high liberal norms and low evaluation in St Petersburg. We might speculate that residents of this region have historical reasons for supporting free speech which are connected with the traditions of the city in particular; it is not surprising that the standards of free speech and organisation in practice in Russia failed to satisfy their expectations.

Table 6.5 **Predictors of nationalism and attitudes toward Western involvement**

| | Nationalism | | Western involvement | |
	Model 1	Model 2	Model 1	Model 2
Organisation	.03	.03	.01	.01
Trade Union	.03	.02	.03	.02
Communist	−.09**	−.06	−.08*	−.06
Churchgoing	−.03	−.02	.01	.04
Entrepreneur	−.02	−.05	.01	−.01
Intelligentsia	.09**	.03	−.01	−.04
Manager	.05	.03	−.03	−.04
Peasant	−.02	−.02	.01	.01
No class	.02	−.04	.03	.00
Coop	.04	.02	.05	.04
Private	.07*	.05	.04	.02
Other	.04	.04	.07*	.07*
Benefit	−.04	.02	−.02	.04
Income	.13**	.09*	.08*	.04
Ethnic	.06*	.06	.08*	.07*
Earth	.01	.02	.00	.00
Novgorod	−.04	−.06	−.10**	−.11**
East Siberia	.06	.05	.12**	.12**
West Siberia	.00	.00	−.07*	−.08*
Volga	.04	.03	−.09*	−.09*
Caucasus	−.14**	−.14**	−.01	−.02
Urals	.05	.04	.03	.03
St Petersburg	−.00	.01	−.01	−.01
education		.06		.04
atheist		.06		.05
age		.16**		.16**
gender		.08*		.01
Adjusted r^2	.07	.10	.06	.07

*significant at p > .05
**significant at p > .01

Interestingly, the effects of more socially located factors are generally not the same in the case of nationalism or Western involvement. There is almost a statistical effect for former Communist Party membership – in both cases the direction of the coefficient is negative. Higher income is also connected with less nationalistic positions. However, the main specific factor influencing attitudes on these dimensions is again region. Those in the Caucasus, despite the otherwise liberal direction of their normative commitments, appear to be much more nationalist than others, but this is the only region to show a significant effect. With respect to Western involvement, regional differences in evaluations appear to be far more prevalent: as was the case with a number of other evaluative dimensions, those in Novgorod and the Volga (joined this time by Western Siberia) are all notably negative. Again, only Eastern Siberia appears to be significantly more supportive in its judgements.

The results presented in this section certainly suggest great complexity in the social bases of support for, and opposition to, reforms in Russia. None of the changes commands overwhelming support and many of them face stiff opposition. However, society is clearly highly differentiated in its response. Some social differences are easily predicted; age, income, education, and religious belief structure attitudes, especially on normative matters. Class identity is surprisingly weak and sector appears most important on issues of the market and private property.

However, other differences are more difficult to explain because they are rooted in local and regional experiences and traditions. Indeed, on many dimensions of reform, regions appear to explain more of the differences among Russians than any other social factor. The direction of regional support and opposition, however, does suggest a pattern. Where reforms are weakly implemented they are supported as norms; where reforms have been implemented badly, they are negatively evaluated; only in one region is there evidence of normative commitment being related to a positive evaluation of change.

Political orientation, reform and society

The final question to be addressed in this chapter concerns the relationship between attitudes to reform and the social bases of reform and political allegiances of Russians. The pattern which emerged in the last section suggests a deeply worrying potential 'double whammy' for reform-minded politicians in Russia, who may be failing to satisfy in practice those who want change but don't feel it or feel change but don't like it. How far is this picture justified by data on the voting intentions of Russians in the summer of 1993?

Clearly, voting intentions are likely to be more volatile in Russia than attitudes towards reform itself. For one thing, a number of the candidates for president chosen by respondents in July were in prison following the events of October 1993. However, it is probable that any tendencies present in the analysis presented below were likely to have been intensified by developments leading up to the elections and, as such, the picture in Table 6.6 still casts light on the success of the more gradual and anti-reform parties in the December elections.

Respondents were asked to name the presidential candidate for whom they would vote if an election were held tomorrow. Their answers have been recoded into two camps: 'reformers' who were clearly favourable to the line taken by the Yeltsin and Gaidar team, and 'conservatives' who were publicly opposed to it (see Table 6.6). For ease of presentation and, in some cases, because of the small number of respondents, 'centrists' and supporters of Zhirinovskii are not considered here. The ideological and social bases of support for the two camps were then estimated using a logistic regression procedure which is appropriate for a dichotomous dependent variable of this sort.

Table 6.6 **Logistic regressions predicting support for reformers or conservatives**

	Ideological bases	Social bases
Democratic norms	−.23	
Democratic evaluation	−.69**	
Liberal norms	.60**	
Liberal evaluation	.03	
Market norms	−1.03**	
Market evaluation	−.53*	
Privatisation norms	−.32*	
Privatisation evaluation	−.11	
Western involvement	−.05	
Nationalism	−.24	
Organisation		−.23
Trade union		−.02
Communist		.29
Entrep		.11
Intelligentsia		.29
Manager		.10
Peasant		−.36
No class		.01
Coop		.33
Private		−.57
Other		.28
Atheist		.09
Churchgoing		−.09
Ethnic		−.30
Earth		.07
Novgorod		1.18**
East Siberia		−1.59*
West Siberia		.33*
Volga		.63*
Caucasus		.76*
St Petersburg		.45
Urals		−1.55**
education		−.08
income		−.11*
age		−.01
gender		.03
-2loglikelihood	660.53	503.33
constant	6.09	16.40

*significant at p > .05
**significant at p > .01
Respondents were asked an open-ended question about who they would vote for if an election were held tomorrow. Answers were then recoded into the two blocs in the table. Conservatives = 308. Reformers = 642. Conservatives are coded 1, reformers, 0. Reformers include: Yeltsin, Shakhrai, Borovoi, Gaidar, Nemtsov, Sobchak, B. Fedorov, Chernichenko, Shumeiko, Iavlinskii. Conservatives include: Rutskoi, Khasbulatov, Baburin, Ziuganov, Isakov, 'Communist', Ligachev, Lipitskii, Ryzhkov, 'Stalanist'.

The first model in Table 6.6 investigates whether there are significant ideological differences between supporters of the two blocs. To achieve this, the scales measuring attitudes towards the various dimensions of reform are included as predictors of support. A negative score indicates support for the reform group.

Significant ideological differences are readily apparent, though not necessarily as expected. First, despite the arrogation of the term 'democrat' by the reform camp, its supporters are not significantly more democratic in their normative orientation than the opponents of reform. These results suggest that the terms of the debate about the base of support for opposition parties and politicians, particularly in the West, have been misjudged. Opponents of the ruling party since 1991 are not less committed to the democratic process as an ideal but they are significantly less appreciative of democracy in practice. This is hardly surprising, given that the ruling group around Yeltsin persistently refused to recognise the right of democratically elected opposition leaders to an effective say in policy-making. This picture is confirmed by looking at the direction of the effect for liberal norms which shows that 'conservatives' are actually more likely to support freedom of speech and organisation than are supporters of 'reformers' – which is also hardly surprising given the efforts of reform politicians in this period and after to deny rights of access to the media, to association (particularly of former communists) and to the electoral process.[16]

Second, there are significant differences between the two camps on economic issues at both the normative and evaluative level. 'Conservatives' are less committed to the market and private property and evaluate the market less favourably than those in the reform group. However, this is more a matter of 'normal' politics ranged along a left–right axis. As argued earlier, there may well be a number of tenable normative positions between state intervention and the free market to which anti-reform politicians are appealing. Clearly they are also picking up votes from those whose experience of the market in practice has been negative. Third, it is notably that there is no contribution to support for 'conservative' politicians from opposition to Western involvement or nationalism once the other reform dimensions have been taken into account. Left–right issues and the practice of political reform are what appear likely to structure electoral choice in the summer of 1993.

The social bases of preference for 'conservatives' or 'reformers' offer some support for the negative effect of reform on the prospects of reform-oriented politicians. It is notable, first, how few social factors are at work in structuring electoral choice. Neither camp appears to be picking up votes among particular social groups, though

16. As with the bivariate relationships shown in Table 6.3, so the zero-order relationships of ideology to vote are at times at variance with the picture in Table 6.6. This is not surprising given the correlations among reform dimensions shown in Table 6.2. Thus, at the zero-order there are no significant differences between supporters of 'reformers' and 'conservatives' with respect to liberal norms; however, these appear as soon as differences between the two groups on their evaluation of the market are controlled for. Conversely, 'conservatives' appear at the zero-order to be less committed normatively to democracy; this difference is removed as soon as differential experience of democracy is taken into account. Similarly, the 'conservatives' appear more negative about privatisation in action, more nationalist and more anti-West. These differences, however, are only removed when a range of other dimensions are included.

reformers do find significant support from those on higher incomes. Notably, though education, age and income are clearly associated with the reform dimensions above, they do not appear to be strong – or even weak – bases for the vote of 'reform' politicians.

Once again, however, it is regional differences which play the greatest role. The reformers appear likely to pick up votes in Yeltsin's political base, the Urals and, in support of the argument made above, in Eastern Siberia where high levels of normative and evaluative support for reform was evident. But the 'conservatives' are favoured in three predictable places: in the Caucasus where reforms have proceeded slowly despite the evidence of higher normative commitment to them presented above; and in the regions around Nizhny-Novgorod and St Petersburg where reforms have proceeded faster but, in the eyes of the local inhabitants, badly. Though these results do not correspond exactly with the regional pattern in the December elections of 1993, there is still a high degree of overlap, particularly if the Zhirinovskii vote is added to those of the 'conservatives' considered here. Commentators were surprised by the strong showing of the Liberal Democrats (i.e. Zhirinovskii supporters) and 'conservatives' in Nizhnii-Novgorod and the Leningrad *oblast*, though the ideological evidence provided here suggests they should not have been. The Caucasus went as predicted to 'conservatives' and the Urals to 'reformers'. Only in the Black Earth region around Voronezh was the result significantly at odds with the analysis above; 'conservatives' fared far better than respondents' ideological orientations or voting intentions would have suggested.[17]

Conclusion

Clearly, Russia is in transition. Evidence derived from a single survey can give only a snapshot of the Russian people at a single moment in time rather than measuring the dynamics of change. Nonetheless, the analysis does point to a high degree of variegation in the opinions, norms and judgements of Russians. It also indicates where sources of stable support for change may be found: among the young, educated and secular; among those in the private sector and among those who are doing relatively well in terms of income; and, on some dimensions, among non-Russians. However, it also suggests that support for reform is very much a function of how the reform is being conducted, particularly in the regions. And it also indicates how 'reform' politicians have failed to find a secure ideological and social base among those committed to change.

17. See Mary Cline 'Nizhnii Novgorod: A regional view of the Russian elections', *RFE/RL Research Report*, 3 (4), 1994, pp. 48–54; E. Teague 'Russia's local elections begin', *RFE/RL Research Report*, 3 (7), 1994, p. 2; *Current Digest of the Soviet Press*, 51, 1994, pp. 7–8.

Appendix A: Questions and reliability of scales

Responses to each of the questions below have been coded to create five-point scales indicating strong agreement (1), agreement (2), neither agreement nor disagreement (3), disagreement (4), strong disagreement (5). These were then recoded so that, regardless of the direction in which the question was put, pro-democratic, pro-market, pro-privatisation, pro-Western, and anti-nationalist responses scored highly.

The scale for *normative commitment to values of democracy* consists of two items:
How do you feel about the *aim* of introducing democracy in the county, in which political parties compete for government? (Strong supporter, supporter, opponent, strong opponent, neither supporter nor opponent.)
Democracy is a good means of solving social conflicts. (Strongly agree, agree, disagree, strongly disagree, neither agree nor disagree.)
The items correlate at 0.35, which is reasonable for survey research.

The *democratic evaluative* scale consists of six items:
How would you evaluate the *actual practice* of democracy in (Russia) so far? (Very positively, positively, negatively, very negatively, neither positively nor negatively.)
In respondents's country,
> The government acts for the benefit of the majority of the society.
> Everyone has an influence on the election of the government.
Elected officials don't care much what people like me think.
On the whole, what governments do in this country reflects the wishes of ordinary people.
There is no point in voting because the government can't make any difference. (Strongly agree, agree, disagree, strongly disagree, neither agree nor disagree.)
Cronbach's alpha is = 0.64.

The *normative commitment to liberalism* scale consists of four items:
Tell me whether and to what degree these characteristics are necessary for what you would consider a *good* society:
> Freedom to create social, economic, political and other organisations.
> Freedom of speech and the right to publicly express different opinions.
> Limits put on the public expression of opinions that are opposed to the feelings and opinions of the majority of the people.
> Limits put on the public expression of opinions that are opposed to the views of the authorities.
Cronbach's alpha for the scale is 0.52. Factor analysis shows the existence of two significant factors which are the result of question direction effects.

Evaluation of liberalism is measured by a single item.
Please say how much you agree with the following statement:
> There is freedom of speech and organisation.

The *normative commitment to the market* scale consists of five items:
Thinking next about economic reform, how do you feel about the aim of creating a market economy with private ownership and economic freedom to entrepreneurs?

(Strong supporter, supporter, opponent, strong opponent, neither supporter nor opponent.)

The Western market economy is a good example for (Russia) to follow.

Tell me whether and to what degree these characteristics are necessary for what you would consider a *good* society:

      Central management of the economy.

      Free economic competition, market-based economy.

There should be no government interference with business and trade.

The scale is slightly unbalanced – three pro-market, one anti-market and one neutral item. However, factor analysis shows that there is only one dimension of attitudes at work. Cronbach's alpha is = 0.60.

The *market evaluation scale* consists of four items:

And how would you evaluate the *actual experience* of the market economy in (Russia) so far?

The market economy gives too much freedom to individuals.

The market economy improves the standard of living of ordinary people in (Russia).

The market economy leads to more social conflict.

Cronbach's alpha for the scale is = 0.59.

The scale of *normative commitment to privatisation* contains three items:

Consider the following pair of statements and say which one comes closest to your views.

      The government should take all major industries into state ownership.

or

      The government should place all major industries in private ownership.

Private enterprise is the best way to solve (Russia's) difficulties.

Major public services and industries ought to be in state ownership.

Cronbach's alpha for the scale is = 0.65.

The *evaluation of privatisation* scale contains three items:

Privatisation is just a means of handing out the wealth of the country to people who are already rich and well-connected.

Privatisation gives ordinary people the opportunity to develop the economy.

Privatisation increases social divisions.

Cronbach's alpha for the scale is = 0.65.

The *nationalism* scale consists of four items:

We have a lot to learn from other countries in running (Russia's) affairs.

(Russia) should cooperate with other countries even if it means giving up some independence.

People should be free to emigrate even if (Russia) needs their skills.

Consider the following pair of statements and say which one comes closest to your views.

      Foreign ownership of enterprises might be accepted if it improves the state of our economy.

or

      It is better that we should own our own enterprises even if it means more hardship in future.

Cronbach's alpha for the scale is = 0.43. Although the alpha for the scale is relatively low, factor analysis shows that there is only one dimension of attitudes at work.

Attitudes towards *Western involvement* are measured using a single double-headed item:

Western institutions have been helpful and supportive of our country.

or

Western institutions have been interfering in our affairs and using our difficulties for their own advantage.

Appendix B: Coding of independent variables

1. Civic society
(a) Membership in any of the following: business association, professional association, farmers' association, church group, local or community group, sports or social club, armed forces organisation, political party, ethnic organisation, factory committee. N = 305.
(b) Member of a trade union. N = 854.
(c) Was a member of Communist Party before 1991. N= 257.
(d) For those with religious beliefs, there was then a religious intensity indicator from 'church attendance once a week' to 'never attend'.

2. Class identity, sectoral and source of income cleavages
(a) Dummies for class (self-identified): entrepreneurs = 87; managers and administrators = 133; intelligentsia = 506; peasants = 131; no class identity = 362. The reference category is manual workers = 650.
(b) Dummies for sector: cooperative (collective farms and cooperatives) = 84; private firm (private firm, leased firm, self-employed) = 193; other sector = 219. The reference category is the state sector = 1,263.
(c) Benefit: Those receiving state benefit (students, unemployed, retired, disabled) = 1; those receiving income = 0.

3. Regional, religious and ethnic identities
(a) Dummies for region: Eastern Siberia (Irkutsk) = 154; Volga-Vyatskii (Nizhnii-Novgorod) = 120; Urals (Ekaterinburg) = 145; Earth (Central Chernozem-Voronezh) = 110; North Caucasus (Krasnodar) = 224; Volga (Saratov, Kazan) = 361; Petro (St Petersburg) = 193. The reference category is Moscow (Moscow, Vladimir) = 416.
(b) Dummy for religion: atheist = 809, Orthodox = 990.
(c) Dummy for ethnic group: Non-Russian = 196, Russian = 1,671.

4. Education, income, age and gender
(a) Respondents were asked to name the highest educational qualification achieved. Responses were then coded as a 13-point scale: no qualification/never attended school = 3; primary school = 82; secondary school = 306; high school = 315; professional course = 71; vocational school = 38; technical secondary = 153; vocational post-school = 124; technical college = 279; incomplete higher education = 79; higher education = 392; additional training = 25; degree = 10.
(b) Income.
(c) Age.
(d) Gender: Women = 1,008, Men = 864.

115

Part Two

THE POLITICAL ECONOMY OF CHANGE

Chapter 7

PRIVATISATION AND THE NEW BUSINESS CLASS[1]

Lynn D. Nelson and Irina Y. Kuzes

In this chapter we review the evolution of Russia's economic reforms up until the conclusion of voucher privatisation in mid-1994, with particular attention to the place of entrepreneurship in the reforms and the implications of the privatisation programme for entrepreneurship. In addition to utilising primary and secondary data from various sources, this analysis draws from research we carried out in four Russian cities (Moscow, Ekaterinburg, Voronezh and Smolensk) during the time that the features of voucher privatisation were being finalised in 1992 and after voucher privatisation was well under way, in the summer of 1993.[2]

In the first section we describe key features of the new era for entrepreneurship that was ushered in under Gorbachev. Next, we discuss the reorientation of reforms which accompanied Yeltsin's political ascendancy – one which emphasised monetary policy more than enterprise efficiency and which focused more on privatisation procedures than the creation of a climate favourable to entrepreneurial activity. We then examine the role of the state bureaucracy in the ongoing struggle of entrepreneurs to gain stable footing in Russian economic life. Next, we turn to such impediments to entrepreneurship as confiscatory taxation and regulatory provisions which invite bribery. We conclude the chapter by considering the importance of regional issues and interest group politics in the post-voucher privatisation phase of Russian reforms.

1. The work leading to this report was supported from funds provided by the National Council for Soviet and East European Research; the Center for Institutional Reform and the Informal Sector; and the International Research and Exchanges Board, with funds provided by the Andrew W. Mellon Foundation, the National Endowment for the Humanities, and the US Department of State. None of these organisations is responsible for the contents or findings of this report.
2. Our 1993 project included 5,019 respondents in several categories: political and opinion leaders at the federal and local levels, directors of privatised enterprises, privatisation administrators, and general population sub-samples in each of the four cities. The sample of directors includes all production enterprises that had begun or completed privatisation by June 1993 in Voronezh and Smolensk, most in Ekaterinburg, and about half of the Moscow total. In the 1992 study, 5,872 interviews were conducted among privatisation officials, enterprise directors (state, privatised and private), and non-mangerial enterprise personnel. Details about these projects are provided in Lynn D. Nelson and Irina Y. Kuzes *Property to the People: The Struggle for Radical Economic Reform in Russia* M.E. Sharpe, Armonk, New York 1994; and Lynn D. Nelson and Irina Y. Kuzes *Radical Reform in Yeltsin's Russia: Political, Economic and Social Dimensions*, M.E. Sharpe, Armonk, New York, in press.

Prelude to the Yeltsin reforms

Before the end of the Soviet period, an approach for moving the USSR toward a market economy was developing an identifiable shape, although these innovations were being hammered out in a context of lively discussion about preferred directions and were accompanied by repeated setbacks to the agendas of the country's most determined reformers. The core idea that had crystallised under Gorbachev was that both new business start-ups and the privatisation of state enterprises would proceed together, with the hope that wrenching dislocations could be avoided in the economy and the production system. The evolving economy would include a mix of state and non-state enterprises to replace the tired and inadequate command system. Ryzhkov's 1990 economic reform proposal called for the government to 'consistently, step by step, reduce the scale of direct, inflexible state influence on the economy and expand the sphere of market relations'.[3] Pavlov's anti-crisis initiative a year later proposed 'to move consistently toward the freeing up of prices in all spheres of the economy'.[4] There were sharp divergences in the proposals that were being developed during this period, but the overarching perspective of the '500 Days' programme that was created by Stanislav Shatalin's task force illustrates a prevalent perspective of that time. 'Everybody has a right to choose', the preface to the programme stated, 'whether to become an entrepreneur, an employee of the state apparatus, or a manager at a stock company, to engage in individual labour, or to become a member of a coop.'[5]

Early in the 1990s, both the parliaments of Russia and of the Soviet Union were beginning to underscore more decidedly than ever before their support for entrepreneurship. A stream of legislation that was passed in the USSR during the late 1980s had established principles for cooperative enterprises – a development which was justified by Soviet leaders as being consistent with the idea of 'socialist enterprise'. This attempt to avoid breaking with party orthodoxy, however, soon ended. Most cooperative heads actually wanted to be private business people. Workers, while preferring non-state to state employment, had a strong preference for forms of private business activity other than cooperatives – private firms or joint ventures, for example.[6] The RSFSR Law on Ownership was approved on 24 December 1990 and accorded private ownership equal standing with state, municipal and other forms

---

3. 'Ob ekonomicheskom polozhenii strany i kontseptsii perekhoda k reguliruemoi rynochnoi ekonomike', *Pravda*, 165, 25 May 1990, pp. 1–4.

4. *Current Digest of the Soviet Press* (hereafter, *CDSP*) 43, 22 May 1991, p. 3; from *Pravda* and *Izvestiia* 23 April 1991, pp. 2–3.

5. Stanislav Shatalin *et al*. 'On the programme developed by the task force headed by academician S.S. Shatalin', in G. Yavlinsky, B. Fedorov, S. Shatalin, N. Petrakov, S. Aleksashenko, A. Vavilov, L. Grigoriev, M. Zadornov, V. Machits, A. Mikhailov and E. Yasin *500 Days* (*Transition to the Market*), St Martin's Press, New York 1991, p. xii.

6. Lynn D. Nelson, Lilia V. Babaeva and Rufat O. Babaev 'Perspectives on entrepreneurship and privatisation in Russia: policy and public opinion', *Slavic Review* 51, Summer 1992, p. 278.

of public ownership.[7] The next day, the Law on Enterprises and Entrepreneurship was approved. This law outlined several permissible forms of property ownership, including private enterprises.[8]

In April 1991, Gorbachev signed the Law on Principles of Entrepreneurship, which embodied similar thinking at the Union level regarding both entrepreneurship and the legitimacy of private property. The law pointedly endorsed 'initiative-taking, self-development by citizens that is intended to obtain income or profit . . . and is performed for oneself and at one's own risk and property responsibility, or is performed on behalf of and at the property responsibility of a legal person – an enterprise'. The law also recognised 'the equity of all forms of ownership'.[9] This was a decisive break with the tentativeness about individual initiative that characterised the Law on Individual Labour Activity adopted in November 1986 (effective May 1987) which had specified that private activity was to be part-time only – and not an alternative to state sector work. This law had stated that enterprises could not make use of hired labour, and it had also required that participants obtain licences. These licences were often difficult to obtain, and because they were valid for only five years, the requirement underscored the long-term uncertainty of non-state enterprise in the Soviet Union.[10] And although the February 1987 decree 'On the Creation of Cooperatives in the Service Sphere for the Population' permitted the establishment of cooperatives, a significant restriction was the provision that cooperatives could be created only under the authority of local government commissions or state enterprises or organisations.[11] While the 1988 Law on Cooperatives had been more supportive of non-state enterprise, it did not go as far toward legitimating private entrepreneurial activity as many had wanted it to. Economist Vladimir Tikhonov, for example, who had helped to draft the Law on Cooperatives, stated in an August 1991 interview that he had tried to include regulations which would have permitted private entrepreneurship because, as he explained his reasoning at the time, private entrepreneurship is 'a great deal more effective economically than cooperative ownership'. Although the Law on Cooperatives did not go as far toward recognising private ownership as Tikhonov had wanted, it did permit the hiring of full-time workers at fixed salaries and gave cooperative heads the

7.   See 'Annotatsiia osnovnykh zakonodatel'nykh i normativnykh aktov, reguliruiushchikh otnosheniia sobstvennosti i privatisatsiiu gosudarstvennykh i munitsipal'nykh predpriiatii v Rossiiskoi Federatsii', *Delovoi mir*, 131, 10 July 1992, p. 7. This legislation stood in contrast to the USSR Law on Ownership passed earlier in 1990, which contained an ambiguous definition of property. See Anthony Jones and William Moskoff *Ko-ops: The Rebirth of Entrepreneurship in the Soviet Union*, Indiana University Press, Bloomington, 1991, pp. 124–25.
8.   'O predpriiatiiakh i predprinimatel'skoi deiatel'nosti', *Ekonomika i zhizn'* 4, January 1991, pp. 16, 17.
9.   'Ob obshchikh nachalakh predprinimatal'stva grazhdan v SSSR', *Izvestiia* 86, 10 April 1991, p. 2.
10. International Monetary Fund, The World Bank, Organisation for Economic Cooperation and Development and European Bank for Reconstruction and Development *A Study of the Soviet Economy: Volume 1*, OECD, Paris, 1991, p. 22.
11. 'O sozdanii kooperativov po bytovomu obsluzhivaniiu naseleniia', *Sobranie postanovlenii Pravitel'stva SSSR* (otdel pervyi) 11, art. 43, 1987, pp 227–32.

right to decide how to use their profits without state interference.[12] But subsequent legislation had restricted entrepreneurship in other ways by forbidding or limiting cooperative enterprise in some sectors of the economy, allowing local Soviets to fix maximum prices for cooperative products, and levying special charges on cooperative purchases.[13]

Expanding its focus on entrepreneurship and recognition of private ownership in April 1991, on 1 July the USSR Supreme Soviet approved the Law on the Basic Principles of the Destatisation and Privatisation of Enterprises, which specified target dates for removing enterprises from state control, some of which would initially be leased and others converted into joint stock companies.[14] According to the plan, about half of the fixed production assets of state enterprises were to be shifted outside the sphere of direct state management by the end of 1992.[15] It was expected that this sector of the economy would grow to between 60 and 70 per cent by 1995.[16]

Two days later, on 3 July the Law On Privatisation of State and Municipal Enterprises was passed in the RSFSR Supreme Soviet.[17] This legislation specified that enterprises could be privatised in several ways. An entire enterprise could be sold through auction or competition.[18] It could be transformed into a joint stock company and its shares sold.[19] Finally, leased enterprises could be redeemed by their management and workers.[20]

The same day another law was passed in the RSFSR, On Personal Privatisation Cheques and Accounts,[21] which stated that privatisation 'investment accounts' would be available in state banks for all citizens. With these accounts, citizens could acquire property from the state. Over the summer, the Russian legislature issued a series of normative documents outlining privatisation plans of different departments.

---

12. Irina Kruglianskaia 'Na polnoi skorosti k rynku', *Izvestiia*, 187, 7 August 1991, p. 3.
13. See International Monetary Fund *et al. A Study of the Soviet Economy: Volume 1*, p. 30. A review of earlier legislation regarding non-state enterprise is provided in Jones and Moskoff, *Ko-ops, op. cit.*
14. 'Ob osnovnykh nachalakh razgosudarstvleniia i privatisatsii predpriiatii', *Izvestiia* 188, 8 August 1991, p. 3.
15. See A. Stepovoi and S. Chugaev 'Konets monopolii gossobstvennosti', *Izvestiia*, 156, 2 July 1991, pp. 1–2; and 'Ob osnovnykh nachalakh razgosudarstvleniia i privatizatsii predpriiatii', *Izvestiia*, 188, 8 August 1991, p. 3.
16. *ibid.*
17. 'O privatizatsii gosudarstvennykh i munitsipal'nykh predpriiatii v RSFSR', *Zakony RSFSR o privatisatsii gosudarstvennykh i munitsipal'nykh predpriiatii, zhil'ia* Sovetskaia Rossiia, Moscow, 1991, pp. 3–36.
18. In a competition, potential buyers would submit a plan for their use of the enterprise and the amount of their investment, and the relative merits of the proposals would be evaluated by a commission created for each individual enterprise.
19. Workers of enterprises transformed into joint stock companies would have the right to buy shares for 30 per cent less than their face value and to pay for them over a three-year period. The proportion of an enterprise's shares which could be purchased in this way was to be decided later in the State Programme for Privatisation which would be reformulated each year. These shares were not to be sold for three years.
20. They could be transformed into joint stock companies if the option of buying the leased enterprise were not exercised.
21. 'Annotatsiia', *Delovoi mir*, 131, 10 July 1992, p. 5.

In sum, both the Soviet Union and the Russian Republic were clearly pointed in the direction of radical economic reform by mid-1991. The legislation adopted between December and July showed that the ideological centre of the country had decisively shifted. The state was now encouraging the establishment of new private businesses, as well as cooperatives and joint ventures. By August more than 111,000 cooperatives were in operation,[22] and for the year the cooperative sector accounted for six per cent of the Soviet Union's gross national product[23] – about 17 times greater than the cooperative contribution in 1988.[24] Seven million people worked in cooperative enterprises at that time,[25] and the number of non-cooperative private enterprises was growing rapidly.[26]

The legislation crafted in the parliaments of both the USSR and the RSFSR during 1991 had aimed at increasing the efficiency of production and the viability of the economy through both new business ventures and privatisation. The RSFSR legislation had also included a pronounced emphasis on equity, in recognition of the deprivation that Soviet citizens had endured under the banner of collectivisation. But the August 1991 coup abruptly ended the process of formulating a coherent economic policy for the Soviet Union. The economic programme which eventually emerged under the leadership of Egor Gaidar had very different priorities from those that had crystallised before the coup.

Implications for entrepreneurship of the deficit reduction emphasis

The introduction of price liberalisation in January 1992, and the imposition of higher taxes, were intended to overcome the budget deficit problem. But these initiatives drove many non-state firms out of business. In 1991, as private entrepreneurship was becoming accepted in the USSR, the inaccessability of many materials needed for production outside the state sphere had made it difficult for private businesses to venture far beyond retail and intermediary agent activities. (More than 50 per cent of small enterprises were in the service, retail and wholesaleing spheres in 1989 and 1990.[27]) This was one reason why private business people were frequently accused of being primarily speculators. Thus most of the capital of new entrepreneurs was kept in the monetary sphere.[28] By the beginning of 1992, many private entrepreneurs had

22. Many more cooperatives than this were registered but not operating. In August 1991, Tikhonov reported that 255,000 cooperatives had been registered. See Kruglianskaia, 'Na polnoi skorosti k rynku', *op. cit.*
23. Lidiia Belokonnaia 'No faith in the future', *Business World Weekly*, 2, 27 January 1992, p. 3.
24. *CDSP* 43, 11 September 1991, p. 23; from *Izvestiia*, 7 August 1991, p. 3.
25. Vladimir Tikhonov 'Vlast' i rynok', *Vek (Delovoi mir* supplement) 11, 22–29 October 1992, p. 6.
26. Valentina Sal'nikova 'Pul's malogo biznesa Rossii', *Delovoi mir*, 134, 15 July 1992, p. 5.
27. Andrei Orlov 'Ne khlebom edinym zhiv malyi biznes', *Nezavisimaia Gazeta*, 53, 23 March 1993, p. 4.
28. Ol'ga Osetrova 'Podderzhit li gosudarstvo predprinimatelia', *Torgovo-promyshlennye vedomosti* 5, November 1992. See also N. Palkina 'Podderzhka malykh predpriiatii v Rossii', *Ekonomicheskaia gazeta* 39, September 1992, p. 16.

large reserves of capital which they were ready to invest in production enterprises,[29] but their capital lost most of its value nearly overnight with the advent of price liberalisation. It was difficult in Russia's now tumultuous economic environment for entrepreneurs to borrow money for business development. When money was available it nearly always took the form of short-term loans at steep interest rates.

Writing in *Delovoi mir* during that period, editor Yurii Kirpichnikov blamed the government for this development: 'Because the state is not supporting small businesses, it did not make it possible for them to secure financial, material and natural resources for production,' Kirpichnikov complained, 'Thus their main field is selling and buying – not production'. This was the most serious problem in the Russian economy, Kirpichnikov insisted.[30] Leonid Lopatnikov clarifies the reasoning that prompted many Russian analysts to favour state participation in small business development, rather than letting entrepreneurs find their own way by themselves. He argues that 'We need to take into account Russia's realities', which include 'decades of pressure from the system which kills initiative' and a structure 'which was fashioned *to create* obstacles'. It is important to remember, Lopatnikov urges in July 1994, 'that many people are still in prison who had been charged with "private entrepreneurial activity". This fact cannot be quickly eliminated from the public's consciousness.'[31] Ironically, the actual number of small businesses declined during 1992, as Yeltsin's reforms were developing their distinctive character.[32]

The virtual impossibility for private business people to secure long-term loans at manageable interest rates was consistent with the government's overall economic agenda. 'After the [April 1993] referendum, it became possible to increase control over monetary and budgetary policy', Gaidar stated in August 1993. 'In particular, it was then possible to direct the Central Bank to increase interest rates – something that we were unable to do from May 1992 until April 1993. [Following the referendum], the interest rate was raised from 100 per cent to 110 per cent, then 120 per cent. Now it has reached 170 per cent – about the current level of inflation. Unfortunately, the process is slow. We would, of course, prefer a more radical solution', Gaidar indicated.[33] Thus the government severely constricted the lifeline of the entrepreneurial class who could generate the competitive vitality, and tax revenue, that drive a market economy.

A month before Gaidar wrote of this strategic 'success' in getting interest rates up to the level of inflation, economist Vadim Medvedev, head of the Economic Analysis Group in the Gorbachev Foundation, described the effect of these interest rates on private business. Loans were too costly for most entrepreneurs to obtain them for

29. Fedor Rusinov and Mikhail Ioffe 'Rossiiskoe predprinimatel'stvo', *Delovoi mir* 6, 14 January 1993, p. 12.
30. Diaz Zamilov 'Nishcheta i blesk malogo predprinimatel'stva', *Delovoi mir* 48, 11 March 1992, p. 6.
31. Leonid Lopatnikov 'Podderzhka malogo predprinimatel'stva', *Delovoi mir* 153, 18–24 July 1994, p. 1.
32. See Orlov. 'Ne khlebom edinym zhiv malyi biznes' *op. cit.*; and Tikhonov 'Vlast' i rynok' *op. cit.*
33. Egor Gaidar 'Na karte – budushchee ne tol'ko Rossii', *Delovoi mir* 161, 26 August 1993, p. 11.

capital investment, Medvedev insisted. Further, banks were reluctant to make loans for longer than three months – which made it virtually impossible to use loans for investment in production.[34] In mid-1994, economist Pavel Bunich reported that 96 per cent of all money available for loans went for short-term purposes.[35]

Within Russia, criticism of orthodox macroeconomic policy has often been grounded in the realisation that the planned Soviet economy, having been developed to function independently of supply and demand pressures, could not be expected to react to anti-inflationary measures in the same way that a mature market economy would. Thus, Yavlinskii's YABLOKO faction stated in April 1994, 'Purely monetary methods to fight inflation must be supplemented with real reform which can eliminate the causes of inflation.'[36] Evgenii Yasin, appointed economics minister in November 1994, suggests that monopolism and Soviet-style enterprise behaviour are important sources of inflation which monetary policy alone cannot correct.[37] Thriving entrepreneurship, however, could effectively deal with these problems, as many critics argue.[38]

Entrepreneurship and the privatisation programme

The Russian government put most of its hope for entrepreneurship in the privatisation of state enterprises – hoping thereby to create efficient ownership which would be the core of a new market economy. But not all of the objectives of privatisation were compatible one with another. The reformers wanted privatisation to facilitate the realisation of monetary goals. Divestment would reduce the state's financial obligations to enterprises, many of which were inefficient, and thus help to lower the budget deficit while reducing the state's involvement in the economy. Selling state property to investors – which was the planners' initial idea – would also contribute to deficit reduction by bringing in revenue.[39] But the realisation of efficient ownership required more than loosening the state's hold on enterprises. Managers of privatised enterprises needed many of the same things that private entrepreneurs were lobbying for – favourable terms for loans, for example, and a reasonable taxation policy. In our 1993 interviews with 514 directors and vice-directors of privatised enterprises,[40] 77 per

34. Vadim Medvedev 'Proidena li nizhniaia tochka ekonomicheskogo krizisa?' *Nezavisimaia Gazeta* 136, 22 July 1993, p. 4. See also Vil' Dorofeev 'Znaki vozrozhdeniia', *Nezavisimaia Gazeta* 171, 9 September 1993, p. 5; Aleksandr Ioffe 'K nam – milosti prosim', *Ekonomika i zhizn'* 4, February 1994, p. 8; and Prokopii Drachev 'Malyi rossiiskii biznes i bol'shoi zapadnyi kapital', *Delovoi mir* 95, 2–8 May 1994, p. 12.
35. Pavel Bunich 'Glavnoe seichas – ozhivit' investitsii', *Ekonomika i zhizn'* 15, April 1994, p. 7.
36. 'Novyi biudzhet: ni vashim, ni nashim', *Novaia ezhednevnaia gazeta*, 68, 14 April 1994, p. 2. The Duma faction of YABLOKO deputies represent the bloc headed by Yavlinskii.
37. Evgenii Yasin 'Starye diskussii i novye problemy', *Segodnia* 5, 12 January 1994, p. 9.
38. See, for example, Grigorii Yavlinskii 'Inaia reforma', *Nezavisimaia Gazeta* 26, 10 February 1994, p. 4.
39. See Oleg Bogomolov 'Razdaetsia nicheinoe bogatstvo', *Nezavisimaia Gazeta* 13, 23 January 1993, p. 4.
40. The sample includes 382 directors and 132 vice-directors.

cent indicated that high taxes were 'a very serious problem' for their enterprises. For 47 per cent, a shortage of working capital was also a major obstacle, and 46 per cent stated that it was 'very difficult' to obtain loans at a reasonable interest rate.

As privatisation was originally conceived in the Parliament of the RSFSR during 1991, it would be primarily oriented toward equity and toward increasing the efficiency of production and the viability of the economy. There were problems here, because the lawmakers' equity concerns did not mesh well with their emphasis on increasing enterprise efficiency. The features of their legislation that were oriented toward equity, such as the creation of personal privatisation accounts, were not optimal for improving management decision-making – which could have been more adequately realised by selling enterprise shares to outside investors.

The Gaidar planning team ultimately retained the concept of free distribution of property to citizens as a keystone of their programme. They accepted this approach because the way in which state property would be distributed was not nearly as important as ensuring that there could be secondary redistribution, through the buying and selling of vouchers or enterprise shares. In this way, they believed, 'efficient owners' would surface. Thus efficiency considerations gave way to the priority of rapid privatisation, and in the process of negotiating with the Parliament to realise the goal of a rapid privatisation pace, 'insider privatisation', in which an enterprise's personnel could acquire 51 per cent of its shares, was permitted. This variant was strongly supported by the directors' lobby and was ultimately incorporated into the programme (see also Chapter 8). Among the enterprise directors and vice-directors we interviewed in 1993, insider privatisation was preferred over the sale of enterprise shares or distribution to outsiders through voucher auctions by a margin of about two to one.[41] This privatisation variant became the most popular approach to allocating enterprise shares and was ultimately utilised by about three-quarters of enterprises that were transformed into joint stock companies before the conclusion of voucher privatisation in June 1994.

During May 1992, we discussed the new variant which permitted insider privatisation with Dmitrii Vasil'ev, a deputy chair of the State Property Management Committee (Goskomimushchestvo, GKI). This alternative had just been worked out, and would be approved by the Supreme Soviet the following month. Vasil'ev estimated at that time that about half of all directors opposed the privatisation of their enterprises, and he suggested that they were the ones who were most urgently calling for collective ownership among enterprise personnel. 'That is the way to insure that the director stays in control', Vasil'ev noted.

That week, we also interviewed Petr Filippov about the new proposal to allow workers to own 51 per cent of privatising enterprises. Filippov was then chair of the Subcommittee on Privatisation of the Russian Supreme Soviet. (He later became a close Yeltsin adviser.) 'It is obvious to any economist that the most important need now is to bring in outside owners', Filippov argued. These would be owners 'who are interested in new opportunities and can make enterprise operations more efficient. If we permit workers to keep 51 per cent of the shares of their enterprises,

---

41. See Lynn D. Nelson and Irina Y. Kuzes 'Evaluating the Russian voucher privatisation programme', *Comparative Economic Studies* 36, Spring 1994.

then those enterprises will have no chance of outside investment – either foreign or domestic. Who would want to invest their money under those conditions?' Filippov acknowledged, however, that pressure was strong from directors who wanted to retain control of their enterprises. 'The interests of different layers of the population became transparent during the first stage of privatisation', Filippov said, 'and the battle to satisfy these different groups quickly became more severe.' In early 1994, Filippov reflected on that watershed change in the privatisation program. 'We agreed to this new privatisation variant because the alternative was to give up on privatisation entirely', he stated. 'This was our concession to the Supreme Soviet.'[42]

'Rapid privatisation creates problems', privatisation head Anatolii Chubais told us in August 1993, 'but a slower pace would create more problems. We have had a narrow window of opportunity. The Parliament started to accept the idea in 1991, but their support faded entirely by the end of 1992.' Cubais thus reflected the perspective of the Yeltsin reformers more generally in seeing privatisation as the *starting point* for reform. The 'Economic Policy Memorandum' and the 'Economic Strategy of the Russian Government', which were released in early 1992, had underscored this emphasis. These had been the first documents to make public the short-term reform plans of Yeltsin and Gaidar. They had discussed monetary policy and emphasised the strategy of rapid privatisation. Entrepreneurship had been mentioned only in terms of investment in privatised enterprises. New businesses had not been highlighted as being an important part of the government scenario during this initial phase of reforms, because it had been thought that liberalisation and stabilisation were prerequisites to effective entrepreneurship.[43] The preoccupation with monetary policy and privatisation that were reflected in these documents can partly be attributed to the fact that they were intended to satisfy IMF (International Monetary Fund) expectations, and thereby increase the likelihood of IMF membership for Russia and the opportunity to use Fund-provided resources.

Over the spring and summer of 1992, the government worked on a new 'Programme for Deepening Reform', which outlined longer-term reform priorities, broken down into three stages which spanned the period from mid-1992 until 1997. The planners envisioned the emergence of entrepreneurial activity as a strong force after the first 'crisis stage' ended around mid-1993. By that time, the budget deficit and inflation were expected to be under control and the ruble exchange rate stable. After that time, according to the government's proposal, entrepreneurship would be appointed in a variety of ways that would facilitate the entry of new firms and promote the creation of a competitive market environment.[44]

Underscoring the government's stated interest in entrepreneurship, a new Committee for the Support of Small Enterprises and Entrepreneurship was created within GKI. According to the committee's chair, Petr Miagkov, the committee

---

42. Petr Filippov 'Kuda poshel protsess?' *Delovoi mir* 26, 7–13 February 1994, p. 19.
43. 'Osnovnye napravleniia ekonomicheskoi politiki Rossiiskoi Federatsii', *Kommersant* 9, 24 February–2 March 1992, p. 22; and 'Ekonomicheskaia strategiia pravitel'stva Rossii', *Biznes, banki, birzha* 12, 1992, p. 1. Continued in *Biznes, banki, birzha* 14, 1992, pp. 1, 15. The documents also addressed social protection concerns and inter-republican trade relations.
44. 'Programma uglubleniia reform', *Izvestiia* 224, 9 October 1992, p. 2.

was organised to help entrepreneurs 'stand on their own feet'. Government help was needed to support small enterprises and entrepreneurs, Miagkov suggested, because of the monopoly conditions that prevailed. The committee proposed to provide technical, legal, organisational and financial support to emerging businesses – to assist entrepreneurs in confronting the particular difficulties of the Russian business environment.[45]

But the lawmakers had become increasingly restive over the summer, as Yeltsin and Gaidar's predictions of an economic turnaround seemed ever further from realisation, and the Programme for Deepening Reform was never approved by the Parliament. Further, interest groups representing entrepreneurs were dissatisfied with the Committee for the Support of Small Enterprises and Entrepreneurship and other government overtures that had been intended to register support for private business, arguing that nothing concrete was being done. They maintained that private businesses were dying due to the unavailability of materials and supplies in Russia's monopoly environment, excessive taxation, unduly high interest rates and an inadequate legal basis for private business.[46]

With the beginning of large-scale privatisation and voucher auctions, crises surrounding the reforms became even more acute, and the government's focus shifted almost entirely to privatisation-related issues, along with the continuing focus on monetary policy.[47] Yet interest groups which represented entrepreneurs continued to press for measures which would benefit small businesses. In October 1992, a coalition of several of these organisations developed a draft for a presidential decree that would make it easier for entrepreneurs to start their own businesses. The proposal was to provide tax relief, to make loans more readily available for small businesses and to simplify licensing procedures.[48]

The private business community waited anxiously for the government's response. A number of prominent entrepreneurs organised the Entrepreneurs' Political Initiative in the autumn of 1992, and in November they published an open letter to the government urging a timely response to their request for governmental action. 'We want to live and work in Russia', the letter said, 'despite all of the attempts from the government and the Parliament to force us to take our ability and our capital abroad.'[49] On 30 November a Yeltsin decree was issued. But rather than providing relief to entrepreneurs from critical obstacles to business development, it offered only encouraging words – with no specific initiatives which would facilitate business

45. Palkina 'Podderzhka malykh predpriiatii v Rossii' *op. cit.*
46. See, for example, Boris Krotkov 'Bez etogo – ne vyzhit'', *Delovoi mir* 100, 27 May 1992, p. 1; Igor' Krylov 'Malyi biznes nadeetsia na Yeltsina', *Radikal* (*Delovoi mir* supplement) 46, December 1992, p. 9; Viktor Voloshin 'Ne khochu byt' malen'kim!' *Delovoi mir* 236, 8 December 1992, p. 1; and Mark Masarskii 'Gde sidit pravitel'stvo reformatorov', *Nezavisimaia Gazeta* 225, 21 November 1992, p. 4.
47. See Igor' Gritsenko 'Polgoda bez Gaidara', *Chastnaia sobstvennost'* (*Izvestiia* supplement) 15, 26 May 1993, pp. 1, 3.
48. 'Ukaz Prezidenta Rossiiskoi Federatsii: "O vremennykh merakh po podderzhke malogo biznesa" (proekt)', *Radikal* (*Delovoi mir* supplement) 46, December 1992, p. 11.
49. 'Predprinimateli rezko kritikuiut pravitel'stvo, no schitaiut, chto ego kurs poddaetsia ispravleniiu', *Izvestiia* 255, 24 November 1992, p. 2.

development. Writing about the decree on 12 December, analyst Igor' Krylov noted that 'the text of the presidential decree . . ., besides constantly repeating the words "support for small and medium-size businesses", has nothing in common with the draft document' which was submitted for the government's consideration. 'The President's administration gave birth to a document which . . . is a mockery of common sense', Krylov continued. 'They do not understand that small business and the middle class that it creates are the main sources of support for reforms.'[50]

Criticism of Yeltsin's 30 November decree was widespread among Russian analysts.[51] For example, Mark Masarskii, an adviser on entrepreneurship to the Moscow government, emphasised that new businesses which had begun to flourish during the early days of reform were, by that time, 'on the edge of disaster' in many cases. Gaidar's response to this development, Masarskii said, was 'So what? One who is dying deserves to die.' But in reality, Masarskii answered, 'the ones that are dying never had a chance to stand on their own feet'.[52]

Dysfunctional outcomes of the reformers' overriding concern with privatisation, as an alternative to the emphasis on entrepreneurship which had become prominent before the breakup of the USSR, are signalled in the analysis of Andrei Shleifer and Maxim Boycko – both economic advisers to the Russian government. (Boycko was also director of the Russian Centre for Privatisation, an agency of the Russian government under GKI.) Shleifer and Boycko describe how the interests of 'stakeholders' (people and groups with credible claims to control over assets being privatised) were addressed in the privatisation programme. 'Unless these stakeholders are appeased, bribed, or disenfranchised, privatisation cannot proceed', they suggest.[53] And as they see it, the privatisation programme provided a viable solution to the appeasement of enterprise directors. According to the provisions of the programme, they note approvingly, 'Any manager in Russia today can use the programme to become rich and remain in control'.[54] Not surprisingly, then, about nine-tenths of the directors of privatised enterprises remained in their former positions at the conclusion of voucher privatisation.[55]

50. Igor' Krylov 'Gora rodila mysh'', *Delovoi mir* 240, 12 December 1992, p. 9.
51. See Voloshin, 'Ne khochu byt' malen'kim!', *op. cit.*
52. Leonid Shinkarev, 'Chastnoe delo millionov', *Izvestiia* 6, 14 January 1993, p. 5.
53. Andrei Shleifer and Maxim Boycko 'The politics of Russian privatisation', in Olivier Blanchard *et al.* (eds) *Post-Communist Reform: Pain and Progress*, MIT Press, Cambridge, Massachusetts, 1993, p. 39.
54. *Ibid*, p. 64. This statement is in the context of a discussion about how 'enterprise managers were successfully enticed to cooperate in privatisation'.
55. Åslund, citing the figure of 'over one-tenth' replacement, argues in an autumn 1994 article that this means 'enterprise managers are now being replaced on a large scale'. What he fails to note is that the trend has been for directors to *solidify* their hold over their enterprises during this period, rather than for them to lose control – a development which has been widely reported by researchers. See Anders Åslund 'Prospects of the new Russian market economy', *Problems of Post-Communism*, special issue, Fall 1994, p. 19. Economist Carol Clark, for example, writes of the 'concentration of ownership' during this period. See Carol Clark, 'New trade unions, workers' response and post-soviet labour relations', paper presented at the annual meeting of the American Association for the Advancement of Slavic Studies, Philadelphia, 17–20 November 1994.

With Russian privatisation, formal ownership was changed, but most directors retained their jobs – as did most workers. Not only were new businesses, which could have injected competition into the system, not strongly encouraged, but most 'privatised' enterprises were not actually freed of state control. In March 1994, the first vice-president of Stanislav Shatalin's Reforma Foundation, Stanislav Assekritov, pointed out that 'The transformation into joint stock companies changed the form of ownership, of course, but this does not at all mean the complete independence of enterprises from those who own controlling shares. Upon opening the Goskomstat [State Statistics Committee] report [for 1993], one can see that in 81 per cent of the joint stock companies at the federal level, a controlling share is in state hands.'[56]

Thus privatisation, which was Russia's main hope for business development from 1992 through 1994, avoided mandating fundamental restructuring within the enterprises that had been products of the Soviet command economy, and at the same time it further confused the economic linkages which had been severely disrupted by the demise of the Soviet Union.

The most problematic of these developments for the economy was the sharp decline in production that accompanied privatisation – a drop that continued until late 1994. Although estimates of the magnitude of decline vary, by any adequate measure the rapid worsening of the Russian economy after late 1991 was catastrophic – and an outcome which was arguably brought on in part by the reformers' inattention to new business start-ups, which could have made up for part of the output decline in state and privatising enterprises. And a substantial proportion of this new business production would probably have been in the consumer goods sphere, which was hard-hit by the economic crisis that intensified from 1992 onward.[57]

The neglected entrepreneur

During our summer 1993 interviews with political and business leaders and analysts, we continued to hear the complaint that, as Konstantin Zatulin emphasised in July, 'Gaidar never took notice of the entrepreneur'. A prominent Moscow businessman and state Duma deputy following the December 1993 elections, Zatulin was frustrated, maintaining that 'Gaidar showed no sign that he saw entrepreneurship as being critical to economic reform'.

Similarly, when we interviewed economist Niklai Shmelev in June he argued, 'Gaidar, Chernomyrdin, the Bolsheviks – *all* have artificially kept a lid on the natural energy of entrepreneurship.' Shmelev stated later, in a *Nezavisimaia Gazeta*

---

56. Stanislav Assekritov 'Iur'ev den' privatisatsii', *Delovoi mir* 65, 28 March–3 April 1994, p. 21.
57. See, for example, Evgenii Vasil'chuk 'Prodolzhenie reform trebuet peresmotra roli gosudarstva', *Finansovye izvestiia* 45, 4 October 1994, pp. 1–2; Liudmila Biriukova 'Spasti sittsevuiu Rus'', *Delovoi mir* 203, 'Region' 1, 15 September 1994, p. 12; Lidiia Malash 'Vse khorosho, prekrasnaia markiza', *Megapolis-Express* 26, 21 September 1994, p. 14; Goskomstat Rossii 'Sotsial'no-ekonomicheskoe polozhenie i razvitie ekonomicheskikh reform v Rossiiskoi Federatsii v 1992 godu', p. 14; and Goskomstat Rossii 'O sotsial'no-ekonomicheskom polozhenii Rossii v 1993 godu', *Ekonomika i zhizn'* 6, February 1994, p. 7.

interview, that the Yeltsin reformers had 'not changed anything' in the private sphere. 'They made it even worse, somehow, than it used to be', he continued. 'You could be put in prison for private activity earlier, but economically it isn't any easier now. There was a lot of talk, but the current powers continued to control – even worse, they made more difficult – the process of securing authorisation to open a business.'[58]

'It would be as difficult to open my own production enterprise today as it was 60 years ago,' Shmelev maintained in our interview, and added, 'Gaidar talked about promoting private initiative, but he did nothing.' Consistent with Shmelev's assessment, Natal'ia Shuliat'eva, president of the Russian Union of Small Enterprises, argued in February 1993 that 'Today, the lack of state support for small enterprises is shown in the fact that there are fewer and fewer private production enterprises. Only a naive person would start a production enterprise now.'[59]

We have shown elsewhere that the private sector also became hostage to the intrusions of criminal groups as the reforms continued. An important reason for this development was the loosening of state control in ways that permitted organised crime to step into the resulting coordination vacuum.[60] Gaidar saw this slackening of the reins as 'a methodologically new advance in Russia's history' which would make it possible for 'the invisible hand of the market' to 'begin pulling the wagon out of the mud'.[61] But a 1994 study that was prepared under the direction of Yeltsin aide Petr Filippov found that at least 70 per cent of privatised enterprises and commercial banks had connections with organised crime, and that, unlike the situation in Western Europe and the United States, 'In Russia, organised crime controls all kinds of activity'.[62] Another 1994 study concluded that 55 per cent of enterprise capital and 80 per cent of voting shares of enterprises were in the hands of criminal groups.[63] The implications of this development for a successful Russian transition to a competitive market economy may be grim, analyst Louise Shelley concludes. 'The pervasiveness of organised crime may lead to an alternative form of development', she suggests – 'political clientelism and controlled markets.'[64]

If Russia's reformers did not create conditions favourable to normal entrepreneurship this outcome was not seen as alarming by some of the more prominent Western advisers to the Russian government. Jeffrey Sachs's 'main pillars' of

58. Dorofeev 'Znaki vozrozhdeniia', *op. cit.*
59. 'Malyi biznes v ozhidanii' (round-table discussion) *Ekonomicheskaia Gazeta* 7, February 1993, p. 4.
60. Nelson and Kuzes, *Radical Reform in Yeltsin's Russia*, *op. cit.*
61. Egor Gaidar 'Novyi kurs', *Izvestiia* 26, 10 February 1994, p. 4.
62. 'Rossiiskaia mafiia sobiraet dos'e na krupnykh chinovnikov i politikov', *Izvestiia* 15, 26 January 1994, p. 1. See also Terrorism, Narcotics and International Operations Subcommittee of the Senate Foreign Relations Committee, 'Drug trafficking', 103rd Cong., 2nd sess., 20 April 1994. Available from Federal Information Systems Corporation, Federal News Service. In Mead Data Central, Inc., LEXIS/NEXIS (database online).
63. Boris Krotkov 'Duma otkryvaet pokhod protiv korruptsii', *Delovoi mir* 99, 14 May 1994, p. 1. See also Stephen Handelman 'The Russian "Mafiya"', *Foreign Affairs* 73, March–April 1994, p. 88.
64. Louise I. Shelley 'Post-Soviet organised crime: implications for economic, social and political development', *Demokratisatsiya* 2, Summer 1994, p. 341.

economic reform for Russia, for example, failed to emphasise initiatives which could have promoted the private business sector, and Anders Åslund, who had a great deal to say about stabilisation and privatisation of state enterprises, devoted only minimal attention to the subject of entrepreneurship.[65] By trying to treat an infant market as if it were a mature one, these advisers neglected the extraordinary opportunity that had developed by late 1991 to encourage vigorous expansion of Russia's private sector. As Masarskii describes this situation, 'During the last two years, due to the efforts of our monetarists, hundreds of thousands of enterprises in the private sector were destroyed – enterprises which could have become the basis for efficient production.'[66]

Entrepreneurship and the state bureaucracy

A Yeltsin decree had established the Council on Entrepreneurship, an independent think tank comprised of Russian business executives, in March 1992. It was ostensibly created to provide a business perspective for governmental decision-making, but its early members protested that its advice was largely ignored.[67] In 1993 Ivan Kivelidi was the chair of the council. Kivelidi had become a businessman in 1987, when he organised a cooperative and turned his first small business into an empire. These accomplishments had made him a leading proponent of entrepreneurship, but he had been frustrated in his efforts to help insure that business people in 1993 would have the same opportunities he had enjoyed in 1987. In a July interview, Kivelidi charged that entrepreneurship seemed to be, for the government, only 'an abstract idea, and even dangerous. It is a threat to their existence.' In the Yeltsin government, Kivelidi argued, initiatives which had been announced with the stated goal of promoting entrepreneurship had actually been created for the benefit of 'quick bureaucrats who seized a piece of our proposal in order to find "a warmer place" for themselves'.[68]

In our interviews with Russian business and opinion leaders, the focus of responsibility for the government's neglect of entrepreneurship was wide-ranging. Viktor Shchekochikhin, President of the Russian Union of Private Owners, told us in July 1993 that 'the post-Communist regime which is declaring its commitment to the market doesn't want to see private entrepreneurship develop. These people want to create pseudo-entrepreneurs . . . *Gosplan* entrepreneurship is now developing.'

Even the World Bank and the European Bank for Reconstruction and Development do not work with entrepreneurs, Shchekochikhin maintained, although they say that they want to support entrepreneurship. 'They go through state structures, which aren't interested in promoting private business', Shchekochikhin charged.

---

65. He did complain, however, that entrepreneurs often had to pay bribes. See Anders Åslund 'The gradual nature of economic change in Russia', in Anders Åslund and Richard Layard (eds) *Changing the Economic System in Russia*, St Martin's Press, New York, 1993, p. 21.
66. Mark Masarskii 'Ia skorbliu po pogibshim predpriiatiiam', *Delovoi mir* 235, 22–28 November 1993, p. 1.
67. See Mikhail Glukhovsky 'Yeltsin's council means business', *Delovie lyudi* 26, September 1992, pp. 20–21.
68. Larisa Il'ina and Ivan Kivelidi 'Biznes pridet k vlasti ne ran'she 2000 goda', *Delovoi mir* 124, 3 July 1993, p. 9.

'Thus, in practical terms, Western help doesn't often reach private entrepreneurs. And foundations that were organised according to Russian government decisions only *pretend* to represent private entrepreneurs', he added. This criticism was pointedly directed against Gaidar's All-Russia Association of Private and Privatising Enterprises, which was created before the April 1993 referendum.[69] Zatulin agreed with Shchekochikhin's conclusion, arguing that Gaidar's new association was no more than 'a decorative supplement' to GKI.[70]

The privatised sector 'is still close to the state sector', Shchekochikhin stated – closer to it than to the private sector. 'Private entrepreneurs have nothing to do with the privatisation of state enterprises.' To Shchekochikhin, the privatisation programme was achieving only one goal: that of 'dividing property into parts, which is just a continuation of the old socialist idea'. The privatisation planners neglected what should have been their main priority in privatisation, he suggested, which is how to create a real market and real entrepreneurship through the distribution of the vast holdings under state control. That is a task, he concluded, which is entirely different from the one they undertook.

Masarskii insists that Gaidar understood from the beginning that the government's policies would have a dampening effect on entrepreneurship. Masarskii attributed his pursuit of initiatives that were unfavourable toward entrepreneurs as stemming from Gaidar's position. 'He represents the interests of the state', Masarskii argues. 'That means the "apparatus" – the power which has suppressed the civil society until now.'[71] This conclusion is underscored by a report prepared by a panel of prominent economists for *Novaia Ezhednevnaia Gazeta* at the end of 1993 which stated that, although the command system was swiftly demolished with Gaidar's reforms, no satisfactory alternative system was created. Instead, the study finds, the state bureaucracy came to see 'in the emerging entrepreneurial class a threatening competitor'.[72]

During 1993, Western governments and international financial institutions began to demand more insistently that Russian reforms attend more closely to the requirements of effective entrepreneurship. Although most of the aid that G-7 leaders pledged to Yeltsin in advance of the April 1993 referendum was not forthcoming following his referendum victory,[73] the entrepreneurship component of promised Western assistance remained a prominent lever of influence in the West. In May 1994, for example, Assistant Secretary of State Strobe Talbott underscored the Clinton administration's 'special emphasis' on assistance for new Russian businesses in a hearing of the House Appropriations Committee, and Representative Robert

69. See Elena Kotel'nikova 'Chubais reshil ukrepit' svoi pozitsii "sverkhu" i "snizu", *Kommersant-daily* 169, 4 September 1993, p. 3.
70. Stepan Kiselev 'Konstantin Zatulin: "My dolzhny prizvat' k vlasti novykh liudei'", *Moskovskie novosti* 24, 13 June 1993, p. A10.
71. Masarskii 'Ia skorbliu po pogibshim predpriiatiiam', *op. cit.*
72. 'Krizis v Rossii budet preodolen v . . . godu', *Novaia Ezhednevnaia Gazeta* 57, 2 December 1993, p. 3.
73. Sachs estimated in January 1994 that perhaps $4 billion of the $28 billion announced in 1993 had actually arrived. See Jeffrey Sachs 'Betrayal', *The New Republic*, 31 January 1994, p. 14.

Livingston likened Russia to 'a burned-out forest', whose young entrepreneurs 'are like the seedlings coming up through the ashes . . . We want to make sure that they are cultivated and encouraged to whatever degree possible', Livingston said, 'and I guess that's really the essence of our programme of assistance to Russia.'[74] In a similar vein, an April 1994 statement in St Petersburg by the chair of the European Bank for Reconstruction and Development (EBRD) emphasised that the EBRD was changing its loan strategy and would now shift support to specific entrepreneurial projects in different cities and regions of Russia – with particular emphasis on small and medium-size enterprises.[75]

In the context of these clear signals, a number of Russian analysts have suggested that the Russian government's continuing, if reluctant, attention to entrepreneurship in 1994 was partially a response to pressure from the West. Writing in *Kommersant-daily*, for example, Sergei Viktorov noted in May 1994 that Western governments and financial organisations 'traditionally demand from Russia's leaders support for small private entrepreneurship, in particular, as proof of their adherence to the course of reform'.[76]

Although entrepreneurship was still being prominently encouraged with words in 1994, as it had been from the start of Yeltsin's radical reforms, the lack of useful measures which could have positive effects for entrepreneurship continued to elicit criticism from analysts. Thus, when the Russian government's budget proposal for 1994 was submitted to the state Duma, Yavlinskii was one of many who objected to its priorities. 'The draft for the federal budget does not conform to the necessary priorities in economic and social policy', the April statement by the YABLOKO faction argued.[77] These deputies agreed with Aleksandr Ioffe, chair of the Moscow government's Council of Experts on Small and Medium-Sized Businesses, that 'Only the state is able to start the engine of entrepreneurship, to supply money for small businesses.'[78] YABLOKO objected that the portion of the budget aimed at supporting small business was less than 0.01 per cent of the total. This amount needed to be increased 50 to 100 times, the lawmakers argued.[79] In the budget proposal 'the share of state expenditures for institutional transformation is extremely low', according to the April YABLOKO statement. 'The urgent tasks for economic

74. Foreign Operations, Export Financing and Related Programs Subcommittee of the House Appropriations Committee, 'The Former Soviet Union and Eastern Europe', 103rd Cong., 2nd sess., 10 May 1994. Available from Federal Information Systems Corporation, Federal News Service. In Mead Data Central, Inc., LEXIS/NEXIS (database online).
75. Irina Vasil'eva 'Evrobank meniaet strategiiu', *Megapolis-Express* 14, 27 April 1994, p. 13. See also Mikhail Loginov 'Evropeitsy vydelili eshche \$10 mln rossiiskomu biznesu', *Kommersant-daily* 196, 15 October 1994, p. 6.
76. Sergei Viktorov 'Vlasti reshili, chto nuzhny melkim predprinimateliam', *Kommersant-daily* 87, 14 May 1994, p. 3.
77. Boris Krotkov 'Biudzhet, god 1994: situatsiia arkhislozhnaia', *Delovoi mir* 81, 16 April 1994, p. 1. See also 'Novyi biudzhet: ni vashim, ni nashim', *Novaia Ezhednevnaia Gazeta* 68, 14 April 1994, p. 2.
78. Ioffe 'K nam – milosti prosim', *op. cit.*
79. Grigorii Yavlinskii, Mikhail Zadornov, Sergei Ivanenko and Aleksei Mikhailov 'Biudzhet – 94', *Nezavisimaia Gazeta* 70, 14 April 1994, p. 4.

policy today are institutional and structural transformation. From this point of view, the 1994 budget does not provide the necessary vehicles to realise the most important economic priorities.'[80]

During May 1994, Russia's government completed a document aimed at showing support for small businesses. The Federal Programme of State Support for Small Entrepreneurship proposed 'to create good economic, legal, and organisational conditions' for small business.[81] But details of the programme were not encouraging to entrepreneurs. 'It seems that the initial goal of those who developed the programme was not so much to support entrepreneurs as to support those bureaucratic structures which want to continue leading and managing entrepreneurs, the same way they used to oversee state production', Lopatnikov said.[82]

Several federal-level organisations had been created by 1994 which were devoted to entrepreneurship. There was a Federal Foundation to Support Entrepreneurship and Develop Competition, and there were four departments in different ministries which were aimed at promoting private business. But the significance of these initiatives was contested by analysts. Alla Aloian of the Federal Foundation argued in June that, 'In spite of its repeated declarations, the government does not consider the development of small business as one of its priorities.'[83] And speaking of the deliberations within the government which surrounded development of the Federal Programme developed in May 1994, Aloian charges that it 'was not discussed with much interest'.[84] Yet Viacheslav Prokhorov, chair of the government's Department of Property Management and Entrepreneurship, believed in mid-year that, in spite of regional obstacles to the development of entrepreneurship, 'the state has now actually turned its face toward small business. Both in the government and state Duma I see a positive attitude toward its development.'[85] But Ivan Grachev, chair of the state Duma Subcommittee on Small Business, stated in October that 'the people who hold state power in the country today still do not understand the role of small business in a market economy. They see it as secondary.'[86] And Prokhorov, also, was concerned about the implications of decentralisation for the business climate, insisting in May that the heads of local administration would need to 'restrain regional tendencies toward restrictive surveillance over entrepreneurship and excessive licensing requirements'.[87] We will return to the question of regional control in the concluding section of this chapter.

80. Novyi biudzhet: ni vashim, ni nashim', *op. cit.*, p. 1.
81. Igor' Skliarov 'Malyi biznes: namereniia i vozmozhnosti', *Ekonomika i zhizn'* 25, June 1994, p. 1.
82. Leonid Lopatnikov 'Chinovnikam – milliardy, predprinimateliam – obeshchaniia', *Delovoi mir* 2, 10–16 January 1994, p. 2. See also Leonid Lopatnikov 'A tsifry? Ikh prosto vycherknuli . . .', *Delovoi mir* 89, 25 April–1 May 1994, p. 11.
83. Alla Aloian 'Malyi biznes: problemy i prioritety', *Delovoi mir* 133, 25 June 1994, p. 5. See also Lopatnikov 'A tsifry? Ikh prosto vycherknuli . . .', *op. cit.*
84. Aloian *op. cit.*
85. Skliarov 'Malyi biznes: namereniia i vozmozhnosti', *op. cit.*
86. Igor' Skliarov 'Malyi biznes: kakova vlast', takova ego podderzhka', *Ekonomika i zhizn'* 41, October 1994, p. 1.
87. Elena Kotel'nikova, 'Pravitel'stvo predlozhilo regionam podderzhat' chastnikov', *Kommersant-daily*, 89, 18 May 1994, p. 3.

The tax system and other impediments to entrepreneurship

A confiscatory taxation system took shape in Russia near the end of 1991 – one formulated to achieve specific goals. Hyperinflation was threatened, and high taxes were seen as a way of preventing it. The state also needed revenue, and profits from private businesses were viewed as a ready source. But the result for business activity, economist Larisa Piiasheva maintains, was that 'all the honest and upright people . . . went broke the first year of Yeltsin's reforms. All the rest began evading' the enforcement of governmental regulations.[88] Andrei Orlov, president of the Academy of Economics, adds detail to this assessment. He describes a study of tax problems faced by Russian business people which he completed in the spring of 1994. Orlov found that all levels of taxation, from local to federal, collected from 80 to 90 per cent of reported profits from private businesses.[89] 'Private entrepreneurship has come over time to be treated as a cow which is being milked but not fed', the Moscow Union of Independent Workers complained in a statement they released in mid-1994.[90] This outcome prompted Zatulin to charge that 'Gaidar's government . . . pushed entrepreneurs into tax evasion, which meant bribing tax collectors and corrupting state institutions.'[91]

Frequent changes in tax regulations compounded this problem for business people.[92] Just to keep up with the changing regulatory picture would be a full-time job, analyst Sergei Pepeliaev insists, and would require near-constant revision of a firm's business practices.[93]

Russia's licensing requirements and regulatory provisions directed at private businesses present formidable barriers to new businesses development. Orlov argues that state policy toward small businesses is oriented both toward increasing state revenue and providing a source of income for state bureaucrats (because of the maze of regulations that invite bribery).[94] The director of the State Anti-monopoly Committee's Moscow branch, Oleg Novikov, observes that licensing requirements in Moscow 'create barriers to any entrepreneurship activity in the city', which, he maintains, do not work in the interest of either owners or consumers.[95] When we interviewed Novikov in June 1993, he interpreted such impediments as strategies to preserve monopoly control. 'There is monopoly at every level of government', Novikov insisted, 'and people want to keep it that way.'

88. Larisa Piiasheva 'Svobodu Sergeiu Mavrodi!'. See also Mikhail Deliagin, 'Fiskal'naia politika gosudarstva meshaet rynochnym reformam', *Finansovye izvestiia* 44, 29 September 1994, p. 4.
89. Yurii Chirkov 'Malye shansy dlia malogo biznesa', *Delovoi mir* 127, 18 June 1994, p. 4.
90. Leonid Lopatnikov 'Podderzhka malogo predprinimatel'stva', *Delovoi mir* 153, 18–24 July 1994, p. 1.
91. Kiselev 'Konstantin Zatulin: "My dolzhny prizvat' k vlasti novykh liudei"', *op. cit.*
92. See Mark Goriachev 'Den'gi reshaiut vse', *Izvestiia* 166, 2 September 1993, p. 4.
93. Sergei Pepeliaev 'Nakazat' ili obobrat'?', *Ekonomika i zhizn'* 25, June 1994, p. 3.
94. Chirkov 'Malye shansy dlia malogo biznesa', *op. cit.*
95. *Ibid.*

Conclusion: two phases of reform

Regional issues

Following the end of voucher privatisation in June 1994, the process of comprehensively implementing policies to sustain the course of reforms was just beginning. To the centrifugal tendencies in Russia that had already strengthened regional autonomy was added an extension in the domain for local discretion in the implementation and consolidation of reforms in the post-voucher phase. Thus, the potential influence of both official elites and private interest groups had substantially increased since the beginning of reforms under Yeltsin. Not only privatisation but also private entrepreneurship would face formidable challenges as the consolidation phase of reforms began. Conditions favourable toward private business activity had not been realised, even though a number of measures had been announced from 1992 onward with the stated goal of promoting entrepreneurship. Entrepreneurs faced a daunting tangle of licensing requirements and regulatory provisions, an inadequately developing legal system, burdensome taxation policies that changed frequently, credit policies that were unfavourable to business growth, and vulnerability to organised crime.[96] And as with privatisation, initiatives oriented toward the expansion of entrepreneurship were certain to be contested in cities and regions, where the effectiveness of their implementation would depend on the political actions of competing interest groups at those levels.

Philip Hanson observes that in Russia, not only do the interests of local elites frequently diverge from those of central administrators, but the potential for regional differences in the implementation of reform policies is also great, and reflects variations in economic conditions, technological factors and the availability of natural resources as well as policy orientations among local leaders. Public spending needs vary from region to region, as do tax contributions. In the absence of a standard formula for redistributing budget revenues, *ad hoc* arrangements have been worked out between the centre and individual regions. The weakness of the centre contributes further to the 'disorder in relations between the centre and the periphery' Hanson observes,[97] and these conditions in combination offered exceptional opportunities for local interest groups to shape economic reforms, as structural adjustment to early reform initiatives began to accelerate.

Edward Carmines and James Stimson suggest that local variation in issue resolution is to be expected when control from the centre is limited.[98] Consistent with that

---

96. See Nelson and Kuzes, *Radical Reform in Yeltsin's Rusia, op. cit.*; Chirkov, 'Malye shansy dlia malogo biznesa', *op. cit.*; Seifali Akhundov 'Chinovniki nastupaiut', *Obshchaia Gazeta*, 22, 3–9 June 1994, p. 3; 'Malyi biznes khochet vyiti iz podpol'ia. Kto protiv?', *Tsentr plius*, 18, 1993, p. 3; Medvedev 'Proidena li nizhniaia tochka ekonomicheskogo krizisa?', *op. cit.*; Dorofeev 'Znaki vozrozhdeniia', *op. cit.*; Ioffe 'K nam – milosti prosim', *op. cit.*; Drachev 'Malyi rossiiskii biznes i bol'shoi zapadnyi kapital', *op. cit.*; and Yavlinskii 'Inaia reforma', *op. cit.*

97. Philip Hanson, 'The centre versus the periphery in Russian economic policy', *RFE/RL Research Report* 3, 29 April 1994, p. 28.

98. Edward G. Carmines and James A. Stimson, 'On the evolution of political issues,' in William H. Riker (ed) *Agenda Formation*, University of Michigan Press, Ann Arbor, 1993, p. 155.

general perspective, regional differences in the implementation of reforms were already evident in Russia at the conclusion of voucher privatisation,[99] as local officials and interest groups pursued their diverse political objectives with varying degrees of success.[100] In late 1994, then, it was becoming clear that assessments of the evolving climate for entrepreneurship and the continuing direction of privatisation needed to be region-specific.

Beyond state autonomy

The initiation phase of Russian economic reform under Gaidar was guided by a policy-making group that illustrates central characteristics of the 'change team' approach described by John Waterbury, in which relatively autonomous technocrats are partially protected from interest group pressure by the head of state.[101] This strategy is intended to weaken anti-reform coalitions, and the Russian reformers' approach enjoyed at least limited success in achieving that short-term goal.[102] Waterbury suggests, however, that 'top-down change without the support of organised constituencies probably cannot be sustained'.[103] Consistent with this position, Peter Evans argues that the state autonomy which offers advantages in the initiation phase of reforms should give way in the consolidation phase[104] of structural transformation to a broader organisational autonomy. Taking into account the perspectives of Alexander Gerschenkron[105] and Albert Hirschman,[106] which highlight the role of the developing state as a 'surrogate entrepreneur' and provider of investment-promoting incentives, Evans concludes that what is called for under such circumstances is 'a

99. See Nelson and Kuzes, *Radical Reform in Yeltsin's Russia, op. cit.*; Elizabeth Teague 'Russia's local elections begin', *RFE/RL Research Report* 3, 18 February 1994, pp. 1–4; Richard Sakwa *Russian Politics and Society*, Routledge, New York, 1993, pp. 189–200; Vera Shirobokova 'Nalogovaia voina regionov s Tsentrom ugrozhaet Rossii razvalom', *Finansovye izvestiia* 60, 24–30 December 1993, p. 1; Il'ia Shkabara and Andrei Skvortsov '"Sil'nye" regiony Rossii poluchat dopolnitel'nye sredstva', *Segodnia* 89, 14 May 1994, p. 3; and Ol'ga Senatova and Aleksandr Kasimov 'Chto za strana nakhoditsia za Moskovskoi kol'tsevoi dorogoi?' *Novaia Ezhednevnaia Gazeta*, 95, 25 May 1994, p. 5.

100. Stephan Haggard and Steven B. Webb 'Introduction', in Haggard and Webb (eds) *Voting for Reform: Democracy, Political Liberalization, and Economic Adjustment*, Oxford University Press, New York, 1994, p. 16.

101. John Waterbury 'The heart of the matter? Public enterprise and the adjustment process', in Stephan Haggard and Robert R. Kaufman (eds) *The Politics of Economic Adjustment: International Constraints, Distributive Conflicts, and the State*, Princeton University Press, Princeton, 1992, pp. 190–92.

102. See Lynn D. Nelson and Irina Y. Kuzes 'Coordinating the Russian privatisation programme', *RFE/RL Research Report* 3, 20 May 1994, pp. 15–27; and Nelson and Kuzes, 'Evaluating the Russian voucher privatisation programme', *op. cit.*

103. *Ibid*, p. 192.

104. In this second, consolidation phase, reformers try to 'stabilise expectations around a new set of incentives and convince economic agents that they cannot be reversed at the discretion of individual decision-makers' (Haggard and Kaufman, *The Politics of Economic Adjustment, op. cit.*, 19).

105. Alexander Gerschenkron *Economic Backwardness in Historical Perspective*, Belknap Press, Cambridge, 1962.

106. Albert Hirschman *The Strategy of Economic Development*, Yale University Press, New Haven, Connecticut 1958.

state that is more embedded in society than insulated'.[107] Evans's comparative analysis of several countries at different stages of development indicates, however, that embedded autonomy is more likely under certain societal and institutional conditions than others.[108] Further limiting the applicability of the statist perspective is the fact that the state is often not a unitary actor. State agencies in Russia sometimes operate at cross purposes, and at the regional level different officials – presidential representatives, heads of administration, and local Duma deputies, for example – often have divergent interests in economic reform and issues concerning privatisation and entrepreneurship more specifically.[109]

The clearest alternative to Evans's concern with neocorporatist interest group systems is pluralist theory, which views political influence as emanating from diverse groups, whose actions are often independent of the state.[110] Pluralism directs attention to interest group influence which extends well beyond that which is found under conditions of embedded state autonomy, but as representatives of the statist perspective have pointed out, it often exaggerates the degree to which state actions are constrained by societal interests.[111]

107. Peter Evans 'The state as problem and solution: predation, embedded autonomy, and structural change', in Haggard and Kaufman (eds) *The Politics of Economic Adjustment, op. cit.*, p. 148. Evans points out that this view makes the relationship between state capacity and autonomy more ambiguous than it would seem to be from a Weberian or a neo-Marxist point of view (*ibid*). Evans's orientation exemplifies 'third wave' thinking regarding development and the state – less optimistic about the state as a carrier of development than were first wave post-war development perspectives, and less visionary regarding the possibility of sharply curtailing the state's role than were the later minimalist theories of the state. See also Theda Skocpol 'Bringing the state back in', in Peter Evans, Dietrich Rueschemeyer and Theda Skocopol *Bringing the State Back In*, Cambridge University Press, New York, 1985, pp. 3–37; Stephen D. Krasner 'Approaches to the state: alternative conceptions and historical dynamics', *Comparative Politics* 16, January 1984, pp. 223–46; and Eric A. Nordlinger 'Taking the state seriously', in Myron Weiner and Samuel P. Huntington (eds) *Understanding Political Development*, Little, Brown, Boston, Massachusetts, 1987, pp. 353–90.
108. *Ibid.* See also Philippe Schmitter and Gerhard Lehmbruch (eds) *Trends Toward Corporatist Intermediation*, Sage, Beverly Hills, 1979; and Gerhard Lehmbruch and Philippe Schmitter (eds) *Patterns of Corporatist Policymaking*, Sage, Beverly Hills, 1982.
109. See, for example, Nelson and Kuzes's discussion of property management committees and property funds in Russia (Nelson and Kuzes, 'Coordinating the Russian privatisation programme, *op. cit.*).
110. See Robert A. Dahl, *Who Governs? Democracy and Power in an American City*, Yale University Press, New Haven, Connecticut, 1961; Robert A. Dahl, *Pluralist Democracy in the United States: Conflict and Consent*, Rand McNally, Chicago, 1967; and David B. Truman *The Governmental Process: Political Interests and Public Opinion*, Alfred A. Knopf, New York, 1971. Of course, neocorporatism itself encompasses divergent schools of thought. See, for example, Noel O'Sullivan 'The political theory of neo-corporatism', in Andrew Cox and Noel O'Sullivan (eds) *The Corporate State: Corporatism and the State Tradition in Western Europe*, Edward Elgar, Aldershot, 1988, pp. 3–27; and Alan Cawson, *Corporatism and Political Theory*, Basil Blackwell, New York, 1986.
111. See Eric Nordlinger, *On the Autonomy of the Democratic State*, Harvard University Press, Cambridge, Massachusetts, 1981; and Skocpol 'Bringing the state back in' *op. cit.* For a discussion of the limitations of the statist perspective for the analysis of interest group politics, see Pierre Birnbaum, *States and Collective Action: The European Experience*, Cambridge University Press, Cambridge, 1988.

Stephan Haggard and Robert Kaufman propose an approach to the analysis of economic reform politics which transcends the limitations of neocorporatism's embeddedness emphasis while avoiding the tendency of pluralism to exaggerate the power of interest groups. Haggard and Kaufman point out that the 'politics of initiation', in the first phase of a reform programme, tend to allow for the insulation of 'politicians and their technocratic allies from particular interest group constraints'. But in the second phase, the 'politics of consolidation' demand 'a somewhat different balance between state autonomy and the representation of interests' – one which requires studied constituency building and the crystallisation of alliances among affected interest groups.[112]

Aleksandr Radygin, head of the privatisation department in Egor Gaidar's Institute for the Economy in Transition and one of the authors of the Russian privatisation programme, observed in May 1994 that the administrative elite still controlled the levers of Russian enterprise, and that 'the formation of the new property structure – which is the objective that was presented as being most important in the privatisation process – is still ahead.'[113] In a like vein, Evgenii Yasin, head of the Analytic Centre of the Administration, wrote in June 1994, 'There is no so-called "effective" owner yet, and in this sense privatisation has not achieved its aims'.[114] And Boris Fedorov, former Minister of Finance, cautioned in July, 'The danger now is that . . . local powers – communists and other interest groups – will start the last battle to stop privatisation. There are signs of that in the Parliament, in the regions, and in the government.'[115] Gaidar describes the current situation in similar terms, especially emphasising the importance of regional politics. 'Capitalism cannot, in reality, be stopped', Gaidar maintains. 'But the dilemma is bureaucratic (*nomenklatura*, state) capitalism or democratic (civic, open) capitalism.' The potential of bureaucratic elites to derail the reforms is especially strong in the regions, where they 'retain absolute power', he continues.[116]

These developments suggest that future research into Russian reform should attend closely to the significance of interest group politics for initiatives from both the centre and localities. In a country such as Russia, where political parties are weak, interest group analysis not only gives the researcher a good vantage point for examining features of the state–society linkage but also can offer suggestive clues to the kinds of citizen responses and concerns which are likely to shape the evolution of party politics, since it seems clear that strong interest groups may be closely allied with strong parties in countries with mature political party systems.[117] Even more basic

112. Haggard and Kaufman, *The Politics of Economic Adjustment, op. cit.*, pp. 19–20.
113. Aleksandr Radygin 'Delo Chubaisa zavershit tol'ko vtorichnyi rynok', *Moskovskie novosti* 22, 29 May–5 June 1994, p. B1.
114. Evgenii Yasin 'D'iavol – v detaliakh', *Literaturnaia Gazeta*, 22, 1 June 1994, p. 1.
115. Boris Fedorov 'Konets vaucheram. Nachalo privatizatsii', *Izvestiia*, 123, 1 July 1994, p. 2.
116. Egor Gaidar 'Fashizm i biurokratiia', *Segodnia* 110, 15 June 1994, p. 10.
117. See Graham, K. Wilson *Interest Groups*, Oxford, Basil Blackwell, 1990, pp. 33–34. Wilson also discusses the controversy over whether or not there is an inverse relationship between the strength of interest groups and of political parties (pp. 156–72).

to the importance of interest group development for future political arrangements in countries undergoing structural change, Metin Heper suggests, is the likelihood that the particular configuration of relations between the state and civil society in earlier stages of national development exerts strong influence on the dominant pattern of interest group politics that are subsequently insitutionalised.[118] The significance of these dynamics for the long-term success of entrepreneurship in Russia is obvious.

Russia's reform results through late 1994 underscore Merilee Grindle and John Thomas's point that, 'However difficult and politically risky it is to decide to introduce a reformist initiative, the process of implementing and sustaining that decision is likely to be even more fraught with difficulty and risk.'[119] It is at this point that the fit of state initiatives with interest group concerns that are effectively voiced becomes critical to maintaining the direction and momentum of reforms. Thus associations which represented entrepreneurs were in a good position at the end of 1994 – perhaps their best position since the dissolution of the Soviet Union – to exert strong influence on the continuing evolution of Russian reforms.

118. Metin Heper 'The state and interest groups with special reference to Turkey', in Heper (ed.) *Strong State and Economic Interest Groups: The Post-1980 Turkish Experience*, Walter de Gruyter, New York, 1991, p. 6.
119. Merilee S. Grindle and John W. Thomas *Public Choices and Policy Change: The Political Economy of Reform in Developing Countries*, The Johns Hopkins University Press, Baltimore, Maryland, 1991, p. 121.

Chapter 8

PRIVATISATION AND THE STRUGGLE FOR CONTROL OF THE ENTERPRISE[1]

Simon Clarke and Veronika Kabalina

The fundamental difference between privatisation in the East and the West is that in the West privatisation is the culmination of an extended process of restructuring and refinancing to secure the initial profitability and medium-term prospects of the object of privatisation. Without such preparatory work, there would be no possibility of finding buyers for the object of privatisation.

In the former Soviet bloc privatisation is essentially a formal process, with little or no substantive preparation, which involves no more than the legal definition and demarcation of the assets of the enterprise, its incorporation as a private enterprise, usually in the joint-stock form, and the issue and distribution of shares. Privatisation in Russia is not about capitalist transformation, but about the constitution of property rights.

The politics of privatisation in Russia

The transformation of state ownership was an inevitable consequence of the attempt to replace 'administrative' by 'economic' methods of regulation which lay at the centre of Gorbachev's reform programme. The programme of *perestroika*

1.   This chapter is based on our primary research and that of our collaborators, supplemented by monitoring of the local and national Russian press. The collaborative research project, funded until April 1994 under the East–West Programme of the ESRC, on 'the restructuring of management and industrial relations in Russia', is directed in Britain by Peter Fairbrother and Simon Clarke, with Russian research teams coordinated through the Centre for Comparative Labour Studies in Moscow, directed by Irina Kozina (Samara), Petr Biziukov (Kemerovo), Olga Pulyaeva and Kostya Burnishev (Novokuznetsk), Veronika Kabalina (Moscow), Vladimir Ilyin and Pavel Krotov (Syktyvkar). Additional discussion and case studies of privatisation can be found in the following papers published on the basis of this research: Simon Clarke 'Privatisation and the development of capitalism in Russia', *New Left Review*, 196, November/December 1992, pp. 3–27; Simon Clarke and Petr Biziukov 'Privatisation in Russia: the road to a people's capitalism?', *Monthly Review*, 44(6), November 1992, pp. 38–45; Simon Clarke, Peter Fairbrother, Michael Burawoy and Pavel Krotov *What about the Workers? Workers and the Transition to Capitalism in Russia*, Verso, London, 1993, Chapter 9; Veronika Kabalina and Alla Nazimova 'Privatisation through labour conflicts: the case of Russia', *Economic and Industrial Democracy*, 14, 1993, pp. 9–28; Simon Clarke 'The politics of labour and capital', in S. White, A. Pravda and Z. Gitelman (eds) *Developments in Russian and Post-Soviet Politics*, 3rd edn., Macmillan, London, 1994, pp. 162–186; Simon Clarke, Peter Fairbrother, Vadim Borisov and Petr Bizyukov, 'The privatisation of industrial enterprises in Russia: four case-studies', *Europe-Asia Studies*, 46 (2), 1994, pp. 179–214; Vadim Borisov 'A very Soviet privatisation', *Labour Focus on Eastern Europe*, 47, 1994, pp. 31–36.

was based on a fundamental contradiction: although *perestroika* was based on democratisation and the decentralisation of responsibility, these were seen only as the means to strengthen centralised control which would be asserted by economic and ideological rather than administrative means. This contradiction ran through both policy and legislation between 1987 and 1991, until it finally broke the whole system.

The basis of the process of privatisation in Russia was the 'destatisation' of property, which expressed the disintegration of the monolithic administrative-command system to leave independent enterprises, associations and concerns, cooperatives, leasehold and shareholding companies and individual entrepreneurs, all appropriating and using, buying and selling state assets over which the central state apparatus had lost control, but over which no single individual or corporate entity had established clear ownership rights. This 'destatisation' of property left the enterprise directorate in control of the means of production, with all rights but none of the responsibilities of ownership. They disposed of the assets under their control at will, but had no obligation to meet their liabilities, which were still nominally those of the state.

In the absence of a strong state, whose disintegration had been the other side of destatisation, there was no alternative but to give juridical recognition to the control of the industrial *nomenklatura* over the assets of the enterprise. However, the purpose of establishing juridical recognition of the rights of private ownership of the means of production was not to give *carte blanche* to those who had already in practice gained those rights, but to impose on them the responsibilities of private ownership in an attempt to subject them to the 'discipline' of the market and to the levers of fiscal, monetary and financial regulation. The general conception of privatisation in Russia as a process of freeing enterprises from the shackles of state control is the inverse of the truth. Privatisation in Russia has been dominated by the attempt to restore central control over the economy by establishing a juridical framework within which enterprises could be subjected to the instruments of government economic, financial and monetary policy.

The All-Union Law on Destatisation and Privatisation, which was approved on 1 July 1991, allowed the conversion of state enterprises to leased, collective, cooperative, joint-stock or private ownership. The labour collective was given a preferential right to shares, and had the power to determine the form and procedure for privatisation. However, the Law was not so much about the transfer of state assets to private ownership, as about the transformation of state property into other forms of corporate property, and particularly to the form of the joint-stock company. Thus the law did not define any procedures through which privatisation could be achieved in practice.

While the contending forces in the state apparatus saw privatisation primarily as a means of transforming and reconstituting state power over the economy, enterprise directors had quite different ambitions. Enterprise directors had established their independence as the system disintegrated around them, and saw privatisation as the means of securing juridical recognition for this independence. They were not going to sit quietly by and see themselves placed under the control of new owners. However, they did not press their claims in their own name, but in the name of the people, in the form of the 'labour collective' of the enterprise.

First steps in privatisation – Russia's managerial revolution

Privatisation proceeded slowly through 1990 and 1991. However, some enterprise directors were able to exploit the provisions of the various property laws to assert their independence, resting on the support of their workforces to press their claims against those of external economic and political structures to carry through the first stage of Russia's 'managerial revolution'.

The pioneers of privatisation were those enterprises which had already established *de facto* independence on the basis of their transformation into cooperatives or, more often, leasehold (*arenda*) enterprises. Whether privatisation went via the cooperative or the *arenda* form the pattern was the same. The valuation of the enterprise was based on the discounted historic cost of its assets, which meant that it was sold at a price that was very low even in 1991. Typically shares would be sold to employees at a discounted price, subsidised from the profits of the enterprise, with the enterprise offering cheap credit to finance share purchases. Share allocations would generally take account of a worker's grade and/or earnings, length of service and, sometimes, disciplinary record.

This form of privatisation appealed to both workers and managers. Workers were attracted by the offer of high dividend payouts, the end of centralised control over wages and the implied promise of job security attached to share ownership. Privatisation provided the managers with juridical guarantees of the independence of the enterprise from state control. The closed type of joint-stock company ensured that control of the enterprise could not pass to outsiders. The relatively equal distribution of shares among the labour force enabled the management to continue to use the well-established mechanisms through which they controlled worker representation, and made it unlikely that they would face any concerted internal challenge.

Privatisation was not simply about transforming public assets into private ones. The process was also very important in making it possible to bring the private commercial and financial activities of managers – which had been conducted through subsidiary or parallel cooperatives and small enterprises, which were often of very dubious legality – into the framework of the law. The pioneers of privatisation were the directors who had most actively explored the new forms of economic activity, not so much because their enterprises were the most advanced or the most capitalistic producers, as because their financial and commercial activity was outgrowing the institutional framework within which it had been born. This was reflected in the typical form of privatised company, in which even the smallest of shareholding companies was effectively a kind of investment trust, which remained distinct from the enterprise or enterprises that it owned, with its own management, constitution and decision-making bodies. The outcome was a symbiotic relationship between the (former) state industrial enterprise and capitalist commercial and financial activities in which the two parts remained distinct, but their relationship ambiguous.

Although this first wave of privatisation embraced relatively few enterprises, mostly of medium size, it was a direct expression of the interests of enterprise directors, and so set the pattern to which the industrial *nomenklatura* as a whole aspired, and to which the privatisation process eventually conformed.

Yeltsin's privatisation programme

The dilemma that faced Yeltsin and his entourage once they had seized power in the autumn of 1991 was that the means by which they had done so had fatally weakened the political, juridical, economic and administrative mechanisms through which they could exercise that power. For all the liberal rhetoric about privatisation and the transition to a market economy, the Yeltsin regime had one overriding priority, which was to restore some control over the disintegrating economy, a priority increasingly dominated by fiscal considerations as the government sought to bring the budget deficit under control. The collapse of the authority of the centralised administrative organs meant that the reestablishment of control could only be based on the use of fiscal and monetary instruments, whose effective implementation implied the immediate liberalisation of prices and the rapid privatisation of enterprises. This was a strategy which was in fact the opposite of that advocated by the neo-liberal economists, who stressed the priority of anti-monopoly legislation as the basis of the subjection of enterprises, not to state regulation (and the associated fiscal appropriation of monopoly profits), but to market competition.

Initially the Gaidar government envisaged privatisation as involving the sale of assets both to raise revenue and to create a new class of owners, while it was implacably opposed to giving assets away for nothing and to handing control to the existing management in the name of the 'labour collective'. In the event, the failure to find buyers, the need to secure popular support, and the need to come to terms with the power of the industrial *nomenklatura* led the government progressively to reverse its position during 1992.

The privatisation programme issued in July 1992 marked an almost total capitulation to the demands of the industrial *nomenklatura*. Enterprises were offered three routes to privatisation, with the choice being a matter for a meeting of the labour collective. The first option allocated 25 per cent of the shares to the workers free in the form of non-voting stock, with a right to buy a further 10 per cent with a 30 per cent rebate (the senior management would have an option on a further 5 per cent). The remaining shares would remain in the hands of the state or regional privatisation committees, to be sold by auction at a subsequent date. The second option allowed the workers to purchase a controlling interest in the enterprise directly, instead of having to bid at auction, on a decision of at least two-thirds of the labour collective, with individual share ownership bid for in a closed subscription at little more than a nominal price, and the remaining shares to be sold at auction. Other options were primarily for the privatisation of small enterprises in trade and services and of bankrupt enterprises. Various measures, including the privatisation vouchers, ensured that workers would have the money needed to buy the shares allocated to them. Effectively the labour force was being offered the controlling interest in the enterprise for next to nothing.

The priority of senior management in the first phase of privatisation was to ensure that control of the enterprise did not fall into the hands of outsiders. In general, the second option was more attractive to management because it ensured that the controlling interest remained within the enterprise, so long as the workers bought the shares allocated to them. Although the bulk of the shares would be held by the workers, the management was very experienced at handling the 'representation' of workers' interests to ensure that its own nominees were elected to the board, while worker share ownership provided a useful prop to the ideology of 'social partnership' through which the industrial *nomenklatura* sought to maintain the stability of the enterprise and to consolidate its political base. However, in enterprises in which it was expected that a secondary market for shares would develop, such as the large automobile factories, there was a risk that workers would be induced to sell their voting shares by outside interests. In this situation the first variant could be more attractive since workers received only a minority of non-voting shares.

The decision as to which variant to adopt was nominally a matter for the labour collective, but in general the drawing up of privatisation plans was a process which did not involve the workers, and which did not give rise to significant conflict within the enterprise. Workers had very little understanding of what privatisation involved, little faith that the purchase of shares would improve their economic position, and little opportunity to develop or express their own opinions. The whole process of approval of privatisation plans was rushed through in a few weeks over the summer of 1992, with intensive propaganda campaigns in the shops, and ritual endorsement by short meetings of the labour collective. Management controlled the channels of information so that their proposals were routinely endorsed through the traditional channels of 'representation'. Management conducted intensive propaganda throughout the enterprise to drum up support, primarily in the attempt to persuade workers to take up their allocation of shares so that they would not fall into outside hands. Workers were induced to subscribe for shares by various means, including in some cases the promise of future dividend payouts, but the most common was the implicit or explicit threat that in the event of redundancy those without shares would be the first to go. Although in almost every enterprise management's plans came under criticism, it was exceptional for the plan to meet with significant opposition from the labour force.

The process of mass privatisation in Russia took place remarkably quickly. However, such speed was possible because the act of privatisation itself was a purely formal process, providing juridical confirmation of the *de facto* control of the enterprise by its management, and transforming the basis of representation within the enterprise from that of labour to that of share ownership. The real process of transformation of the enterprise into a proto-capitalist company, and accordingly the real struggle for control of the enterprise, only began after the formal process of privatisation was completed.

Management control and privatisation to the labour collective

The predominance of privatisation to the labour collective in the second wave of 'voucher privatisation' in Russia inevitably raised the question of whether the fears of the neo-liberals, that Russia will follow the dreaded 'Yugoslav road', would be realised. According to the mythology, held even more strongly in the former Soviet bloc than in the West, supposed workers' control in Yugoslavia was the basis of the 'wage consumption of revenues', as workers paid themselves high wages at the expense of profits, and voted for large dividend payouts at the expense of investment. This pattern of behaviour is certainly very familiar to Western business executives, since they practise it themselves all the time, but it is hardly an accurate picture of the Yugoslav case, since it rests on the unfounded supposition that Yugoslav workers controlled their enterprises.

On the other hand, at first sight this picture does appear to provide an accurate characterisation of the Russian situation. It certainly has been the case that enterprises have given priority to making wage payments, and have used their resources to maintain employment and, if possible, to increase wages and benefits at the expense of investment and even of meeting their current costs. It has also been the case that in a significant number of enterprises workers have voted to replace their director, frequently electing a more compliant director in his (or, rarely, her) place. However the fundamental question is whether this is a consequence of the assertion of workers' control, and indeed of whether it is connected to the form of privatisation. To examine this issue we need to look first at the strategy of enterprise management in the post-Soviet enterprise and then at the forms of control of the enterprise. Our central argument is that support for the labour collective is a feature of management strategy, which has different significance at different stages of the transition process, but that the form of privatisation does not impose significant constraints on that strategy.

The first priority of enterprise management was to keep control of their enterprise, using both the time-honoured methods inherited from the old system, and the more highly developed authoritarian-paternalist methods pioneered by those enterprises which privatised in the first wave. With the collapse of the Soviet system the enterprise directors became the *de facto* owners of their enterprises, but having lost the support of higher bodies they had no guarantees of the security of their position. The director was most vulnerable to a challenge from an opposition faction within the enterprise administration, often drawing on support from external political, financial or commercial structures. In the absence of any established ownership rights the only formal bases of managerial legitimacy were the representative bodies of self-management, and particularly the Labour Collective Council, Sovet trudovogo kollektiva (STK) and the meeting of the labour collective. While these bodies were almost universally under management control, they provided the framework within which an opposition faction in management could try to replace the existing director by mobilising worker dissatisfaction in its support. Thus the director sought to avoid conflict within the enterprise by trying by all means possible to maintain wages and benefits.

The extreme aversion to conflict of enterprise management was not only the result of a fear of being ousted, but was more fundamentally a feature of the established forms of authoritarian management of the Soviet enterprise, with much deeper structural and ideological roots than the relatively recent innovation of 'industrial democracy'. Thus, while the STK and the meeting of the labour collective provided an institutional framework within which a director could be ousted, the threat came not from these institutions but from the fact that conflict, if it developed unchecked, tended rapidly to become generalised, with the director becoming the target or the scapegoat. In the past in such a situation the director would have been removed by the Party Committee or by higher authorities; after 1987 the STK or meeting of the collective provided the framework for a director's removal, and following privatisation it became the board of directors or the shareholders' meeting.

Directors needed to retain the support of the collective not only to secure their positions and managerial authority within the enterprise, but also to reinforce their attempts to extract subsidies and privileges from local, regional and central government bodies, which became increasingly important as the 'transition to the market economy' descended into chaos. However, such lobbying could only be effective if the director could speak convincingly on behalf of the labour collective as a whole. The 1989 miners' strikes had first shown enterprise directors how powerful a weapon a strike could be in extracting such concessions, and the vast majority of strikes in Russia, whatever their origins, have turned out in their effects to have been such 'directors' strikes', with demands orchestrated by senior management and addressed to state bodies of various levels to secure subsidies, tax privileges, cheap state-guaranteed credit, and speedy settlement of debts to the enterprise.

This was the main reason why enterprise directors pursued a strategy of 'authoritarian paternalism' in the period of transition. This strategy was expressed in the rhetoric of 'social partnership', in which the directorate guaranteed to protect the labour collective in return for the workers' passive support for the directorate's ownership claims. The cries of 'social partnership' reached a crescendo during the privatisation campaign as the directorate enlisted popular support for its demand for privatisation to the labour collective.

Far from strengthening the workers' control of the enterprise, privatisation to the labour collective was seen by the enterprise directorate as the means of freeing themselves from that control, and securing their position juridically by establishing themselves as representatives of the 'owners' of the enterprise. Their initial priority in the privatisation campaign was to ensure that the enterprise did not fall into the hands of 'outsiders', and a great deal was made of such a threat in their propaganda campaigns within the enterprise to persuade the workers to adopt the second variant of privatisation, and then to buy their allocation of shares, so that in most cases the allocation was well-subscribed.

Once the workers had subscribed to the share issue the first objective, of keeping the shares in the family, had been achieved. The next stage in the strategy of the directorate was to ensure that the new representative bodies of shareholders were as firmly under their control as had been the traditional organs they replaced. Most enterprises distributed shares on a relatively equal basis, although in enterprises which had opened up wide differentials between workers and managers allocation tended to be in proportion to wages, so that managers ended up with larger holdings. Moreover, senior managers had additional privileged allocations, and were able to buy further shares if the issue was undersubscribed. Nevertheless management usually held only a small proportion of shares in the first stages.

In more traditional enterprises, with no record of worker activism, there was no need for management to take any special steps to ensure that the shareholders' meeting voted through the management programme, and elected management's nominees to the Board of Directors, and indeed the traditional meeting of the labour collective was frequently used in lieu of a shareholders' meeting, that is, no account was taken of who held shares and who did not, or of the size of their holdings. Few enterprises had share registers, and even fewer had such registers open for inspection. In one enterprise which we have been studying, workers were not even issued with share certificates, so they had no proof of their ownership.

Where management was less confident of its control a whole range of measures have been employed to ensure that no problems arise. In large enterprises a general meeting of the shareholders can only be held in a sports stadium, with management on the platform controlling the public address system, the selection of speakers, the submission of resolutions and the counting of votes. In many large enterprises management chooses to hold representative meetings, either using the traditional methods of electing representatives in the shops, or persuading workers to assign proxies to their managers. In these circumstances there is no independent monitoring of the electoral process, whose announced results do not always correspond with the impressions of the participants, and no independent check on the number of proxies claimed by managers. Opposition within meetings is headed off by equally familiar methods, by issuing more or less veiled threats of dismissal and even physical violence against opponents, by controlling the agenda, ruling motions out of order, prolonged discussions of trivial issues in order to close the meeting before completion of the agenda.

In general, although these methods are fairly widespread, this is largely out of habit, since none of them is really necessary. Once the board has been elected by the shareholders' meeting the role of the latter is at an end, at least until the next election to the board. If the shareholders' meeting has passed resolutions which are not to the liking of the president of the shareholding company, the president can reverse them, or the minutes of the shareholders' meeting can be falsified. If the board includes malcontents, the president simply fails to call meetings. Moreover, even the board has little significance for the everyday running of the enterprise. In general, the shareholding company is seen as a financial-juridical body without any management role in relation to the productive enterprise, beyond appointing the enterprise director, normally the same person as the president of the shareholding company. Its main function, where it is not a purely paper body, is to serve as a holding company through which the senior managers coordinate their commercial and financial activities and those of their associates.

In our experience, management, except in the most profitable branches of production, is more interested in control than in ownership of the enterprise, and more interested in profiting from enhanced salaries and bonuses and from commercial and financial opportunities, than from dividend payouts which have to be shared with the worker shareholders. Nevertheless, this does not prevent managers from acquiring shares on advantageous terms, often financed by loans from the enterprise or an associated bank, nor from paying out large dividends to pay off their loans. Senior managers have privileged opportunities to purchase additional shares because they know about their availability, they have access to financial resources to fund their purchases, and they know the dividend policy since they make it.

Managers have access to shares on privileged terms in the first stage of privatisation. Thereafter they have to buy their shares on the open market. However, in the absence of any effective secondary share markets and even of any real knowledge of what a share is on the part of the public, the market is not very open. In enterprises in which we have been researching, workers have been induced to sell their shares to management at or close to their massively discounted nominal valuation by various means, the most common being to offer workers the chance of exchanging their shares for cheap consumer goods, exploiting cash shortage and the non-payment of wages to persuade workers to sell shares, holding down wages to induce workers to sell their shares, and persuading or (illegally) forcing retiring and redundant workers to sell their shares.

There are many ways in which the senior management can establish control over blocks of shares which they do not, at least nominally, own. It is not unusual for a block of shares to remain unissued, with voting rights vested in the director or board. Moreover, it is equally common for a portion of the shares to be sold or allocated to subsidiary companies of the main enterprise, with voting rights vested in the board. Similarly, associate companies, often owned by relatives or close associates of senior managers, will typically buy substantial shareholdings. Finally, the appropriate property committee is free to vest the voting rights attached to its residual shareholding in the existing management or its associates.

These links are connected with another feature of privatisation, which is the changing relationship between the large state industrial enterprise and the new commercial and financial structures which oil the wheels of the market economy, and through which state resources have been diverted into private hands. The majority of commercial and financial enterprises were established in close symbiotic relationship with state enterprises, but this relationship was typically sealed by informal personal relationships in which managers of the state enterprise, their relatives, or their close associates, were partners in formally independent companies. The disadvantage of such arrangements was that the relationship between state and private enterprise at best sailed very close to the wind, and more often was simply illegal. The privatisation of the state enterprise then makes it possible to bring these illegal and semi-legal activities within a secure legal framework, by incorporating the commercial and financial enterprises as partners or subsidiaries of the privatised state enterprise, or in many cases as substantial shareholders in the state enterprise. In this way, paradoxically, privatisation provides a way of consolidating the dominance of the enterprise directorate over the proto-capitalist financial and commercial sector, while also providing the directorate with an exit route if life within the enterprise becomes difficult. Typically, the privatised shareholding company is conceived as a holding company, established on the basis of its majority shareholding in the privatised state industrial enterprise, but soon embracing a number of other commercial and financial subsidiaries, through which it can engage in a variety of speculative undertakings, which in many cases will in their turn be major shareholders in the privatised enterprise, leading to complex networks of mutual ownership.

Privatisation also provides a means of sealing links with local or regional authorities by the allocation of shares to those authorities or, not infrequently, the vesting of the residual state-owned shares in those companies. Far from fostering de-monopolisation and the growth of competition, privatisation provided the means of consolidating monopolistic relationships which linked industrial, financial, commercial and state structures in inter-dependent blocks.

Management strategy in 'worker-owned' enterprises

In the transitional period the enterprise directorate had to remain attentive to the needs and expectations of the labour collective. However, once the shares are issued and the board elected, the directorate's hand is freed from dependence on the labour collective as a whole, and a change of strategy is in order.

Management has effective control of the enterprise, but for what purpose does it exercise its control? We can identify three elements in the management strategy of the post-Soviet enterprise, which coexist in different proportions in different enterprises and at different stages of development of the enterprise.

The first element is the simple desire to survive, which for many enterprises in the contemporary situation is the best that can be hoped for. This ambition is strongly underpinned by the traditional ideology of Soviet management, in which the fate and reputation of the director was tied to the fate and prosperity of the enterprise. Thus to some degree this first element is the foundation of any management strategy. There is still a considerable range of variation within this strategy. The survival of the enterprise is not seen in terms of its financial indicators, but in terms of its survival as a productive unit, and above all, as a labour collective. However, survival might equally involve trying to preserve the highest possible level of employment, at the expense of lower wages, short-time working and reductions in social and welfare facilities, or it might involve trying to maintain wages and social expenditure at the expense of large-scale reductions in the labour force. Nevertheless the primary objective is some notion of devoting the enterprise's resources to securing the short-term reproduction of the enterprise as a unit of productive labour.

The second element is what can politely be called a 'rent-seeking' strategy, in which the senior managers are preoccupied with their personal interests. This will often involve the diversification of the enterprise, usually into financial and commercial activity and often involving subsidiary or associate companies, as managers use the resources of the enterprise for their own benefit and to prepare a place for themselves in the private sector. Such activity often crosses the borders of legality, for example, selling the enterprise's products or assets to oneself at discount prices or borrowing from the enterprise at low rates of interest, and not infrequently amounts to outright theft.

The third element is a market-oriented profit-seeking strategy, oriented to the long-term profitability of the enterprise in the new environment of the market economy. It is this element that privatisation and the entire programme of economic reform was designed to foster.

These three elements are by no means mutually exclusive; differences between one enterprise and another relate to the balance between them. Moreover, it is extremely difficult to identify which of these elements prevails in practice in any particular enterprise. Management may espouse the traditional rhetoric of preserving the enterprise, while in fact pursuing an aggressive strategy of restructuring it, which they may judge to be the best way of preserving the enterprise in the long term. The reverse may also be true – a conservative practice may be masked by the rhetoric of capitalist modernisation. Meanwhile, managers in both enterprises will undoubtedly be covering their options by engaging in 'rent-seeking' activity. Moreover, in conditions of extreme economic and political instability a conservative strategy may be the best way of securing the long-term profitability of the enterprise, while a commitment to an aggressive restructuring may mark the undoing of the enterprise if conditions become unfavourable.

The strategy pursued by management depends on a number of factors. Ideological factors are undoubtedly important, with older and longer established directors on the whole finding it more difficult to adapt, while younger directors are more willing to explore new opportunities and to renounce traditional obligations. However, the substantive differences in strategy are often smaller than the contrasting rhetorics might indicate, because the enterprise is severely constrained by both its informal relationships and external circumstances in what it can do. In particular, the collapse of the market and the extreme shortage of working capital and investment funds has meant that connections with political authorities and with commercial and financial structures can play a decisive role in determining opportunities.

The economic position of the enterprise is the most powerful constraint on the strategy pursued by management. In conditions of extreme political and economic instability any long-term planning is extremely difficult. Labour-intensive enterprises, which can diversify rapidly without incurring major fixed investment costs, can exploit changing market opportunities, while heavy industry lacks the resources to make major investments which can only pay off over years. In a situation in which there is an acute shortage of working capital, and real interest rates have reached 5 per cent per month, not only is long-term investment out of the question, but even investment in inventory is insupportable, putting a huge premium on a rapid turnover and on cash-generating activities.

The economic position of the enterprise is also increasingly closely connected with the maintenance of links with the old system. After three years of reform, enterprises which initially embraced independence with enthusiasm are having second thoughts as they find themselves burdened with debt, facing falling demand and an increasingly demoralised labour force. In these circumstances they are looking to maintain stable links with customers and suppliers, the crisis of mutual indebtedness being the heritage and the price of the maintenance of these connections. Similarly, enterprises are keen to preserve or restore connections with regional and branch state authorities, which provide access to state orders, guarantees of local and regional monopoly and various kinds of subsidies and privileges. In this respect enterprises which struck out on their own in the early stages of reform, breaking old economic links and struggling for their independence against local authorities, now find themselves cut off from this lifeline.

Various conjunctional factors also play an important role in determining the economic position of the enterprise, most notably the ability to export or the strategic importance of the enterprise in the local or national economy, which increases its bargaining power. Similarly, enterprises with well-established financial and commercial subsidiaries and associates are in a stronger position for securing access to markets and finance, including subsidised state loans which are channelled through commercial banks.

As already noted, the three aspects of management strategy are by no means mutually exclusive. Although the 'rent-seeking' element appears to be predominant in the present economic, political and legal environment, the enterprise directorate depends on retaining its position in the enterprise to be able to continue its rent-seeking activities, even if the senior managers are able to leave the enterprise if the going gets tough. Thus the management team has to work for the survival of the enterprise, and in order for the enterprise to survive it also has to adapt.

Although it is difficult to generalise about the pattern of restructuring within the enterprise, some common directions do seem to be emerging. Typically, the first step is to undertake a restructuring of the management of the enterprise, removing or downgrading those branches of management which had been central to the administrative control of the enterprise, and expanding the commercial and financial branches of management which play the leading role in the adjustment to changing market conditions. Typically this restructuring is associated with a dualistic management structure in which the day-to-day management of the productive enterprise remains under the control of the chief engineer and shop chiefs, who are oriented to the preservation and reinforcement of traditional authoritarian management structures, while the management of the shareholding company is dominated by economic and financial branches of management, which are oriented to commercial and financial activity, are the most heavily involved in parallel structures, and tend to favour a 'rent-seeking' strategy. Alongside this restructuring of the management hierarchy there is a substantial widening of pay differentials in favour of management as a whole, and within management in favour of the strategic senior managers, despite the fact that this violates the deeply held 'egalitarian' values of the workers who supposedly own the enterprise.

Privatisation also seems to be closely linked to the introduction of redundancies and the restructuring of the labour force. Although most large enterprises have been threatening redundancies for some time, and many have reduced their labour force substantially, these reductions have largely been through natural wastage, primarily in response to low wages. This is why until 1994 labour force restructuring appeared in the form of a continuing high level of labour turnover, rather than a significant growth in the level of unemployment. The disadvantage of a strategy of 'preserving the labour force' by holding down wages is that the workers who leave voluntarily are the more highly skilled and motivated workers. There has therefore been a growing tendency for management to attempt to maintain or increase the wages of these categories of workers by increasing pay differentials, modifying payment systems (including a move towards individual contracts, loyalty bonuses etc.), and by introducing programmes of compulsory redundancy. This tendency is associated with privatisation since those enterprises and branches of production which remain under state ownership and/or control continue to look to the state to meet the wages bill, pressurising the state by running up wage arrears rather than trying to reduce the wages bill by cutting numbers or wages.

On the whole management has been successful in avoiding resistance to redundancy, despite the fact that it violates the traditional social guarantees, by selecting the most marginal and vulnerable workers for redundancy, and rationalising it on the grounds of the need to pay higher wages for those who remain in order to preserve the 'backbone' of the labour collective intact. In many cases responsibility for selecting workers for redundancy is passed down to the shop, section or even brigade level. Compulsory redundancy has largely focused on older workers (those working beyond pension age), auxiliary administrative and manual workers (especially women), and workers with a poor disciplinary record. Wages and redundancy policy is most closely associated with the attempt to restructure the labour forces in circumstances in which, despite the massive fall in production, there are still felt to be acute shortages of skilled and motivated workers. The managerial ideal is to release older, unskilled and undisciplined workers, and to recruit younger, highly skilled and more highly motivated workers in their place. In our view it is this attempted restructuring of the labour force and the associated competition for skilled, loyal and diligent workers, rather than the power of 'workers' control', that underpins the attempt of management to pay high wages and to provide housing, health and social facilities to attract the desirable quality of worker. While those enterprises able to maintain a high standard of living for their workers achieve such an upgrading of the labour force, less prosperous enterprises find skilled and younger workers leaving in droves to seek opportunities elsewhere.

Despite the promise of the regenerative powers of private ownership, privatisation provides very little incentive to investment in new production facilities, or even to the significant reorganisation of existing production. In the face of the disintegration of the Soviet system, enterprise directors have shown themselves to be extremely flexible and resourceful in exploiting short-term opportunities, using the skills which had been necessary to meet the plan in the face of the shortages and chaos which masqueraded as a planned economy. Enterprises have proved extraordinarily adept at finding new markets and new sources of supply, and at using existing equipment, labour and raw materials to develop new lines of production in response to fluctuating demand. However, in conditions of extreme economic instability, large-scale productive investment, except on the basis of state subsidies for production for state orders, is unprofitable, while the more modest restructuring of production to raise productivity risks provoking dangerous conflict with the labour force, and between senior and line management. It is far more profitable to invest in the exploitation of commercial and financial opportunities, avowedly to earn money to support the labour collective, and to restrict attempts to raise productivity in the sphere of production to the intensification of labour and the restructuring of the labour force indicated above. In this context the workers' scepticism about allocating profits to investment is quite justified, for if management is unchecked such investment will be in financial and commercial affiliates beyond their control, rather than in improving working conditions and developing the productive facilities of their own workplace.

Privatisation to the labour collective has not presented a barrier to the ambitions of the management of privatised enterprises. Management has available the whole range of tried and tested methods of intimidation and manipulation of worker representation. Control is more important to management than ownership, and other means of making profit than through dividends (e.g. higher salaries, profit-related bonuses, subsidiary activities). But at the same time, the process of concentration of share ownership, the purchase of shares by pocket and associate companies, and the vesting of residual and state owned shares in management's hands continues to strengthen the control of management.

Management has been able to pursue its chosen strategy, both before and after privatisation, without reference to the representation of the workers' interests, whether through the STK or the shareholders' meeting. This strategy has included a heavy reliance on authoritarian paternalist methods of management, which include an avowed commitment to preserve the labour collective and to maintain employment and living standards. But this commitment is no more an expression of workers' power than is the commitment of Japanese managers to a superficially similar paternalism. It is an aspect of traditional forms of management, deeply embedded in the expectations of both workers and managers. Far from increasing the power of the labour force, privatisation to the labour collective has seen a rapid erosion of the forms of worker representation that developed under *perestroika*, while worker protest has been demobilised by paternalism and, above all, by the fear of victimisation and unemployment. The payment of high wages is not an expression of workers' power, but of labour market conditions, and the payment of high wages is closely linked to the strengthening of managerial authority, the introduction of individual contracts, much stricter discipline, and increased job insecurity. Similarly, the lack of investment is not a matter of workers' power, but of the absence of investment funding and of profitable outlets for productive investment.

The third wave of privatisation

The second wave of privatisation, dominated by the exchange of shares for privatisation vouchers in closed subscriptions, came to an end on 30 June 1994, with the intention being that the privatisation programme would move fully into the third wave, which is based on the sale of shares for cash payment primarily through auction. The supposed purpose of the third wave of privatisation is to loosen the grip of existing management over large enterprises by diluting their shareholding and bringing in outside investors. Estimates of how many remaining state enterprises are eligible for privatisation by this means vary considerably, but the bulk of auction sales will involve already privatised enterprises. In principle, the third wave should involve the issue of new shares to raise investment funds, but the bulk of the shares to be sold at auction will be the residual holdings in already privatised enterprises that are held by the State Property Fund.

Enterprise directors have managed to consolidate their control of the enterprise in the first two waves of privatisation, and are certainly not willing to cede control in the third wave. In the context of undeveloped secondary markets, management control of information and enterprise resources, and tight formal and informal networks connecting management, regional administration and financial institutions, the existing management is in a very strong position to control the auction and tender process in its own interests and to use it to strengthen that control. Thus it is very common for a large block of the shares sold at auction to fall into the hands of subsidiary or associate companies, often using enterprise profits directly or indirectly for share purchase, and there is more than a suspicion that cartels between buyers to keep the price low are the rule rather than the exception. However, the sale of shares also provides enterprises with the means to cement other connections than those with their subsidiary companies, most notably with customers and suppliers and with state bodies. In this way the third wave of privatisation may paradoxically provide a powerful lever for the further consolidation of state capitalist monopolies.

Hostile takeovers are extremely rare, and most often reflect divisions within the management of the enterprise which links up with outside interests, most commonly local or regional authorities, on the initiative of one side or the other. Banks or other financial institutions play the mediating role in establishing this relationship. In a few cases the outside interests may seek to displace the entire management team. Most attempts on the part of individuals or financial institutions to launch a hostile takeover without the support of an internal management faction or regional authorities have ended in failure. Outsiders are at a clear disadvantage in buying up workers' shareholdings, since insiders are able to mobilise enterprise resources and use various levers to induce workers to sell shares to them.

Secondary share issues are still rare, partly because of the undeveloped character of the secondary market in shares and partly because of management's fear of losing control. Most commonly secondary issues are used to strengthen management's control, either by issuing shares in large blocks to subsidiary companies or affiliates, or in small blocks to disperse ownership. Secondary issues to raise investment finance are confined to large and stable enterprises with secure future prospects and are primarily directed at foreign investors, with foreign consultants organising the share issue, although few such schemes come to fruition.

We have noted above the increasing importance of traditional links for enterprises, and these links can be cemented by the sale or exchange of shares with customers, clients and financial associates, often linked to privileged contracts for purchase and sale or privileged credit terms. Similarly, vesting or transferring a part of the shareholding to local authorities cements the vital political connections of the enterprise. These political connections are by no means in contradiction with the links of the enterprise with 'capitalist' commercial and financial institutions, since links with regional and national state bodies have become equally important to the prosperity of financial and commercial organisations, so that the two kinds of connections are mutually reinforcing rather than being mutually exclusive.

The culmination of these tendencies is the formation of the financial-industrial groups which are proliferating in Russia, and which link industrial enterprises, financial and commercial organisations, and regional or branch state bodies in monopolistic organisations. Although most of these groups exist only on paper at the moment, the tide is running strongly in their direction, a direction which links together in a tight package the three elements of management strategy identified above – the survival of the enterprise and 'rent-seeking' and profit-seeking activities – and the three major players in the transitional period – regional and branch state bodies, large industrial enterprises, and proto-capitalist commercial and financial institutions. The core of this package remains the industrial enterprise, not so much because productive investment is a serious source of profit, but because it is the industrial base of these groups that is the source of local revenue and that provides employment for the local population.

The formation of such a regionalised 'state monopoly capitalist' or 'monopoly state capitalist' economy is still the object of intense conflict between the elite groups at its core and the reformers in the central government, and particularly around the State Property Committee and in the presidential apparatus. The 1994 privatisation programme, approved by Yeltsin in December 1993, focuses on the regulation of cross-shareholdings and the formation of holding companies and financial-industrial groups, which were themselves brought under regulative control in December 1993. In Russia the best sign that a development tendency is becoming dominant is that the central government attempts to block it by legislative and regulative means. Just as the government failed dismally to prevent spontaneous privatisation and privatisation to the labour collective, it also seems most likely that it will similarly fail to block the state monopolisation of the economy. This is particularly the case because the strongest weapon that the federal government can employ in preventing the regionalisation of the economy on the basis of the formation of financial-industrial groups is to counter such developments with the formation of sectoral groupings linking the largest enterprises on a branch basis. Thus the struggle between Moscow and the regions will be reproduced in the struggle between former Moscow ministries pressing for branch monopolisation and regional authorities looking for monopolisation on a regional basis, with control of fiscal and financial resources being the decisive factor in this struggle. It is this conflict that is likely to force the central government back into alliance with the old ministerial apparatus, and to marginalise the State Property Committee.

Conclusion

At one level privatisation has been a disaster. The majority of the productive assets of Russia have been sold off for a song, with the revenues from privatisation almost certainly amounting to less than the administrative costs of the programme as a whole. Privatisation has not established clear rights and responsibilities on the part of owners, while it has been accompanied by an explosion of theft and fraud which has encouraged the criminalisation of fundamental economic activities and relationships. Privatisation in the absence of competitive markets, in the face of a massive structural dislocation of the economy, in the absence of even the most primitive financial institutions or any adequate framework of legal regulation, has been associated with the collapse of production and investment, growing insecurity, widening inequalities and falling living standards alongside a boom in speculation and fraud. Not surprisingly, the crash privatisation programme, which was supposed to secure mass political support for an irreversible programme of reform, has provoked growing disillusionment with the reform process as a whole.

However, privatisation should not be written off simply because it has not provided the magic wand that could turn the Soviet Union into a prosperous capitalist liberal democracy. Although a growing number of people would like to return to the old system, the basis of that system has been destroyed. Mass privatisation may not be a step on the road to liberal capitalism, but it is a step on the road to something.

To help us to speculate about the future it might be worthwhile locating the present privatisation initiative in its historical perspective, to ask what was the purpose of privatisation? If we go back to the beginning of *perestroika*, we see a programme which intended to make enterprises into self-financing units which could then be regulated by financial, fiscal and monetary means, in place of the administrative-command methods of control. In the event it proved impossible to reconcile the freeing of enterprises with the maintenance of centralised control, and the system collapsed into semi-chaos. But this semi-chaos represented the achievement of one side of the programme of *perestroika*. Enterprises have become self-financing, but methods of control have not been put in place. Nevertheless, the enterprise directors have discovered that juridical independence does not mean that they can do what they want, but only that they face a different kind of constraint. Moreover, the disintegration of the economy, and particularly the financial pressures to which they have been subjected by the federal government, has persuaded them that there may be some virtues in state regulation after all. Although they do not want to lose control of their enterprises, they are increasingly willing to enter broader groupings and to accept higher degrees of financial and fiscal regulation as the price to be paid for the restoration of some order and the provision of state support. Thus the programme of *perestroika* is in a sense on the brink of success, as enterprises are forced to accept state regulation for financial rather than administrative-legal reasons.

This process is by no means complete. A degree of economic regulation and stabilisation has been achieved on a regional basis, through the increasing integration of the regional administration, regional financial structures, and commercial, industrial and agricultural enterprises. However, no region is self-sufficient, and the economy cannot be rebuilt on the basis of regional autonomy. While there is some basis for the formation of wider regional groupings and for inter-regional agreements, central regulation of the financial system is the unavoidable basis for the stabilisation of the economic system as a whole, and the focus of the current phase of conflict. This conflict may appear to be a conflict in Moscow between the principles of 'sound banking' and 'financial irresponsibility', but underlying this conflict is the struggle for control over the economy as a whole between Moscow and the regions. In this context the principles of 'sound banking' strengthen the forces of disintegration and regionalisation, within both the financial and the political system, forces which can only be countered by the issue of central credits. This is why the inflationary tendencies of the Russian economy are not simply the result of financial irresponsibility, but are an expression of the struggle for control over the economy between the regional and national authorities.

Chapter 9

THE POLITICAL ECONOMY OF MEDIA DEMOCRATISATION

Ellen Mickiewicz

In post-Soviet Russia, as in the Soviet period that preceded it, television has been considered by the political elite as one of its most powerful political assets. Given an exaggerated perception of the effects the medium could produce on the public, and an underdeveloped knowledge of the complex relationship between viewer and message, the Soviet Politburo had exhibited an obsession with television, discussing it at every meeting and attentive to their own, individual representation on the small screen.[1] For them, as for the later Yeltsin government and its political opponents, television politics was a zero-sum game in which air-time sharing, as well as power sharing, was both illusory and threatening. In the quest for control of the television asset during very volatile times, the leadership attempted to exert a degree of control that, in post-Soviet Russia, became increasingly dysfunctional, both politically and economically. This was illustrated most clearly by the failure of the government's information policy during the Chechnia conflict in the winter of 1994–95.

This chapter discusses the inter-connections between the politics and economics of the most powerful mass medium, television. While television was, quite clearly, at the centre of elite scrutiny virtually since its development as the 'large calibre' medium, it was also, in the radical reform policy largely shaped by Aleksandr Iakovlev in the early Gorbachev years, the instrument used to begin the process of legitimising multiple points of view – or rather, contending positions.[2] That process was to be the foundation of a democratic (or, at least, more genuinely participatory brand of socialist) political culture, and the great socialiser, television, was to carry out the task. Although the course of this great experiment was by no means linear, the fundamental tension between television as most valued and monopolised elite political asset and as the source of the deconstruction of a hitherto unified elite was to affect the course of the political struggle well beyond the demise of the Soviet system.[3] The centrality of television to the contending political elites in post-Soviet Russia was heightened by the profound constriction of the newspaper market.

Tensions in the newspaper market

During the Gorbachev era and after the collapse of the Soviet Union, the vitality and variety of mass media were threatened by economic pressures. With the withdrawal

1. Interviews with Egor Ligachev, Aleksandr Iakovlev, Mikhail Nenashev and Leonid Kravchenko.
2. Ellen Mickiewicz *Split Signals*, Oxford University Press, New York, 1988.
3. For a discussion of these tensions and the policy outcomes, see Ellen Mickiewicz *The Battle for Air*, Oxford University Press, forthcoming.

of state subsidies from these formerly 'budgetary' organisations, many of the most prominent players in the rapidly privatising media market spiralled quickly downward into worsening economic conditions. With the 1990 Law on the Press, the legal foundation was laid for the founding of print entities independent of state direction. These were, by and large, paper transactions in which the newspaper brought together a group of 'founders' who, together with the senior newspaper staff (but mainly its editor-in-chief) determined the policy and content of the paper.

Existing assets were ordinarily simply claimed by those in charge. In the beginning, the founders were very often the 'public organisations' and local government bodies that were now adapting to the new system and diversifying their assets. Until its disbandment, the Communist Youth League (Komsomol) was one such organisation, which used its bank account, particularly at the local level, to convert to new activities. Local governing councils (soviets) were also active in gaining participation in new media enterprises (or conversions of old ones) in their jurisdictions. Later, as television properties sought investors, the same pattern was followed there too.

On the input side then, the new 'independent' media came about through declaration of a new mode of administration and, effectively, seizure of assets. Investments were sought but, at that time, with a heavily state-owned economy, the monies had to come from the institutions that already had discretionary bank accounts for social programmes. This permitted elites with initiative to adapt to change and convert their resources. On the output side, newspapers had to produce newsprint and distribute it to subscribers (most of the circulation was to subscribers). Unfortunately for the papers, these stages of the newspaper economy had not undergone the same process of privatisation; they were firmly in the hands of the state, particularly the printing presses and paper supply. It was impossible, the newspapers found out, to produce a paper simply with writers and editors sitting in newly appropriated offices. For television, the transmission of signals and utilisation of satellite time was also in the hands of the state. Further, the assets the new private entities claimed were often obsolete and required repair or replacement. This was particularly true of high-technology media, such as television.

With these limitations, it is not surprising that the removal of subsidies so dramatically affected the costs of newsprint and distribution services and threatened the survival of many of the most widely read newspapers. Many Russians regarded the sharp increase in charges as an ill-concealed plan for the state to curb the expression of free speech which it had initially encouraged but which had exceeded its expectations. From 1990–91, the price of newsprint escalated five to seven times. In 1992, the Moscow-published newspapers with the largest circulation in the former Soviet Union lost about 18 million subscribers. *Pravda*, the flagship of the Soviet period, went from 10.5 million subscribers in 1985 to 600,000 in 1993. Other papers, particularly the ones that followed bolder reporting, enjoyed peak circulation between 1988 and 1990 before rapidly declining later. The weekly *Argumenty i fakty* was the leader, with over 33 million subscribers in 1990, but 5.1 million in 1993. The daily *Izvestiia*, which struck out on an independent path peaked at 10.4 million in 1988, and *Komsomol Pravda* at 22 million in 1990. Not a single major daily, including the ones that were not left over from the Soviet era, exceeded 1.5 million subscribers in 1993, and most were under a million.[4]

Advertising did not nearly cover operating costs, and although advertising did help to support press independence, it was far less available outside Moscow, thus leaving the provinces more in the grip of local political bosses.[5] By tradition, the campaign for new subscribers and renewals took place twice a year, and the newspaper was, obviously, locked into the price for six months and so could not anticipate the extremely rapid upward thrust of inflation; nor could most readers, increasingly impoverished, dip into sufficiently elastic incomes to match any price increase. In the winter of 1993, just after the subscription campaign had ended, the Russian government without warning substantially raised the price for its monopoly-supplied newsprint. This increase, added to the constraints of the six-months fixed subscription fee, would have driven most papers out of business entirely. In agreeing to strike, the Union of Journalists of Russia, traditionally an arm of the Communist Party for enforcing its policy rather than representing journalists, had achieved collective action in spite of the extremely varied political passions of the members. Although Prime Minister Viktor Chernomyrdin met with the leaders and subsequently rescinded the price rise, many in the union regarded the attempted governmental action as deliberate intimidation.

Having moved to collective action, the union sought to institutionalise its role and set up a strike committee at their annual meeting in January 1994; it also initiated ties to Western, as opposed to the old East-bloc, journalists' organisations. When Boris Yeltsin took over a building called the House of the Press and awarded it to the newly elected upper house of Parliament after the December 1993 elections, dozens of editorial offices and organisations were dispossessed; some saw in this, too, an animus against the press. Whether or not this was true, the symbolism of the removal of the free press from the premises did not represent a strong stand for press autonomy, including the nascent private cable industry.

If subscriptions and advertising revenues did not adequately assure the operation of many of the newspapers, there were other ways. Some newspapers encouraged their staff to take up additional work, such as guiding foreign visitors, the income of which could help to support the paper. But the most common strategy was to approach the government once again. Editors and publishers framed freedom of speech arguments in terms of demands for governmental grants to maintain their voices in the media market. In turn, with governmental subsidies sustaining large numbers of media organs, inevitably there were calls for government oversight of the media. The Russian Supreme Soviet had attempted to institute a news censorship council for all media; this was defeated in the summer of 1992, but was successful the next year, when parliamentary seizure by directive of state television and radio contributed strongly to Yeltsin's disbanding the legislature and the consequent October rebellion. After the October violence, Mikhail Poltoranin's deputy at the

4. 'Circulation of major newspapers', *Post-Soviet Media Law and Policy Newsletter*, 17 November 1993, p. 7.
5. Celestine Bohlen 'Few Russian papers thriving with the new press freedom', *The New York Times*, 26 January 1993, pp. 1, 4.

Federal Information Centre, Sergei Iushenkov, in an interview with the author, criticised what he considered to be the flabby policies of Press Minister Fedotov in granting aid to politically repugnant papers. In sum, as might be expected, those who subsidised the pipers intended to call the tune.

Entrants into the television market: competing with the state system

Political pluralism within highly politicised organisations is virtually oxymoronic – but not entirely. Such a counter-intuitive process had launched *glasnost*, but it was to become temporarily institutionalised only in the spring of 1991, when the opening of Russian Television (RTV) introduced the possibility of a genuinely politically competitive television system, in which fundamentally different political points of view would be disseminated. The pro-Yeltsin and the pro-Gorbachev channels faced each other over a tense political divide. When the divide closed after the attempted coup of August 1991, both national television stations were in the hands of a single political leadership. In a much more dangerous replay of the earlier standoff, opposition to President Boris Yeltsin was centred in the continuing Parliament, which attached an hour daily of RTV for its political messages. Yeltsin had succeeded in gaining control of state-owned television, but the monopoly was about to be broken by new laws laying claim to the state system on behalf of the legislature. It appeared from the difficult history of state television in Russia, that the state-owned, state-run companies could not deviate from their zero-sum path as their beleaguered bosses used television with greater focus and frequency to attempt to govern in the absence of institutions. Genuine competition and genuine diversity apparently could be guaranteed only by the workings of the market, at least until the development of legally enforceable and predictably operating buffer arrangements.

The state channels, though retaining a very significant national audience, increasingly faced an erosion of numbers, particularly in some lively local markets, such as Moscow, St Petersburg, Sverdlovsk, and others. In locales, in apartment buildings, in pockets of homes linked by cable, small television stations began popping up all over Russia. By the spring of 1994, there were about two hundred of them in Moscow alone.[6] Their audiences tended to be quite small by comparison with the numbers of viewers the state-owned system attracted. These 'independent' stations generated their capital initially from investments of 'founders', just as newspapers did. They then charged viewers subscription fees and advertisers airtime assessments. Beginning with mainly entertainment programming, some then added a modest local newsgathering capability. An early exception was the Volgograd-based south of Russia station that in 1992 produced up to 15 per cent of all its programming; locally produced programmes included music shows, children's programmes and public affairs.[7] Equipment budgets were extremely strained for these small companies, since purchases (of Japanese equipment, usually) required foreign currency; foreign aid and investment often

6. Marianna Orlinkova 'Kabelñoe televidenie kamennogo veka', *Izvestiia*, 24 June 1994, p. 9.
7. Valery Kornev, 'Kabel'noe televidenie izbavliaet Volgograd ot provintsial'nosti', *Izvestiia*, 23 January 1992, p. 7.

helped them purchase the new versatile and portable Japanese camera and sound equipment that provided a lower-cost option than the larger and more costly equipment.

Audiences were often attracted to these small-scale stations by the prospect of seeing pirated Western, mainly United States, films. An example of initiative in this regard: when *Jurassic Park* opened in the United States, a filmgoer with a hand-held videocamera taped the film from the screen and within days, it was playing on Russian cable. At the annual film market in Voronezh attended by station directors, including those from the big state stations, it was impossible to detect the provenance of the films.[8] The large state-run channels usually made their deals directly with international distribution firms and observed rights protections; the small, new, mainly cable companies did not. The flow of American films and series on local and national television stations is clearly part of what I term the 'problem of America', part of a larger syndrome of images, messages, and radical change that has had a profound impact on political life. I shall return to this issue below.

In Moscow, as the military gave up some of its frequencies, new entrants in the media market appeared. CNN broadcast its international 24-hour news in English, reaching, in 1993, somewhat more than half a million viewers. Problems had to do with the power of the transmitter and the adaptability of television sets.[9] Moscow viewers could also see private television on the '2X2' Channel, which used Moscow Television Channel's broadcast frequency during its downtime. This channel included in its programming English-language news programmes from CBS and Russian-dubbed news from the BBC.

All of these opportunities pierced the state monopoly and, depending on where they lived, gave viewers some real options. Two ventures, though, represented major moves on the part of former state-television officials and the will to take on the state system in head-to-head competition. On 1 January 1993, Channel Six, the first independent broadcast television station in Russia, began operating under the direction of Eduard Sagalaev. 'The era of monopoly TV, which lasted decades, is coming to an end', said a prominent television critic on the eve of the competition for the frequency.[10] Sagalaev, who had been head of youth programming at Ostankino when Aleksandr Iakovlev and Gorbachev began loosening the restrictions on free speech, won a licence (though initially sharing airtime with a television business school) for TV-6, the Moscow Independent Broadcasting Corporation, in a contest for a low-powered frequency released by the military.[11] At first, received by fewer than a million viewers (due to problems of transmitter power and television set adaptability), TV-6's penetration increased rapidly with the use of satellites and, by late 1993, reached some 30 million viewers in 30 cities of the former Soviet Union.[12]

8. Interview with Gennadii Shmakov, May 1992.
9. Aleksandr Petrov, '24-i kanal', *Sem'dnei*, 13, 1993, p. 3.
10. Elena Karaeva 'Litsenzia-ne pokhvalnaia gramota', *Nezavisimaia Gazeta*, 10 October 1992, p. 5.
11. *Ibid.*
12. Marina Denisova, "TV 6-Moskva" stanovitsia obshcherossiiskim kanalom', *Izvestiia*, 8 April 1994, p. 9.

The TV-6 initiative was begun as a joint venture with the Turner Broadcasting System. From leading Russian filmmakers, Sagalaev received permission to mount retrospectives of an impressive repertory. Nikita Mikhalkov and Rolan Bykov, the two most famous names in recent Russian cinema, made their works available to the new station. For its part, TBS provided films and CNN news; the films (with classic directors such as John Huston, Vincente Minnelli, Preston Sturges) were among the older, often black-and-white, holdings of the Turner film library.[13] By 1994, the Turner connection had been replaced by heavy investment from Russian entrepreneurs, primarily in the automotive industry. This was a notable move away from dependence on foreign investors and foreign products to an indigenous enterprise. It, too, was an expression of the 'American problem'.

The second prominent entrant into the broadcast television market was NTV. Led by Igor Malashenko, who had been Egor Iakovlev's chief deputy at Ostankino and clamorously left when Viacheslav Bragin came, NTV set up shop first on the St Petersburg channel, buying time there for a short period daily, and then acquired, in a bidding competition, Channel 4, formerly the educational channel in Moscow. Viacheslav Bragin's rule at Ostankino had a direct effect on the creation of the new channel; once again, some of the best talent on state television fled political pressure and censorship (and very low salaries) by going over to another channel, this time outside the boundaries of the state-owned system.

Malashenko made Oleg Dobrodeev, the respected head of news for Ostankino, his news director and brought over Evgenii Kiselev, the anchor of the Channel One weekly news analysis programme *Itogi*, and the well-known news anchors Tatiana Mitkova and Mikhail Osokin. Kiselev had made his Sunday evening show the single most popular news programme on television, and he had become a star. In fact, it was because of the drawing power of *Itogi* that Ostankino listed that time slot as the most expensive advertising spot in the week.[14] Malashenko assembled an all-star team and, by the end of 1993, *Itogi* on NTV was attracting a larger audience than the Ostankino competition in Moscow. Success on the new channel was helped by the news stars' ability to bring along as much of the audience as possible; they had used their on-air time at Ostankino as a launching pad for the new venture. On one of his last shows at Ostankino, Kiselev told viewers that 'we are leaving Ostankino because we are convinced that in Russia, genuine news journalism is possible only on independent television that will not be in the pay or the keep of the state – all the more so a state in the present financially calamitous situation.'[15] NTV also began its own news operation and broadcast a rich diet of attractive foreign and domestic films. At the time of its debut, critic Galina Chermenskaia thought the NTV formula

---

13. Sergei Kudriavtsev '"TV 6": interesting to watch, even if you have to hold the antenna in your lap', *Izvestiia*, 6 February 1993, p. 12. translated in *FBIS-SOV*-93-020, 25 February 1993, pp. 56–57.
14. '"Ostankino" Television Channel 1: the price of publicity time from 1 January 1993 till 30 June 1993. Price list distributed by Ostankino Television to prospective buyers.
15. *Itogi*, Channel One, 12 September 1993, translated in *FBIS-SOV*-93-175, 13 September 1993, p. 26.

unbeatable; it had 'the combination of big capital . . . plus high professionalism, plus, one hopes, real independence'.[16]

NTV's method of raising capital to launch the new channel was highly controversial. Malashenko put together large investments from banks; Dobrodeev noted that NTV's bid of 30 million dollars could not be matched by anyone else in the competition for Channel 4.[17] A few months later, assets had grown to 50 million dollars.[18] The Most consortium of banks probably did not purchase NTV to realise a profit very quickly; it would, in fact, take a good deal of time for the new station to turn a profit. Evgenii Kiselev, the anchor, announced that Most's motivation was political stability, which it needed for business success, a sentiment echoed by Malashenko, who noted in an interview that the banks considered television the most important source of social stability.[19] The extraordinary political significance of television had not diminished and was, in fact, in the views of the powerful new entrepreneurs, an important guarantor of the political-economic environment on which their success depended.

In a remarkably brief time, NTV succeeded in creating a reputation among viewers: by mid-1994, 51 per cent of the viewers polled in the European part of Russia said that NTV programmes were the most interesting; 35 per cent said Ostankino programmes were. Just two months earlier, the proportions had been reversed. Even though word-of-mouth favoured the new entrant, viewing habits changed more slowly, and Ostankino was still in the lead, though it was far from holding the commanding lead it had earlier. Individual programmes, such as Ostankino's *Field of Miracles* and *Theme* were still the most popular programmes with great staying power.[20]

However, the crisis of the Chechnia war altered news viewing habits and propelled NTV to the top of the ratings for the areas within its signal range. NTV had sent two teams of correspondents to Chechnia three weeks before any other Russian stations had done so, and the private station's coverage from the front contradicted the materials produced by the Russian government's press centre in Moscow. Bulletins from the press centre announcing the capture of Grozny, a halt to bombing attacks, and distribution of meals to the welcoming Chechen population were all graphically contradicted by pictures from the front. The presence of independent television coverage produced a ripple effect throughout the system and served, in all probability, to usher in a new information environment. Pressure from the government and judiciously produced leaks continually warned NTV of its vulnerability, especially in the transmission of its signals, which depended on governmentally controlled facilities. Nonetheless, the private station continued to function and continued to bring an alternative, but verified, view of events as Russian forces took the Chechen capital.

16. Galina Chermenskaia 'Nezavisimoe televidenie brosaet vyzov', *Izvestiia*, 16 October 1993, p. 12.
17. Interview with Oleg Dobrodeev, October 1993.
18. Tom Birchenough 'Russian TV cuts free from state', *Variety*, 13 February 1994, p. 36.
19. Interview with Igor Malashenko, October 1993.
20. 'Zerkalo dlia TV', *Argumenty i fakty* 28, 1994, p. 12.

The dilemma of state television

Though limited in their viewership and programme production capacity, the new stations did represent an outlet for political pluralism, helped to a considerable extent by the unprofessional administration of the state's Channel One. In 1993, Ostankino, under its director Viacheslav Bragin, had become so partisan and so devoted a micromanager, that journalists attempting to uphold professional standards fled to the new broadcast options. But the problem was not only political; Ostankino, like the Russian economy in general, was in deep financial trouble. State television owned and operated nearly 100 stations across the country. State support was a decreasing percentage of operating costs, in no small measure because of the enormous drain of satellite transmission payments to the state monopoly Ministry of Communications. State stations served most heavily by satellite were the poorest. For example, employees of the distant Chita station, near Lake Baikal, had to turn off the radio transmitters serving Eastern Siberian region because they had not received payment from Moscow for their electricity bills. As of June 1993, they were owed some 400 million rubles.[21] By July 1993, Ostankino owed some eight billion rubles in transmission costs.[22] Russian governmental policy seemed irrationally to be undermining the effectiveness – indeed the very existence – of what it considered to be the prime political asset, to support a ministry that siphoned off not only government funds awarded by television, but also the revenues they succeeded in attracting. By December 1993, transmitters in such regions as Kaliningrad in the west and Kamchatka in the north had been turned off; communications ministry workers were demanding their wages, and the state television and radio companies were not paying.

In February 1994, half of the small screens in Russia went dark. Television was shut off from St Petersburg to Sakhalin, at the extremity of the 11th time zone. The striking communications workers who had pulled the plug complained that charges had been unchanged since 1981, while prices skyrocketed; most had received no wages for several months.[23] Millions of viewers across the country were deprived of news and their soap operas. This was not a trivial action: television had become the principal informational lifeline and connection to the outside world for many now stranded in poverty and deprived communities. The newspaper crisis had accelerated the public's dependence on television, so that as early as May 1991, some 83 per cent of the Soviet Union's population named television as their principal source for news and information.[24] Television was also the only affordable escape from the grinding

---

21. Andrei Fomin 'Chita power engineers switch off transmitters', *ITAR-TASS*, 25 June 1993.
22. Sergei Suntsov 'Novosti', Channel One, 6 July 1993, translated in *FBIS-SOV*-93-128, 7 July 1993, pp. 23–4.
23. Natalya Gorodetskaya and Andrei Nikolaev 'Communications workers intend to stop TV broadcasts', *Segodnia*, 10 February 1994, p. 1, translated in *Russian Press Digest*, 10 February 1994.
24. Data drawn from a survey conducted in 1991 by the Penta survey organisation under the direction of Leila Vasilieva, currently Project Director of the 'Public Opinion' Foundation, Moscow. The author expresses her appreciation to Ms Vasilieva for providing this information.

conflicts of everyday life; television was free. Prime Minister Viktor Chernomyrdin stepped in to order the Finance Ministry to pay the overdue wages.

At the end of 1993, the two channels that attracted the huge majority of viewers, Channels One (Ostankino) and Two (Russian Television), were state-owned and state-run. Politicians had fought over control of them ever since the first cracks of pluralism appeared after 1985, and Moscow went to war over Ostankino in 1993. These two channels, but especially Channel One, were thought to hold the fate of the country, to save or lose Russia in election after election and in crisis after crisis. Television was still the obsession of the administration in power and of its adversaries. That had not changed since the days when Mikhail Gorbachev, Egor Ligachev, and Aleksandr Iakovlev had discussed the medium with their fellow Politburo members at every meeting. But, by the end of 1993, the state could no longer pay very much of the upkeep of its expensive asset, and the government was doling out to Russian Television only 18 per cent of what it needed to operate and to Ostankino, about 25 per cent.

The cuts were having an effect on news reporting. Channel One began closing foreign news bureaus to save money, as had the United States networks in the 1980s, and like the United States networks, Russian television relied much more than it did in the past on purchased footage. Under such conditions, the contribution of the station lies only in what the anchor narrates, but the specific discovery about, and understanding of, events that the station might have made in filming the story itself is absent. Russian television, lacking fresh footage from many domestic locations, relied excessively on file footage, with the unexpected consequence of alarming viewers who, upon seeing a replay of ethnic strife in Russia or a former republic to illustrate a new, entirely different story, took the coverage to mean that violence had broken out anew.

Though downsizing the inflated workforce was clearly in order, it would not solve the deep financial problems in state television. Revenues from the new private sector had to supplement the declining contribution of the state. Advertising was the most logical recourse, and what had been a very limited effort soon mushroomed. The greater the trend toward the market, and the more difficult it was to wring subsidies out of the state, the more attention was paid to programme ratings as a way of establishing advertising rates. Even the daytime audience, hitherto ignored in a nearly full-employment society, began to matter and economic constraints were openly put forward as essential for driving programming decisions. This effect of the market in a television system notoriously insulated from viewer preferences was remarkable. An overall assessment of the viewers of state television fare is startling. With Channels One and Two broadcasting 18 hours a day in 1994, each had more than 20 programmes daily in addition to news, and, in the aggregate Channel One had more than 100 programmes in its schedule. By ratings, beginning with the most heavily watched shows, somewhere around the 40th programme, viewing dropped to 4 per cent or less. On Russian Television, Channel Two, the real audience dropped off after the fifth or sixth show. The rest were 'firing blanks'.[25]

25. Lidia Polskaia 'Esli rezat, to po zhivomu i bez narkoza', *Izvestiia*, 19 February 1994, p. 16.

What did these ratings indicate? It was indeed problematic, because among the beneficiaries of the ratings were such shows as *Love at First Sight*, which roused the critics to angry complaints of vulgarity, while bringing in sponsor and advertising revenues.[26] On the other hand, among the casualties of the ratings was the venerable *Vzgliad (Viewpoint)*. In May 1992, a leading television sociologist noted that whereas the show used to lead with 60 per cent of the audience three or four years before, now a Mexican soap opera attracted 50 per cent of audience figures, while *Viewpoint* was reduced to 8–10 per cent.[27] At about the same time, when asked what kinds of programmes they liked least, most people answered 'political programmes'. The clash of commerce and public interest, of new values and old, of foreign and national images, are all part of the great debate on ratings. With still limited choice among channels and offerings, whose values should be paramount? And where is the emerging 'national identity'?

The dramatic and sudden change from a Communist Party-ruled standardised television to one in which commerce, ratings, and advertising were ubiquitous and, moreover, one that often looked and sounded like the culture of the United States, was surely traumatic. In a very few years, the appearance, tempo, and function of the most powerful medium had been transformed. But the onslaught of the new images and pounding beats was not always welcome and was often confusing. In some ways the new market approach that television trumpeted in its programmes, but even more in its advertising spots, represented a new type of propaganda for an exhausted public; the American-made chocolate bar, Snickers, soon came to symbolise the 'problem of America', the overwhelming dominance of United States commerce and values in a country attempting to sort out the meaning of the loss of great-power status. This context of product advertising on television had, I would argue, an enormous impact on the way that the political parties used their paid and free time in the December 1993 parliamentary election campaign. Russians were divided, not only about the culture of Western or Western-style product advertising on television, but also about the products themselves and about expectations that were raised and then dashed either by unavailability of the product or, more frequently, by astronomical pricing that put it out of the reach of the vast majority of the public. Mainstream newspapers featured complaints about the morality of advertising. Most disturbing of all were the advertisements for foreign foods, an impossible luxury for a population whose basic health needs were unmet. A respected Russian television critic wrote in the autumn of 1993: '. . . how many parents are pushed to rage by the daily whining of their offspring and curse this intrusive advertising of foreign sweets for which most of the adult population of the country simply lack income.'[28]

It is important to note that the form of political advertising adopted by the candidates in December 1993 differed quite substantially and Vladimir Zhirinovskii, for his constituency, clearly made the strategically correct choice in utilising political

26. Irina Petrovskaya 'I Voroshilov v boi na nas idet', *Nezavisimaia Gazeta*, 20 February 1993, p. 5.
27. Interview with Vsevolod Vilchek, May 1992.
28. Irina Petrovskaia 'Kokos na postnom masle', *Nezavisimaia Gazeta*, 11 September 1993, p. 5.

advertising but making sure that it did not appear to relate to product advertising. He deliberately eschewed the rapid tempos, jump cuts, rock music, and modern graphics so characteristic of Western-oriented product advertising and opted, instead, for simple homilies of a spontaneous, personalised, traditional type in a setting of little artifice.[29] Campaigning on taking Snickers advertisements off the air, Zhirinovskii understood that the context of advertising, and its appeal to an American-inspired market ideal with particular cultural dimensions, had sharply divided generations and social strata.

One of the greatest 'success' stories was the advertising for the investment firm, MMM, a paper pyramid scheme that collapsed in 1994. These advertisements were the most frequently broadcast and the most watched on television; some 2,666 spots were aired in March, April, and May 1994.[30] It is clear that state television was largely responsible for the name recognition and financial success of a dubious enterprise against which the government of the same state had warned the population.

The introduction of product advertising also created new, mainly unregulated, channels for the acquisition of funds and influence. Advertising income was the result of individual business arrangements between the production companies and advertisers and the production companies and individual Channel One departments; the administration of Channel One saw very little of it.[31] Moreover, income was not restricted to overt advertising. Much more television airtime was bought by private parties, but it was extremely difficult to identify. Sometimes, 'sponsors' paid for programmes and sometimes they were identified, sometimes not. In addition to 'sponsors', advertising sources included people who bought favours from state television. Sometimes this took the form of kickbacks, and the head of music programmes at Channel One, V.M. Kruzhiiamskii, had his skull crushed with a brick, either because of his involvement in such a scheme, or, since he was new to the job, his refusal to play.[32] A head of music programming at Russian Television said that big pop stars were all tied to organised crime, pushing bribes to have videos shown.[33] Sometimes covert advertising bought news people, a much more dangerous practice for the viewing public. Eduard Sagalaev termed it 'jeans television'; television journalists were bribed to report stories favourable to a factory or product.[34] It was estimated at the beginning of 1993, that some 82 per cent of all television airtime had been sold or 'ordered' by interested parties.

29. Ellen Mickiewicz and Andrey Richter 'Television campaigning and elections in the Soviet Union and post-soviet Russia', in David Swanson and Paolo Mancini (eds) *Politics, Media, and Modern Democracy*, Greenwood, Westport, Connecticut, (eds) forthcoming.
30. 'Na TV emotsii perevodiatsia v tsifry', *Izvestiia*, 17 June 1994, p. 9.
31. Irina Petroveskaia interview with Vsevolod Vilchek, 'Gosudarstvennye telekompanii Rossii segodnia iavliaiutsia mafioznymi strukturami', *Nezavisimaia Gazeta*, 31 July 1993, p. 1.
32. T. Tsyba, '"Chernyi Iashchik" TV, ili chto mozhno uvidet za den'gi', *Argumenty i fakty* 4, January 1993, p. 6.
33. Andrew Solomon, 'Young Russia's defiant decadence', *New York Times Magazine*, 18 July 1993, pp. 16–23, 37–39, 41–2, 51. Citation is on p. 21.
34. Interview with Eduard Sagalaev, October 1993.

Effectively, state television was operating in large part on an unregulated and partially concealed commercial basis within a state-owned framework. Each head of Ostankino in post-Soviet Russia, from Egor Iakovlev to Aleksandr Iakovlev, attempted to take control of the situation, stamp out corruption, and centralise advertising in all its forms. Viacheslav Bragin even closed down the independent studios operating at Ostankino, but he soon rescinded his act when it became apparent that all the popular shows were locked up in the offices he had just sealed. The head of one of the most successful private production companies scoffed at the use of the paired nouns 'state television', since 78 per cent of the programmes on Channel One were made by independent television companies.[35] Network presidents found it difficult to bring to heel the increasingly free-wheeling, almost elemental abandon with which the departments and sub-departments of the financially strapped institution sought funds. A minuscule fraction of these revenues went to support the institutions of governmental television. Ostankino's 1994 creation, 'Reklama-Holding', was another attempt at a centralised advertising authority also aiming to tie advertising revenues to ratings and overhaul the programme schedule, but the venture had to exempt the big programme production companies who preferred, in any case, to keep things as they were.

The Russian public did not have to pay to watch television. Unlike the British model, but like the American, there was no annual fee for broadcast television viewing that then underwrote the operation of non-commercial television. Television programming was, to be sure, supported by the state, from hidden taxes but not overtly. When the state could no longer pay its share, the advertisers, both open and concealed, stepped in. The shrinking family income was not tapped. In the quest for financial independence the notion of a subscription or licence fee was frequently advanced. There had been subscription fees until 1962 and a form of subscription fee was included as a value-added tax on television sets. Some people were willing to pay for subscribing to the new, but not very widespread, cable systems. A more universal call for required viewer contributions was extraordinarily controversial. Many viewers, especially the elderly (for whom television has the most important social function) have incomes so inelastic as to preclude the possibility of even token fees; such viewers would have to be subsidised. Even if fees were collected from all other viewers, the subscription fee would be unlikely to match the advertising revenue currently flowing into the programmes, even though that revenue was itself insufficient. In short, the volume of income generated by subscription fees could not underwrite state television in post-Soviet Russia.

A second argument calling into question the utility of subscription fees related to the extraordinary importance national television had achieved in the turbulent and anxiety-ridden life of the new Russia. As the only institution reaching most people, as the main source of information helping to make intelligible an unpredictable and threatening everyday reality, television performed a social and political role that few, if any, other institutions could duplicate. Few others had the reach and, though

---

35. Russian TV, 9 February 1994, BBC Summary of World Broadcasts, 11 February 1994. See also Irina Petrovskaya '"REN-TV"-nachalo zhizni', *Nezavisimaia Gazeta*, 16 January 1993, p. 5.

declining from earlier levels when television led the way to freedom of speech, the trust. As one analyst put it, 'While trustworthiness and influence may be declining relative to former levels, television remains the most important single medium by which Russians obtain most forms of news.'[36] No government or contender for power wished to deprive itself of this asset. Finally, given the dependence on the population on television as information source as as purveyor of free entertainment, few considered it desirable to risk what they termed a 'social explosion' by pricing the free good out of the reach of the large population of the needy.

The failure of the Russian government to provide the promised subsidies to state television exacerbated the tension and deepened the dilemma of political independence and financial autonomy. Oleg Poptsov, the head of Channel Two, put it to the government forcefully and succinctly: 'If you can't give the money, give the freedom instead, but once you have given the freedom don't complain and don't claim to be governing the state. In other words, having renounced your obligations to finance television and radio, you have to renounce your right to control either of them. Then other forces will control them, not the government and not the President.'[37] As a long-time Yeltsin ally, Poptsov clearly saw the danger to the President's ability to govern were he to be deprived of his television podium. Poptsov also clearly saw that the removal of governmental influence left the way open for what he considered to be in some ways less desirable variants. But the experienced network chief observed the untenable hybrid television had become and the failure of the government to craft a consistent policy in which the policies of the ministries would reinforce and not undermine each other.[38] Most observers of the scene regarded privatisation of most of the government stations as the only viable alternative, and, in due course Ostankino was converted into a 'public television' structure – a form of 'privatisation' by presidential decree – late in November 1994. But there are, of course, degrees and types of privatisation, and the state maintained a controlling interest. The murder of Vlad Listev, to whom this new direction of state television had been entrusted, galvanised the nation early in 1995. He was a figure of such immense on-air popularity that the killing, just a month before the new financial regime was to be inaugurated, brought home the power of the suspected organised crime killers. On the other hand, Listev's death provided an important focus around which to rally the proponents of press autonomy, to which President Yeltsin lent his authority. Paradoxically, Listev's death probably served to strengthen the push for autonomy. It was projected that when the conversion to 'public television' became complete, the need for revenue-producing, overt advertising would be eliminated, at least for a time. What that process might mean for covert advertising, or the growing importance of ratings, or the full financing of programming which both government and private partners could agree on, remained to be seen.

36. Mark Rhodes, 'Russians and television', *RFE/RL Reports* 2(39), 1 October 1993, pp. 5–7. Citation is on p. 7.
37. 'TV and Izvestiia' heads denounce government TV and radio cuts, Radio Moscow, 10 February 1994, translated in BBC Summary of World Broadcasts, 12 February 1994.
38. Poptsov, long an ally of Yeltsin, was nearly fired in 1995 for candid coverage of Chechnia, as well as of President Yestsin's controversial visits to Germany and Ireland in 1994.

Perhaps the underlying and principal concern is not the form of funding or the dispersion of stockholders, but rather the institutionalisation of buffer functions that protect the autonomy of television content decisions and minimise the influence of the funders, state or private. These arrangements are particularly critical during periods in which political leadership is contested. In Russia the frequency of these nationally important elections and referendums is unusually high – averaging more than one a year from 1989 to 1993 – and the consequent pressure on the most powerful medium is, accordingly, significant. In the absence of a developed mediating political party system, the impact of television tends to retard the development of that system without which durable democratic governance is made more difficult.[39]

Conclusion

The status of television, from Politburo obsession to the most desirable of political assets during contested elections, spans the period of Soviet rule and post-Soviet Russian politics. The implosion of the newspaper market heightened the attention paid to the electronic medium that still penetrated all points of the Russian Federation and did much to create nationally known leaders and consumer products. In the absence of regulatory policy and enforcement mechanisms, the development of the most important medium lurched from pluralistic under fragmented elites to more uniform as oppositions were marginalised. Buffer functions that new structures and new agencies can perform are understood as a necessary part of the new legal arrangement, but the development of these buffers requires some period of normalisation for their introduction. The frequency of elections tends to inflate the political currency of television time and produce pressure on the system that the fragile rules cannot withstand. Moreover, the very centrality of television to the electoral process may delay the formation of the political parties themselves and sustain the environment of shifting alliances of highly personalised, Moscow-based political formations termed parties, but not sharing the more important characteristics of parties.

The growing importance of a television market dramatically altered the images and values of contemporary culture and many of the manifestations of the television culture are drawn from the United States model. The 'problem of America' is not only a cultural phenomenon but, more importantly for the issues raised in this chapter, a profoundly political one. As Russian national identity – or more properly, identities, since there will be several from varied sub-cultures and generational strata – coheres, the search entails confronting that other culture that has 'Americanised' both political campaigning and everyday discourse through the most powerful medium.

The rise of the television market through advertising and private investment does, however, provide a basis on which to achieve a more pluralised programming. Even

39. See, for example, Gladys Engel and K. Lang, *Politics and Television Re-Viewed*, Sage, Beverly Hills, 1984.
A reconceptualisation of the development of political parties in the United States may be found in John Aldrich *Why Parties?* University of Chicago Press, Chicago, forthcoming.
A comparison of the impact of television on elections in a number of countries may be found in David Swanson and Paolo Mancini (eds.) *op. cit.*

though this pluralism may be tainted by the pervasive corruption that affects other sectors of Russian society, the fact remains that alternative channels and alternative views of the news have become possible. A buffer to assure press autonomy from commercial sources is as desirable as one to protect from political intrusiveness, and surely must be developed.

The state can no longer afford the rich fare its old ideological monopoly and luxuriously budgeted television industry produced. All the political contenders find the prize of television immensely desirable; some in the opposition attacked television headquarters to gain access to the airwaves in October 1993; some in the government violated the election laws by running anti-Zhirinovskii programmes after the deadline in December 1993. The course of pluralisation is not a smooth one, but in the period of uncertain rule-making and rule-application, without an alternative structure and sources of funding, it would be nearly impossible. Crisis, however, puts television squarely at the centre of appeals to the nation and legitimisation of leaders. Sufficiently strong market alternatives can significantly alter the equation and help to assure the kind of access and multiple points of view that effective socialisation in democratisation requires.

Part Three

CONSEQUENCES OF RADICAL REFORM

Chapter 10

INEQUALITY AND POVERTY

Alastair McAuley

In economic terms, the most obvious feature of the transition period in Russia is the sharp fall in output and the equally sharp increase in differentiation. The collapse of central planning, the collapse of the CMEA, and the disorder that has resulted from the break-up of old state structures and economic relationships has meant that there are no longer customers for the output of many enterprises. The precipitate decline in demand has been accentuated by a general break-down of the monetary system. High rates of inflation, growing indebtedness on the part of many state enterprises, and widespread shortages of banknotes have made a difficult economic situation chaotic. Some individuals have enjoyed windfall gains; most have experienced losses as incipient hyperinflation has rendered savings valueless. Some individuals have prospered through their own efforts, initiative or enterprise. Others have seen their entitlement to even a minimal claim on resources eroded.

This disorderly transition from central planning to a market economy (if that is in fact where Russia is heading) has had a number of social consequences. One of the most significant of these is the growth of poverty. This chapter sets out to describe the nature of poverty in Russia and to show how (and, possibly, why) it has grown since the collapse of the USSR in 1991. It concludes with a few observations on the social consequences of poverty.

What is poverty?

We all think that we know what is meant by poverty. But on closer examination views differ substantially. Over the past 30 or 40 years, economists and others have devoted considerable effort to elucidating some of the hidden assumptions in these different approaches to poverty; they have also spent time in developing ways to operationalise these various concepts of poverty. It is therefore convenient to start with a brief summary of some of the recent work on the topic; this will clarify the terms I use later in the chapter. Here I deal with three issues: the concept of poverty itself; the idea of a poverty threshold and how it has been established in Russia; and, finally, how to measure the level and intensity of poverty.

Alternative concepts of poverty

There are two pairs of distinctions that structure much of the debate on the nature of poverty: absolute and relative; needs-based and rights-based.

For many people, poverty is synonymous with want: the poor are unable to satisfy their most pressing needs – for food, clothing and shelter. At the extreme, their lack of resources can lead to death from starvation or exposure; more generally, their susceptibility to disease is raised. Poverty conceived in this way is both absolute and needs-based.

When one tries, however, to specify more precisely where the threshold lies between want and sufficiency, the precision of the previous concept disappears. Nutritionists can be reasonably sure about how much food the individual must consume if he or she is to remain in good health – and capable of work and so on. Or rather, nutritionists can specify the quantities of fats, carbohydrates and proteins, the vitamins and trace minerals, though they have much less to say about the foodstuffs themselves.

Choice of diet is affected by taste; by availability, and hence cost; by convention and taboo. In this sense, the minimal subsistence diet cannot be specified in ignorance of the society in which it is to be consumed. It is innately relative. When one turns from nutrition to other forms of consumption, the difficulty with specifying an absolute threshold is greater. In fact, it is often regarded as impossible to specify objective minimal levels of consumption for needs like clothing, shelter, hygiene, transport and leisure.[1]

There is another meaning sometimes attached to the concept of poverty. For many people 'poverty is equivalent with an income shortfall from some "fair" income.'[2] This idea is quite widespread. It is linked with T.H. Marshall's ideas on citizenship; it also has connections with Rawls's conception of justice. It lies behind Peter Townsend's identification of poverty with relative deprivation. Individuals in any society can expect to participate in the social and political life of their community. This usually involves the expenditure of resources. Those whose claim on resources is insufficient to allow them to participate fully are deprived; they are deprived relative to the customs and mores of their society. This is a difficult concept to operationalise – but exerts some influence on the thinking of specialists and policy-makers.

There are a number of other approaches to the conceptualisation of poverty which I will not discuss. But I would like to mention the so-called consensual definition. It was pointed out above that needs-based poverty is innately relative; the definition of the threshold is substantially subjective. Given this, economists at the University of Leiden took the next logical step and decided to ask the population what they thought the poverty threshold should be – for their time and culture. They devised a procedure for aggregating the answers and using them to generate a unique estimate of the minimum income needed to avoid poverty.

Determining the poverty threshold

The definition of poverty is usually derived from the needs-based relativist conception. This was certainly the case in the USSR, and it remains true for Russia.

---

1. See A. McAuley, 'Opredelenie i izmerenie bednosti', *Bednost: vzgliad uchenykh na problemu*, Demografia i sotsiologia 10, ISEPN pri RAN, Moscow, 1994, pp. 7–9.
2. M. Jantti, *Essays on Income Distribution and Poverty*, Abo Akademi University Press, Abo, Finland, 1993, p. 27.

In the 1960s, the Nauchno-issledovatel'skii institut truda (NIIT) attempted to specify 'the volume and structure of the necessities of life required for the reproduction of labour power among unskilled workers, *rabotniki prostogo truda*'.[3] Experts decided on the quantities of various foodstuffs, clothing, furniture and so on needed for a notional family of four to maintain a modest but adequate standard of living in the USSR. These were priced at ruling state prices to yield the so-called minimum material security (MMS) budget, *biudzhet minimuma material'noi obespechennosti*. Those whose income fell below this level were defined as *maloobespechennye*, which can be seen as a Soviet euphemism for the poor. The MMS budget was used after 1974 as the entitlement threshold for aid to families with children under the age of seven years.[4] The calculations underpinning the MMS budget were repeated in the late 1970s or the early 1980s, and speaking to Parliament in June 1989 the prime minister of the day, Nikolai Ryzhkov, referred to those whose incomes fell below the revised threshold as 'the poor'. He stated that there were almost 40 million of them.[5]

The approach embodied in the determination of the MMS budget was essentially arbitrary. In the conditions of rapid inflation after 1991, it also gave rise to a very high poverty threshold. For this reason, in 1992 the Russian government commissioned research to determine a new poverty threshold. This was undertaken by Marina Mozhina of the Institute of Socio-Economic Problems of the Population (ISEPN) with technical assistance provided through the World Bank.[6]

The new definition of the poverty standard is based on a basket of foodstuffs that satisfies WHO and FAO standards with regard to the content of fats, carbohydrates, proteins and so forth. Its composition in terms of foodstuffs also corresponds with Russian tastes and the availability of the relevant goods on the Russian market. This basket was priced at ruling market prices. It was, finally, assumed that in the crisis years of 1992–93, the average Russian would spend some 68 per cent of his or her income on food. The cost of the food basket was, therefore, multiplied by 1.47 to give the subsistence minimum. The methods now used in Russia are thus similar to those adopted by Molly Orshansky in the United States in the early 1960s.

In fact, the calculations were somewhat more complicated: the food basket was determined differentially for those who were in work, for pensioners and for dependent children; the share of expenditure devoted to foodstuffs was differentiated for these groups too. On the other hand, no further allowance was made for the composition of households: no attempt was made to introduce ideas of adult equivalence into the determination of the threshold. Nor was any attempt made to vary the composition of the basket to reflect variation in tastes of consumers (or availability of goods) in different parts of Russia. Finally, a unique subsistence

3. G.S. Sarkisian and N.P. Kuznetsova, *Potrebnosti i dokhod sem'i*, Moscow, 1967, p. 18.
4. A. McAuley, *Economic Welfare in the Soviet Union: Poverty, Living Standards and Inequality*, University of Wisconsin Press, Madison, Wisconsin, 1979, p. 282.
5. A. McAuley, 'The welfare state in the USSR', in T. and D. Wilson (eds) *The State and Social Welfare: The Objectives of Policy*, Longman, London, 1991, p. 197.
6. See B. Popkin, M. Mozhina and A. Baturin 'Metody obosnovania prozhitochnogo minimuma v Rossiiskoi Federatsii', *Bednost': vzgliad uchenykh na problemu*, Demografia i sotsiologia No. 10, ISEPN pri RAN, Moscow, 1994, pp. 47–69.

minimum was produced for Russia as a whole. No allowance was made for regional differences in the level and structure of prices.

The subsistence minimum has been adjusted to take account of the inflation from which the country has suffered through the increase in the cost of living index. It has not been reweighted. Some attempt has also been made to estimate its notional value in earlier years, using the retail price index that preceded the present cost of living index. Such calculations are somewhat dubious, however, in view of the significant shortcomings to be found in Goskomstat's price indexes.

The measurement of poverty

The simplest and most direct measure of poverty in any country is the number of households or individuals with an income below the poverty threshold. But such a measure fails to capture the depth of poverty, or to indicate how easy or difficult it might be to eradicate. Such issues have been addressed by economists who have elaborated a variety of more or less sophisticated poverty indexes.[7]

One family of measures, developed by Foster et al., is particularly appealing.[8] To explain what is involved, let $y = \{y(1), \ldots, y(n)\}$ be the vector of incomes of households (or individuals) arrayed in increasing order. Suppose that $z > 0$ is the poverty line and that there are q poor families or individuals. That is $y(j) < z$ $(j = 1, \ldots, q)$. Finally, define $g(i) = z-y(i)$ $(i = 1, \ldots, q)$. $g(i)$ is the income shortfall or poverty gap of the ith individual or family. It is the amount of additional income needed to raise the ith family's income to the poverty line.

Using this notation, Foster et al. define

$$P(0) = q/n \qquad [1]$$

This is the so-called headcount ratio, the proportion of the population that is poor. Define $G(q) = g(1)+ \ldots +g(q)$ as the aggregate poverty gap. Now define $W = G(q)/qz$. W is the ratio between the aggregate poverty gap and minimum total income required by the poor to obviate poverty; it is often referred to as the poverty gap ratio. Foster et al. go on to define

$$P(1) = P(0)W = G(q)/nz \qquad [2]$$

$P(1)$ depends upon both the number of poor individuals or families and on the scale of their poverty. It is a measure of the intensity of poverty. (It, too, is sometimes referred to as the poverty gap. This same term is also used to refer to $G(q)/GDP$.) We can go on to define

$$P(a) = G^a(q)/nz^a. \qquad [3]$$

7. McAuley 'Opredelenie i izmerenie bednosti' op. cit., pp. 19ff.
8. J. Foster, J. Greer and E. Thorbecke, 'A class of decomposable poverty measures', Econometrica 52, 1984, pp. 761–65. See also M. Ravallion, Poverty comparisons: a guide to concepts and methods, Living Standards and Measurement Study No. 88, mimeo, World Bank, Washington DC, 1992.

where $G^a(q) = g(1)^a + \ldots + g(q)^a$ the sum of the individual poverty gaps raised to the power a. For $a > 1$, this increases the weight attributed to the poorest; as a increases, $P(a)$ approximates to a Rawls index.

In this chapter I make use only of $P(0)$ and $P(1)$. As pointed out above, $P(0)$ measures the number (or proportion) of the population that have incomes below the poverty line. It is the conventional measure of poverty. $P(1)$ measures the extent to which the incomes of the poor fall short of what would be needed to eliminate poverty. It measures the intensity of poverty. It is also a measure of the cost of a maximally efficient anti-poverty programme.

Who are the poor?

This section reports on the value of the subsistence minimum and shows how it has changed over the last couple of years. It also provides estimates of the level of poverty during this period. Third, it provides an account of the social composition of the poor and tries to explain why poverty has increased since the beginning of the transition period.

Table 10.1 **The evolution of the poverty standard: Russia 1992–94**

	Subsistence minimum (Rubles)	Minimum consumption budget (Rubles)
1992		
March	1031	2617
June	1639	4097
September	2163	5449
December	4282	10694
1993		
March	8069	20891
June	16527	36984
September	28183	na
December	42800	na
1994		
March	60388	na
June	84100	na

Sources: McAuley, 'Opredelenie i izmerenie bednosti', *Bednost: vgliad uchenykh na problemu*, Demografia i sotsiologia 10, ISEPN pri RAN, Moscow, 1994, pp. 7–23, Table 5.1; A. Surinov and I. Kolosynitsyn, Social inequality and poverty in Russia, mimeo, Institute for the Study of Problems of Economics in Transition, Moscow, 1994, p. 4; *Sotsial'no-ekonomicheskoe polozhenie Rossii. Yanvar'–Aprel', 1994*, Goskom RF po statistike, Moscow, p. 68.

The subsistence minimum

The value of the subsistence minimum, calculated according to the methodology developed by Popkin, Mozhina and Baturin (1994) is given in Table 10.1. The table also reports values for the MMS budget, calculated according to the methodology developed by NIIT in the 1960s.

In March 1992, after the break-up of the USSR and the liberalisation of prices, the subsistence minimum was valued at 1031 rubles a month per capita. By the end of the year, in December 1992, this had increased fourfold to 4,282 rubles a month; by December 1993 it had increased a further ten-fold to 42,800 rubles a month per capita. The nominal value of the subsistence minimum doubled again by June 1994 when it was set at 84,100 rubles a month. Most of this increase in nominal value reflects the very high rate of inflation from which the country has been suffering, but there is evidence to suggest that the real value of the subsistence basket may have increased over the period. The World Bank suggests that in June 1994 it was a third higher than in January 1992. If so, not all of the increase can be attributed to inflation.

In March 1992, the value of the MMS budget was more than 2.5 times as large as that of the new subsistence minimum. It was still more than double the subsistence minimum in June 1993, the last month for which I have been able to obtain figures. According to this standard, poverty would have been more severe than when judged by the official poverty line.

The growth of poverty

The general procedure for estimating the headcount ratio is clear: one compares the poverty line with an estimate of the appropriate distribution of income and obtains an estimate of the numbers in poverty. But there are three general points that I would like to make about this procedure before turning to consider the estimated number of persons in poverty in Russia in 1992–94.

First, as in many other sample surveys, there are differences between the value of incomes and expenditures for individual families in Russia. This gives rise to two different estimates of the headcount ratio. It is assumed that individuals are more likely to underreport income than expenditure, especially if that income accrues in kind or is generated in the informal sector. It is thus inferred that the distribution of expenditures gives a more accurate estimate of poverty than the distribution of incomes. In Russia, in July 1992, according to the Russian Longitudinal Monitoring Survey, some 25 per cent of the population was poor according to the distribution of income; only 21 per cent fell below the poverty line according to the distribution of expenditures.[9] I have been unable to obtain comparative figures for other months.

Second, when a similar exercise was carried out in Kirgizstan, the correlation between the distribution of income and the distribution of expenditure was very

9. World Bank 'Rossiia – bednost', politika i vozdeistvie predvaritel'naia otsenka, 1 Kratkoe izlozhenie Washington, DC, October 1994, Box 2.2.

low – 0.2.[10] I do not know whether the situation was similar in Russia. But if so, then there is a more substantial difference between the two definitions of poverty than is apparent from the aggregate figures: it is not only the level of poverty that changes; the identity of the poor does too.

Third, the calculation of headcounts makes use of the distribution of families and individuals by household per capita income. No attempt has been made to calculate adult equivalent income. Given differences in the physiological needs of persons of differing age and sex and given the possibility of economies of scale in consumption, this will almost certainly result in an exaggeration of the incidence of poverty.

Table 10.2 presents estimates of the growth in poverty in 1991–94. The figures imply that in 1991, the last year of the USSR, a tenth of the population was in poverty. By June 1992 between a fifth and a quarter of the population was in poverty. (According to the Russian Longitudinal Monitoring Survey, in July 1992 some 29 per cent of *individuals* were poor.[11]) In the latter part of 1992, the incidence of poverty declined. It increased again in 1993: according to the table the headcount ratio fluctuated between about a third and a quarter. These figures are confirmed by other sources.[12] The table also suggests that the position improved sharply in 1994. But this claim has been challenged. Surinov and Kolosnitsyn (of the Gaidar Institute) claim that in the summer of 1994, an estimated 23 per cent of the population had per capita incomes less than the subsistence minimum.[13]

Table 10.2 **The incidence of poverty: Russia, 1991–94**

		Poverty line (rubles/month)	Headcount ratio (per cent)	Poverty gap (per cent of GDP)
1991		190	11.4	–
1992	March	1031	23.4	0.59
	June	1639	23.1	1.13
	September	2163	18.9	1.23
	December	4282	15.7	1.85
1993	March	8069	34.7	1.05
	June	16527	24.7	1.43
	October	32400	28.8	3.76
1994	April	66536	(10.7)	

Sources: J. Braithwaite, Old and new poor in Russia: trends in poverty, mimeo, IMF, Washington DC, 1994, Table 1; Gosudarstvennyi komitet Rossiiskoi Federatsii po statistike, *Sotsial'no-ekonomicheskoe polozhenie Rossii* (ianvar'–aprel' 1994), Moscow, 1994, p. 68.

10. J. Falkingham and R. Ackland, 'A profile of poverty in Kirgizstan, October to November 1993', paper prepared for the National Seminar on Poverty and Social Protection in the Kirgiz Republic, EDI, World Bank, Washington, DC, 1994, p. 19.
11. World Bank 'Rossiia – bednost', *op. cit.*, Box 2.2.
12. *Ibid.*
13. A. Surinov and I. Kolosnitsyn, Social inequality and poverty in Russia, mimeo, Institute for the Study of Problems of Economies in Transition, Moscow, 1994, p. 4.

The figures in the last column of Table 10.2 report an estimate of the poverty-gap as a proportion of GDP. This shows that not only is the incidence of poverty increasing but, it appears, so is its intensity. The poor are getting poorer.

The trend of the figures in Table 10.2 is also confirmed by UNICEF's regional monitoring project, although that suggests that poverty in Russia was even more extensive. Cornia defines the social minimum for Russia as 38 per cent of average earnings in 1989; he defines the subsistence minimum as 60 per cent of this. He gives the following figures for the evolution of poverty according to these standards:[14] poor (1990) 11.8 per cent, (1991) 13.3 per cent, (1992) 37.4 per cent; ultra-poor (1990) 2.9 per cent, (1991) 3.1 per cent, (1992) 27.1 per cent. He argues that among the poor – and still more for the ultra-poor – there have been falls in average calorie intake and substitution of less expensive nutrients. Despite this substitution, for some proportion of the poor, calorie intake has fallen below the level recommended by the WHO. Also, there is nutritional imbalance which has had an impact on the health of some young children, pregnant women and lactating mothers.

The composition of the poor

There are a number of ways in which one can approach the issue of the social composition of the poor in Russia. In terms of a general social classification, certain groups figure disproportionately among the poor. First, families with children, especially those with more than two; families headed by a single parent are at particular risk of poverty, as are those where the principal earner is in a low-wage occupation. Second, unemployment is almost invariably associated with poverty – even where the unemployed worker is in receipt of unemployment compensation. Third, the disabled and their families are often in poverty, as are old-age pensioners, especially those who live alone rather than as part of an extended family group. Finally, there are the homeless and those recently discharged from institutions.[15]

Another way of looking at this data is to consider the risk and incidence of poverty among different social and demographic groups. This is done in Table 10.3. The distinction between risk and incidence is as follows: incidence relates to the prevalence of a social characteristic among the poor; risk relates to the probability of poverty among those with a given demographic or social characteristic.

Table 10.3 shows, for example, that children accounted for some 29 per cent of those in poverty in 1992; women over the age of 30 years accounted for 30 per cent of the poor. Thus the incidence of poverty for these two groups is about the same. But the risk is different: children are about a third more likely to be poor than women. To put the same point in a somewhat different way: in 1992, almost a half of all children under the age of 16 years lived in families with per capita incomes below the poverty line; they made up a third of the poor. (The table also shows that about a sixth of all children lived in ultra-poor families and that they made up more than a third of the ultra poor.)

14. G.A. Cornia, 'Poverty, food consumption and nutrition during the transition to a market economy in Eastern Europe', *American Economic Review* 84 (2), May 1994, pp. 297–302, Table 2.
15. World Bank 'Rossiia – bednost', *op. cit.*, paras 2.3–2.6.

Table 10.3   **The incidence and risk of Poverty: Russia, Third Quarter, 1992**

	Incidence of Poverty		Risk of Poverty	
	Per cent of those with income less than 50% of poverty line in social group	Per cent of those with income less than poverty line in social group	Per cent of social group with income less than 50% of poverty line	Per cent of social group with income less than poverty line
Children				
0–5 yrs.	14	11	16	46
6–15 yrs.	22	18	16	47
Adults:				
16–30 yrs.	27	20	13	36
Women:				
31–54 yrs.	17	17	10	35
55+ yrs.	1	13	5	34
Men:				
31–59 yrs.	17	18	9	34
60+ yrs.	1	3	3	22
Total population	100	100	11	37

Source: calculated from A. Illarionov, R. Layard and P. Orszag, 'The conditions of life', in A. Aslund (ed.) *Economic Transformation in Russia*, Pinter, London, 1994, pp. 127–56, Appendix 3; and *Narodnoe khoziaystvo Rossiiskoi Federatsii, 1992*, Moscow, 1992, p. 92.

Similarly, about a third of women pensioners were poor in 1992 and they accounted for about 13 per cent of total poverty. Only a fifth of male pensioners were poor and they made up no more than three per cent of the poor. This discrepancy is explained by the fact that there are so many more women of pensionable age than there are men.

There is one particular group where the risk of poverty is extremely high, even if the incidence is low, and that is the homeless. These are very difficult to identify and include in surveys or censuses, so tend to be ignored. But there is a reasonable amount of anecdotal evidence to suggest that numbers of homeless people have increased during the transition period. This seems to be a consequence, first, of the running down or closure of psychiatric institutions; and second, of the privatisation of housing and the reduction of low-cost residential units in hostels and so on. Homelessness has also been increased indirectly by refugees and migrants from other republics and by the repatriation of Soviet military personnel.

The growth of poverty

As I pointed out at the beginning of this chapter, the transition period in Russia has been marked by two features: a sharp fall in output – and hence in the average real wage; and a significant increase in inequality. The second of these is recorded in Table 10.4 and the first in Table 10.5, if only implicitly.

Table 10.4 **Distribution of money income by population quintile: Russia, 1992–94 (per cent)**

	1992	April 1993	1994
Money income received by:			
first (lowest) quintile	10.6	6.8	7.8
second quintile	15.3	11.6	12.7
third quintile	19.2	16.4	17.3
fourth quintile	23.8	23.2	23.4
fifth (upper) quintile	31.1	42.0	38.8
Total	100.0	100.0	100.0
Gini Coefficient	0.217	0.353	0.311
Ratio of average incomes of first and tenth deciles	3.7	9.7	7.5

Sources: Gosudarstvennyi komitet Rossiiskoi Federatsii po statistike, *Sotsial'no-ekonomicheskoe polozhenie Rossii*, ianvar'–aprel' 1994, Moscow, 1994, p. 66.

Table 10.4 shows that in 1992, the bottom 20 per cent of income recipients received about a tenth of total money income; in 1994, their share had fallen to less than eight per cent. The shares of the next two quintiles also fell. The share of the fourth quintile remained constant at a little under a quarter. Over the same period, the share of the top 20 per cent rose from less than a third of total income to almost two-fifths. This is really a very sharp and rapid increase in inequality. It is not surprising that it has resulted in a sharp increase in measured inequality: the Gini coefficient rose by more than two-fifths, from 0.22 to 0.31. And, since individuals in both tails have experienced income change, it has been associated with increased poverty.

One of the features of the measure of poverty $P(0)$ is that it can be broken down into changes due to population change, income growth (or decline) and increases/decreases in inequality. In a recent paper, Branko Milanovic provided such a breakdown for Russia. Milanovic defines poverty relative to a constant poverty line over the period 1987–93. This is set at $ppp4.00 a day in 1990 prices.[16] (This

16. $ppp4.00 refers to the purchasing power parity equivalent to US$4.00 as derived from the Heston/Summers international comparison project analysis.

Table 10.5 **The value of wages and pensions: Russia, 1992–94** (as per cent of the subsistence minimum)

	Real value of subsistence minimum Jan. 1992=100	Wages		Pensions	
		Average	Minimum	Average*	Minimum
1992					
March	109	264	33	42	33
June	118	309	55	80	55
September	116	341	42	62	42
December	110	375	21	81	52
1993					
March	110	292	28	91	53
June	134	287	26	89	49
September	120	287	27	98	52
December	116	330	34	98	61
1994					
March	117	273	24	88	43
June	133	247	17	90	46

*Average pension is only available quarterly; this column relates average pension for the succeeding quarter to the subsistence minimum for the last month of the preceding quarter. This overstates the real value of the average pension.

Sources: 'Rossiia – bednost', politika i vozdeistvie – predvaritel'naia otsenka', 1, kratkoe izlozhenie, mimeo, World Bank, Washington, DC, 1994, Tables 2.1 and 2.4.

was equivalent to some 54 rubles a month in 1987 prices, but by 1992–93 it was much closer to the subsistence minimum.) According to this standard, the headcount ratio increased by 28.3 percentage points over the relevant period. This increase can be attributed to the following factors:[17] decline in income 8.5 per cent, growth in inequality 18.9 per cent, and demographic change 0.9 per cent. Thus two-thirds of the increase in poverty can be attributed to increased inequality and less than a third to the fall in income. In this, Russia appears to differ from much of the rest of the FSU and from Central and Eastern Europe.

A final feature of the recent rise in Russian poverty is that almost two-thirds of poor families are headed by someone who is in work. There is a large and growing stratum of the working poor. Table 10.5 presents some of the data needed to understand what has been happening on the Russian labour market and how one can account for this development.

As a minimum, one might expect that the average wage would be twice the subsistence minimum. This would allow the average worker to support one dependent at a level equal to the poverty line. Thus, an average family with two wage-earners

17. B. Milanovic, Income, inequality and poverty during the transition, World Bank, Washington DC, forthcoming.

and two dependents would be able to stay out of poverty. More realistically, one might expect the average wage to exceed the subsistence level by a somewhat larger multiple, say 3–3.5. Furthermore, one might expect both the minimum wage and the minimum pension to be at least as large as the subsistence minimum.

Table 10.5 shows how – and how far – Russia failed to come up to these expectations over the period 1992–94. First, while the average wage rose from 2.6 times the subsistence minimum in March 1992 to 3.75 times the subsistence minimum in December, it fell again for most of 1993 and by mid-1994 was back below the level of March 1992. On this basis, it must be increasingly difficult for any worker on average or below average earnings – say 60 per cent of the labour force – to maintain family per capita income above the poverty line. The table also shows that at no time in the last two or three years has the minimum wage been sufficient to keep those earning it out of poverty. Instead, it has only once exceeded a half of minimum subsistence; more generally it has been about a quarter of the poverty line or less.

There are millions of Russian women employed in positions where they earn the minimum wage, or a salary that is linked to it. They make up a significant proportion of the so-called 'budget sphere'. The government's failure to index the minimum wage satisfactorily has condemned them and their families to poverty. This is especially so if such women are single parents.

The table also includes figures on minimum and average pensions, although I have significant reservations about the meaning of the figures on average pensions. However, taking the figures at face value, the table suggests that average pensions more or less tracked minimum subsistence; on average, pensioners were being kept close to – but just below – the poverty line. But the minimum pension fell well short of the value of minimum subsistence. Even though Parliament (which was responsible for setting the minimum pension) did better than the government – responsible for the minimum wage – it still was not able to raise the minimum pension above three-fifths of the poverty line; for much of the time it was closer to a half. This failure too must have condemned millions of elderly people to poverty.

Conclusion

In the last two or three years, Russia has witnessed an enormous increase in the number of persons living in families whose per capita income is below the poverty line. This poses both social and political problems.

There is both old and new poverty in Russia; but, as Table 10.4 above demonstrates, most of it is new. This means that in many respects the poor – and particularly the new poor – do not differ from the non-poor. Although I do not have firm data to demonstrate it, the new poor households have much the same stock of durables as the non-poor, durables that they have inherited from the former Soviet system; they have much the same stock of human capital. In principle, therefore, it should be relatively easy to transform them back into non-poor. This is even more likely to be true for those who are not very poor: for these, a small increase in transfers may be sufficient to lift them over the poverty threshold.

The longer that the new poor remain in poverty, however, the more likely they are to develop a separate 'culture of poverty', and the more likely they are to diverge from the non-poor in terms of the stock of durables that they possess (both because those inherited from the Soviet period will have worn out and because those who remain in employment and above the poverty line will have had opportunities to restock). Further, they may also acquire attitudes towards work that make it more difficult for them to be reintegrated into employment. Finally, after a considerable time spent in poverty and, possibly, unemployed, whatever human capital they once possessed will have depreciated.

The transition period in Russia has been accompanied by a very sharp increase in inequality. There is no reason to believe that this will be reversed in the near future. Hence, if and when the economy begins to grow, it is likely to remain unequal. This implies that relatively high levels of poverty are likely to persist and may prove difficult to eliminate.

Chapter 11

THE POSITION OF WOMEN

Olga Zdravomyslova

The ascendency of the reform government under Boris Yeltsin which came to power in August 1991 has marked the beginning of a new era. The enormous conflicts with the newly emerging system, a loss of orientation, and disenchantment with 'pro-Western' liberal policies have affected all aspects of society and made an impact on the position of all social groups. Women are no exception. Processes of radical social transformation which began back in 1985 continue to unfold. Each of these processes has its own history and its own logical development. Taken as a whole, these processes mark a new level of emancipation of women in Russia.

Underpinning this new level is, on the one hand, the mobilisation of women as a result of a break in traditional structures and the opening up of new possibilities in the professional, political and business spheres. The new level is, on the other hand, the result of a clearly visible retrospective trend in which Soviet values are being reassessed. After August 1991 both of these divergent tendencies grew stronger.

'Moving backwards'

When Soviet Russia vanished, so did its slogans, including 'Women are active builders of Socialist society'. The new philosophy is, increasingly, 'A woman's place is in the home'. In 1992 a Russian Federation bill which concerned 'preservation of the family, motherhood, fatherhood and childhood' was discussed in the Supreme Soviet. A dominant theme in the proposal was a 'rebirth of family traditions' through, first of all, a 'reestablishment of child-rearing as a priority' among women and mothers.[1] In the opinion of feminist researchers, 'the myth of a "woman's mission" which has so rapidly replaced the old myth about emancipated Soviet women is, like the earlier myth, only a cover-up for discrimination that women face both within the family and on the job'.[2]

Evidence of these changes is shown by the fact that in 1990 the Council of Ministers adopted two resolutions on measures to improve conditions for women. They were to support motherhood and childhood by introducing benefits for working women to facilitate the fulfilment of their domestic obligations. These legislative proposals reflected a trend in both employment policy and ideology: the belief that women should be oriented toward family and child-rearing, this being the female 'natural role', which was 'distorted' during the Soviet years.

---

1. Proekt zakona RF *Ob okhrane sem'i, materinstva, ottsovstva i detstva*, Moscow, 1992.
2. *Gendernye aspekty sotsial'noi transformatsii, Itogovyi otchet ZGI*, Moscow, 1992, p. 153.

According to the results of research conducted in Russia at the beginning of the 1990s, the position of women in contemporary Russian society can be summarised as follows:

> Under the existing conditions of a high level of female employment, a division between female professions and male professions has become fixed and permanent. Women find themselves in a disadvantageous position with regard to salary level and opportunities for advancement. So, in 'male' fields (such as metallurgy, oil industry, coal industry – in which many women are engaged), women have, on the average, one-and-a-half to two times fewer and/or lower qualifications, and lower positions according to the 1989 professional census, and experts believe the situation has remained unchanged in the ensuing five years. Accordingly, women earn less.[3]

Unemployment has become one of the indicators of the true state of women in the professional sphere. The figures showed that the actual unemployed total was still relatively low: 800,000 listed as jobless by the end of 1993, that is about 1 per cent of the total employed population. The proportion of women among the unemployed fluctuated from 70 per cent in 1991 to 68 per cent in 1993.[4] At the beginning of 1993, among the unemployed with higher education, women accounted for 73.5 per cent; among those with secondary technical training 78.3 per cent; those with special secondary training 66.8 per cent; and those with incomplete schooling only 54.4 per cent.[5]

At the end of 1993, in a survey of 1,157 unemployed, in seven cities of Russia, 84 per cent were women, and two-thirds of these jobless women had become materially dependent on their relatives. The study also showed that because they were without jobs, the women had become burdened with more household duties. The results showed that 70 per cent of the women and 38 per cent of the men started doing more housework after losing their jobs; 46 per cent of the women and 16 per cent of the men reported spending more time taking care of the children. The question 'What is most difficult for a person who has lost a job?' revealed how men and women react differently to being unemployed. 'Shortage of money' and 'financial dependency' were the top two difficulties listed by both men and women. However, an 'insecure future' causes depression 1.5 times more often in women than in men.[6]

E. Mazentseva, who conducted interviews of both male and female leaders in major Russian cities in 1992, discovered that more than 40 per cent of those surveyed believed that female employment would decline over the next two to three years; 35 per cent believed there would be no change; only 14 per cent believed that the proportion of females employed would rise.[7] Fifty per cent of those questioned belonged to the category of leaders who 'see only positive aspects in the drop of

3. M. Baskakova 'Professional'naia zaniatost' zhenshchin', *Osnovnye tendentsii sotsial'nogo razvitiia Rossii 1960–1990*, Moscow, 1994, p. 39.
4. *Rossiiskaia federatsiia v tsifrakh v 1993 godu*, Moscow, 1994, p. 88.
5. M. Baskakova 'Sotsial'noe polozhenie bezrabotnykh: semeinyi aspekt', *Lichnost' i sem'ia v epokhu peremen*, Moscow, 1994, p. 86.
6. *Ibid*, p. 91.
7. E. Mezentseva 'Kadrovaia politika predpriiatii i perspektivy zhenskoi zaniatosti', *Gendernye aspekty sotsial'noi transformatsii*, Moscow, p. 41.

female employment'. The only negative factor, they noted, was 'the difficulty of filling jobs unattractive to men that women occupy now'.[8]

The most obvious gender difference is evident in a comparative analysis of the occupational structure. Statistics as well as sociological studies show that women are relegated to positions of at best secondary and as a rule, tertiary importance, far from direct participation in policy-making and the attendant advantages in performing executive or organisational functions. The small number of women in leading posts in government is evidence, as noted in an official government document, of 'the presence of elements of discrimination on the basis of sex'.[9] It is not surprising that in the opinion of enterprise managers, surveyed by E. Mezentseva, women are better suited to executing tasks that do not require high qualifications or education.[10]

The stereotypical role is clearly articulated in one of the main characters of a play by Maria Arbatova, a writer of the generation now in its forties. 'A full-fledged woman must mop floors, stand in line, copy recipes for the salads in fashion, gossip, read detective novels at bedtime, keep count of what's left of the paycheque and be glad she has the chance to do it all.'[11] This pecularity in contemporary socialisation of girls and young women has been noted by M. Arutunian. In response to the question 'Who am I?', the most important issue for young women seemed to be 'Will I be liked?'. By contrast, when young men were asked to define their identity, their responses had to do with who they were as members of society, for example, 'Will I be able to influence society in some way?', 'Will I be able to gain a highly visible role in society?'. It becomes evident that, as in times past, the real blow to a woman's self-esteem occurs when she fails in the limited roles of beloved wife and mother.[12] Interviews with the families of 'new Russian' businessmen carried out by I. Bylantseva in 1993 showed that parents want their daughters to get married and have a child by the age of 25. In their opinion, the most important thing for a woman is a good husband, although it does not hurt to have an interesting profession either. The same parents see their sons at 25 quite differently: single, plenty of work, lots of interesting things in life, an excellent education, friends, and so forth.[13]

It is clear that from the point of view of a vast majority of contemporary researchers, the position of women in post-Soviet society reflects a trend which has grown more marked since the beginning of reform: a return to traditional relationships based on gender in all areas of life.

Post-socialist countries: women's perception of their family and professional experience

This 'movement backwards' is profoundly Russian in nature. It is related to particular characteristics of gender relationships and to conflicts in the 'detraditionalised' psyche

8. *Ibid*, pp. 42–44.
9. G. Sillaste 'Sotsiogendernye otnosheniia v period sotsial'noi transformatsii v Rossii', *Sotsiologicheskie issledovaniia*, 1994, 3, pp. 15–22.
10. E. Mezentseva *op. cit.*, p. 45.
11. M. Arbatova *P'esy dlia chteniia*, Moscow, 1991, p. 54.
12. M. Arutiunian 'Kto ia?' *Zhenshchina i sotsial'naia politika*, Moscow, 1992, p. 139.
13. I. Bylantseva 'Sem'i predprinimatelei: vozvrat k traditsionnoi modeli?' *Lichnost' i sem'ia v epokhu peremen*, p. 104.

of the women themselves, who grew up in a country where, for several generations, women were workers and the role of housewife was reduced to a minimum. As women attempted to establish themselves in non-traditional roles, traditional prejudices against them remained. Some of the features of women's psyche are revealed in a European comparative study carried out at the end of 1991 in five cities of European Russia, as well as interviews conducted in 1992–93. Married and single women with pre-school children, as well as married men with pre-school children took part in a survey developed jointly with sociologists from the German Institute for Youth in Munich.[14] In Russia, a total of 800 men and women were questioned. At the time of the survey, all of the respondents were employees of state enterprises. The research took place concurrently in West and East Germany, Poland, Hungary and Russia. The number of persons interviewed in all countries totalled 6,000.

In gathering comparative material on family and work experience among women who until very recently lived in a 'different' socio-economic system, we expected to find, first of all, that there were essential differences in their description and perception of this experience, and, second, that these differences might be explained in the light of the major social, cultural and political differences between respondents living in Western and Eastern Europe. Our expectation was confirmed, but of far greater interest was our finding that the essential differences in women's experience were not so much tied to the fact that Russian women were born, grew up, and raised families under the 'socialist experiment' while others (West Germans) did not. Rather, the differences seem to be more related to deeper cultural and historical roots. Therefore, women from West Germany and East Germany displayed more commonality of experience than German women as a whole shared with Russian women. In turn, Hungarian women, Polish women and Russian women were quite dissimilar in their perceptions.

One problem was shared by all of the women surveyed in post-Socialist European countries: balancing work and family. German women and Hungarian women were polar opposites on this issue. In East Germany, 11 per cent of the women classified themselves as having a professional orientation; in Hungary only 0.6 per cent identified themselves this way. Thirty per cent of East German women – as opposed to 12 per cent of Hungarian – listed career as among 'the most important values'. Sixty per cent of Hungarians responded that they work out of necessity and that their commitment is 'from 9 to 5'. Only 22 per cent of East German women echoed those sentiments.

What we gleaned from the answers were two differing images: the family-oriented woman (Hungarians) and women oriented toward working outside the home but also successfully managing family and children (East Germans).

Polish women listed work as one of their 'most important' values in life less often than East Germans or Russians. At the same time, however, fewer Polish women (22 per cent) than Russians or Hungarians would want to remain housewives if their husbands earned big salaries. Poles also registered the highest proportion of women who would still work full-time, even if their husbands earned high salaries (25 per

---

14. The working group of Family Policy (DJI Germany): Dr Gisela Erler, Dr Monica Jaeckel, Dr Juergen Sass.

cent as opposed to 11 per cent for East Germans, 13 per cent for Hungarians and only 8 per cent for Russians). A greater number of Polish women expressed a desire to build a career. The Polish respondents, therefore, more fully accepted the model of a professionally oriented working woman who has a family and is rearing children.

In contrast to East Germans, Poles and Hungarians, Russian women have been nurtured toward the workplace from their earliest years. Nonetheless, judging from their responses, Russians have conflicting perspectives on their experiences. In our study, married Russian women least frequently stated that their job is 'very important' and that they are 'deeply involved in it'. More than respondents from any other country in the survey, Russian women stated that they work 'from 9 to 5' because their job is 'not very important'. Russia also registered a high proportion (43 per cent) of women who rejected the idea of building a career. One-third of Russians responded that 'if the husband earns enough', they would prefer not to work at all (the figure is about the same as in West Germany, but significantly higher than in Poland and particularly East Germany). In Russia the highest proportion of women surveyed agreed that 'if the husband earns enough and there are few jobs available, the wife should not seek a job'.

At the same time, 40 per cent of the Russian women surveyed said that they have not achieved their career aspirations (the highest percentage of all the respondents in all the countries). Twenty-five per cent of Russians want to build careers, a percentage surpassed only by Poland, with 33 per cent. Russian respondents voiced a belief that female influence in the occupational arena is almost equal to male influence and they would like to see women's influence increase. It was also in Russia that we found the highest percentage of women (8 per cent) who categorised themselves as job-oriented and not family-oriented. In other countries the number of women who identified themselves accordingly ranged from 0.1 per cent (Hungary) to 4 per cent (West Germany). Among Russians, 21 per cent listed occupation as one of the 'most important' values (only in East Germany was the figure higher – 30 per cent – and in the remaining countries the figure was significantly lower).

As it turned out, Russian women were quite consistent in their support of the life choice of housewife, but they were equally affirmative of the option of occupational orientation. In other words, we found two groups of women who have made or are attempting to make a choice in favour of family or career. The Russian respondents appeared to be less successful in combining the two than women in other countries: 14 per cent of Russians said they are completely unable to maintain a balance between family and career. (In other countries, the proportion of women answering similarly ranged from 0.4 to 4 per cent.)

We also discovered that the two groups under comparison (i.e. professionally oriented and family-oriented women) have reacted differently to the changes which occurred after August 1991. Family-oriented married women (F group) working full-time often stated that social change had no impact on their lives, either positive or negative. Professionally oriented married women (P group) are more polarised. They often categorise change as positive or negative. Each group has its own causes for concern.

Professionally oriented married women are concerned about family issues: 43 per cent of such women say it is difficult to raise children according to their views (32 per cent for F group); for 43 per cent of the P women it is difficult to maintain a balance between family and work (33 per cent for the F group). Also, it is harder to live with 'uncertainty about the future' for P group as compared to F group (72 per cent and 64 per cent respectively).

Thirty-seven per cent of the P group (against 26 per cent of the F group) noted that they found it hard to accept that society is becoming 'Westernised'. Thirty-five per cent (in contrast to 25 per cent of the F group) found it most difficult to change their views and to retrain.

Married and single professionally oriented women experienced more hardship in the transition than family-oriented married women. The latter group has suffered fewer difficulties because, in keeping with their family orientation, they have been relatively shielded from the economic and social crisis. Further, they are happier than professionally oriented women with both their marriages and life in general.

The underlying reasons for this are the distinctive features of gender relationships in Russia, based on a traditional and at the same time conflicting model which has not lost its meaning or influence, despite several decades of 'the teaching of equality'. Our findings that follow are evidence of this.

Compared with respondents from other countries, Russian women and men were noticeably less content, most often registering a feeling of dissatisfaction with life in general. In other countries, the response of 'complete dissatisfaction' was hardly encountered. The proportion of respondents who reported that they are 'very satisfied' with life in general in other countries under investigation was two to three times greater than in Russia. The Russian women particularly noted dissatisfaction with various aspects of family life: the most common complaint was inadequate participation by the husband in child-rearing and household duties.

In other countries the question 'Do you consider your husband a good father?' drew almost no negative responses. But 7 per cent of Russian women felt this way. Further, Russian respondents expressed the least satisfaction in the relationship with their spouse, with 8 per cent of women and 6 per cent of men reporting that they are 'completely dissatisfied'. This position was hardly encountered among respondents from other countries in the survey.

Russian women: a special case

What is the reality behind a virtual 100 per cent employment rate among several generations of women (a situation strikingly unique to Russia)? Here one can trace a particular type of attitude toward work, occupational education and career which only gradually changes from generation to generation. Useful here are excerpts from the following interviews with a mother and daughter conducted by the author in 1993.

The mother, born in 1942:

> Life was very hard for my mother, and all she thought about was how to feed us, how to clothe us. Only one thing mattered to her – how to get us on our feet. I really didn't want to go to college and decided to work for a while at the Central Studio for Documentary Films. I became an editor of documentary films. This came about quite naturally – Mother had worked for the studio at one time. I earned very little money. What seemed like a temporary job turned out to be permanent. . . . I would

like my daughter to be educated, of course, but I have never known what she should be. I wanted her to enrol in the Institute of History and Archives, because there are lots of women there – a pleasant group – and she would be surrounded by people she would feel at home with. But as it turned out, she chose the university.

The daughter, born in 1969:

My parents didn't know that I was going to study philosophy. I didn't know it myself. I just went to the university and saw that there was a philosophy department. I didn't know what philosophy was . . . much less what I should expect in the philosophy department and later on. For me it was simply a fabulous profession, the most interesting and most promising. Up until the last three or four years money never occurred to me as an issue. Then I began to realise that money exists and that you have to earn it – this happened in the last three or four years – I was extremely surprised.

In these interviews three types of working women are readily apparent. The grandmother, the mother, and the daughter represent three generations of women who were born and grew up in the Soviet era. The first-generation grandmother had to work to survive and to feed her children, with no room for thoughts about occupational orientation or education. The second generation hardly chose a job but went instead where it was easy to get one – through her mother's connections, as the mother had once worked at the film studio. Nor did the third generation choose a profession that would make her financially independent and become a serious endeavour. Rather, she chose to attend the most prestigious university in the country because it would allow her to lead an interesting life.

The first conclusion that we can draw from these experiences is that the jobs which drew women of the older generation, as well as the education to which their daughters and granddaughters aspired, did not reflect any occupational and career orientation in the true sense.

It is significant that in our studies Russian women most often listed as a 'negative' result of their professional growth the need to work more (64 per cent). The second most frequently listed disadvantage (46 per cent) was the necessity of becoming more involved in matters at the enterprise where they work. The third deterrent to professional growth listed was the impossibility of combining work and family (30 per cent).

On the positive side, both married and single respondents saw the prospect of a more interesting job as a benefit from career advancement. It is remarkable, however, that women ranked growth in power and influence in the workplace last in a list of possible rewards resulting from occupational advancement. In listing more interesting work as the main reward, perhaps the respondents were attempting to cast off the negative connotations that have long surrounded the description of someone making a career – 'careerist' (kar'erist). That has been accompanied by a widespread ambivalence in Russian society toward women who are building careers or even simply have the desire to achieve creative goals and professional success.

These results, gathered at the beginning of the 1990s can be correlated to a finding from earlier sociological studies: although an overwhelming majority of women are oriented toward combining work and family, only a tiny fraction give thought to actually pursuing career. This can be explained by the fact that women have less opportunity for occupational advancement than men. Further, because women sense that they are destined to economic stagnation, because they are increasingly encouraged by society to make family, children and husband their career – a 'woman's' career – a certain type of 'woman worker' has evolved, from which no particular career achievements are expected.

The essential character of the stereotypical female role appears confirmed in studies by G. Sillaste, who described a current phenomenon in which a majority of the female population rejected the idea of women leaders.[15] The same distinctive feature of public opinion has been noted by T. Zaslavskaia. 'When the Centre for Public Opinion was first established, we gave readers of the newspaper *Trud* a list of issues and asked them to select those that they felt merited research and discussion. Among the topics we proposed was "the role of women in management and government". That issue was the first the readers would exclude.'[16] It is not surprising that women's paths to political careers in the *perestroika* years and after have been uneven, with many setbacks along the way. Significantly, women politicians who are otherwise quite different share similar opinions as to the causes, as the following interview excerpts show.

Larisa Piiasheva, economist, former Deputy Mayor of Moscow: 'This is the way men have always thought: All the men first, then the most intelligent woman. They fight madly for these positions; they compete among themselves and lose their human dignity. I don't want to be a politician with dirty hands. Of course, at play here is a strong tradition of "politics – that's man's work".'[17]

Irina Khakamada, a deputy in the State Duma: 'Before men saw me as a serious competitor, it was all very simple – niceties, smiles, compliments. When they began to sense that behind this charming exterior is a person who takes and upholds her own position, the hard fighting started. In politics and in business, it's tough.'[18]

Sazhi Umalatova, former chairman of the permanent presidium of the Congress of People's Deputies of the RSFSR: 'Men here are power-hungry. They find it offensive when a woman is able to outdo them.'[19]

Ella Pamfilova, a deputy in the State Duma, former Minister for Social Protection in Yeltsin's government, also recalled that male ministers were friendly until she starting challenging their interests. After that, their expressions became steely stares.[20]

Conclusion

The experience of Russian women at the beginning of the 1990s demonstrates, on the one hand, tremendous changes in the occupational roles of women and, on the other, the extreme resistance of traditional family values to any radical change. In this

15. G. Sillaste 'Sotsiogendernye otnosheniia' *op. cit.*, p. 20.
16. Interview with T. Zaslavskaia.
17. Interview with L. Piiasheva.
18. Interview with I. Khakamada.
19. Interview with Sazhi Umalatova.
20. *Moskovskii Komsomolets*, 6 March 1994.

sense, it seems more fitting to speak not of a 'moving backwards' or of a 'patriarchal renaissance' (the term most often used to describe the current position of women in Russian society), but of a growing depth in essentially conflicting trends characterising the Soviet period. These trends have been dramatically revealed over the last two or three years.

The radical changes of the 1990s increase the vulnerability of women who are actively engaged in the world outside home through their occupational orientation. It might be observed that Russia's period of transition has deepened the conflict between the career and family roles of women and put them in a position of having to choose between the two.

When women enter into open competition, particularly in politics, they violate the rules of the game in a society in which non-traditional behaviour, expressed by the rule of 'all women work', exists alongside an almost universal acceptance of the traditional division of roles not only in the family, but in the professional sphere and in the political arena.

Chapter 12

SOCIAL POLICY AND THE WELFARE STATE

Nick Manning

The limited achievements of social policy in the Soviet era may be characterised as the pursuit of the gross expansion of 'intermediate' welfare indicators, such as the numbers of doctors, nurses and teachers, numbers of flats available, or the early retirement age. The figures for these were proudly displayed as signs of the inexorable upward growth of 'developed socialism'. However, in practice these were subject to the restraint of the 'residual principle' whereby capital investment was first directed towards industrial goals, while housing, the raising of living standards and other improvements in people's lives only received what remained.[1] Thus 'final' welfare indicators, such as the meeting of social needs, or the quality of the goods and services provided, or the kind of social relationships that were produced or reproduced, were not so impressive.

There was a strong link between work history and social security, which was essentially geared to entitlements carefully accumulated as a result of a good employment record. By contrast the 'social assistance' function, designed to provide income in response to a test of need, was unsystematically developed. This helps to explain why the social security system was neglectful of a number of 'pure need' groups, such as poor children, the disabled, and the unemployed. Health care, by contrast, seems at first to have been a great achievement. There were more doctors, nurses, and hospital beds per capita than any other major industrial country.[2] However, resources devoted to health care by comparison with international trends, even compared with the UK which is at a relatively low level, were extremely meagre: about 4 per cent of NMP (equivalent to about 2.5 per cent of GNP calculated on a market basis), compared with 6 per cent of GNP in the UK, and 10 per cent of GNP in the United States.[3]

Turning to other elements of Soviet social policy, housing provision was a continuous source of dissatisfaction from the October revolution onwards. This shortage of space had a number of consequences on domestic life. Young couples could rarely find their own flat to begin married life in, and normally had to

1. A. Aganbegyan *The Challenge: Economics of Perestroika*, Hutchinson, London, 1988, pp. 15–16.
2. E. Mezentseva and N. Rimachevskaya 'The Soviet Country Profile: health of the USSR population in the 70s and 80s – an approach to a comprehensive analysis', *Social Science and Medicine*, 31 (8), 1990, pp. 867–77.
3. C. Davis 'National health services, resource constraints and shortages: a comparison of Soviet and British experiences' in N. Manning and C.J. Ungerson (eds) *Social Policy Review 1989–90*, Longman, London.

share with one set of parents. In addition a significant proportion of tenants remained in communal flats, sharing cooking and bathing facilities. This stressful situation stimulated divorce, and inhibited reproduction.[4] The chance to escape these constraints through a better job were highly dependent on educational success. Education was regarded with pride in the Soviet union. As in the case of health care, the size and scale of the education sector, including nurseries, was impressive. The main problem in education stemmed from the simple point that the main access to more desirable jobs and social status was the higher education system, yet the main work available was in blue-collar production. There was thus an inevitable conflict between the aspirations of the majority of pupils and the reality of working life for most of them, that is, between the two functions of human capital investment and social reproduction. Competition for the scarce resource of higher education was intense, and for a variety of family-based reasons a steep class gradient appeared in the opportunities available.[5]

Overall, Soviet welfare was, in Titmus's terms,[6] largely reminiscent of occupational welfare. Social policies were not so much a compensation for social risks as an adjunct to the labour market. While coverage was in some areas impressive, particularly in the Central Asian republics, benefit and service levels were low. Many benefits were distributed through the workplace, either directly as enterprise services (e.g. housing, health care, and food) or managed through official trade unions (benefit claims and holidays). Strictly speaking this was entirely compatible with the socialist principle of 'to each according to their work', with social need being the guiding principle for distribution only under future communism. To make it more oriented to need would have been to break the links with the labour market.

Recent changes

In this section a general discussion of the changing environment and shape of social policy will be presented, before a more detailed review of specific areas. Clearly the environment within which social policy exists has changed dramatically: the USSR has collapsed, there is a new constitution, public administrative structures and budgetary arrangements are in turmoil, industrial production has shrunk, prices and wages are free, and domestic and industrial property is being privatised. On the other hand the structure of health and education has changed little, many of the same individuals administer services, major enterprises are still in effect being subsidised through soft financial accounting arrangements, unemployment appears to be low, and living standards have stabilised.

Reaction to the old system favoured reduced planning control in favour of markets, and reduced central control in favour of decentralised and democratic administration.

4. V. Shlapentokh *Public and Private Life of the Soviet People*, Oxford University Press, Oxford, 1989; J. Chinn *Manipulating Soviet Population Resources*, Martin Robertson, Oxford, 1977.
5. M. Yanowitch *Social and Economic Inequality in the Soviet Union*, Martin Robertson, Oxford, 1977.
6. R.M. Titmus 'The social division of welfare' in *Essays on the 'Welfare State'*, Allen and Unwin, London, 1958.

In theory this should overcome the key technical failure of the old system, which suffered from an overload of, and hence loss of, information as a result of central decision-making.[7] In addition, the release of self-interest and a new sense of political empowerment should reinvigorate a demoralised and passive population. These gains may indeed appear in time, but the changeover has brought with it some very sharp social costs. Widening incomes have left more women, children and old people in poverty, and undermined the security of public sector workers such as doctors and teachers. Classic social problems such as infectious disease, alcoholism, prostitution, and crime have grown, and consequently birth rates have dropped while death rates have climbed. Pressures on social services have escalated at the same time as inflation and tax evasion have reduced the resources available to them, and administrative and legal capacities have shrunk.

The policy options here are stark.[8] In the short run, a total absence of social support might enable the quickest restructuring of the economy, but it could only be possible with either the use of a draconian suppression of social unrest (hardly possible now in Russia), or where the economy was ready for 'take off' (for example in the Czech Lands, where Klaus has been sympathetic to this idea). The alternative is to take a slower path to economic change, and to target help as sharply as possible in the short term, with the longer-term goal of a Western mix of social insurance and private provision.[9] Russia appears to have opted for the latter, although benefits are still closely tied to enterprises and poorly targeted; with the new set of policy reforms of 1994, it was just the beginning of a medium-term reconstruction of the finance of social policy along corporatist social insurance lines.

In legal and administrative terms the most significant development has been the new constitution proposed and adopted at the end of 1993. Social policy issues are covered in a variety of proposals, but there are also omissions. The constitution has to be read against a background of more detailed social policy proposals issued by Yeltsin in November 1993 in the run-up to the December referendum. The constitution, many observers have noted, is heavily weighted towards the powers of the President. While ministers will take responsibility for managing various parts of the domestic policy programme, for example in ministries for labour, social protection or health, presidential decrees will continue to take the lead in policy initiatives. The formation of the President's council for social policy in May 1994, charged with overseeing the development and implementation of a series of proposals set out in November 1993, is a key body in this respect.

The constitution retains policy for health, education, and social security at the Federal level (articles 39, 41, 43), leaving only housing to the various republics, territories, regions, and federal cities (articles 130, 132). However, since budgetary provision for these services has moved away from central provision (as detailed in

7. M. Ellman *Socialist Planning*, 2nd edn, Cambridge University Press, Cambridge, 1989.
8. U. Gotting 'Destruction, adjustment, and innovation: social policy transformation in East Central Europe', Centre for Social Policy Research, University of Bremen, 1994, pp. 8–12.
9. N. Barr (ed) *Labor Markets and Social Policy in Central and Eastern Europe, the Transition and Beyond*, Oxford University Press, Oxford, 1994, pp. 26–27.

the separate service sections below), locally raised finance (taxes, charges, insurance, mortgages, charities, and so on) will assume increasing importance, with a consequent growth in regional inequity.

On 3 November 1993, a month after the October confrontation, Yeltsin published his review of policy goals. While it can be read partly as an election manifesto, the review appears to form the basis of current social policy plans:

We are now working together to prepare a package of social decrees:

- on a system of minimum social guarantees;
- on introducing allowances for those who are inadequately provided for;
- on measures to ensure that social protection for the population reaches the right people;
- on a minimum living standard;
- on a minimum wage;
- on a minimum pension;
- on charity and other measures.[10]

The then Council of Ministers agreed to prepare a number of measures during 1994 to deal with uprating various social benefits including family allowances, and to revise the contribution structures for the Pension Fund, the Social Insurance Fund, and the Employment Fund, and to prepare for the first time details of a mandatory medical insurance scheme. These proposals, as they have begun to appear, have been the subject of some sharp disagreements between the State Duma and the President, notably in the summer of 1994 when the Duma agreed an increase of 50 per cent in the basic pension. In view of the pressure on the budget, however, the President decreed an increase of only 15 per cent. This resulted in some pensioners receiving a 15 per cent increase and others a 50 per cent increase, and the resignation of the Minister for Social Protection.

This kind of administrative hiccup is an inevitable consequence of an unstable administrative system. This is the result of two main factors. First, many competent personnel are no longer in the civil service, either pushed out for close association with the old order, or pulled out to more lucrative jobs in the private sector.[11] Second, there has been an element of policy-making on the run, with a concomitant fluidity of administrative organisation. Part of this is the inevitable result of the political struggles that have characterised the period from 1991 to early 1994. Part of it, however, is also the result of the dominance of Yeltsin over government affairs, and the attempt to give administrative form to his changing policy agenda.

Underlying these factors is a deeper tension. This is the simultaneous thrust towards decentralisation of policy development, implementation, and finance, together with a growing centralisation of power in the presidency. Government by decree from Moscow may have advantages for cutting to the heart of issues quickly where there are clear and identifiable national problems, and no doubt this applies to the erosion of pensions by inflation. However, the inequities of the widening income distribution,

---

10. *Current Digest of the Post-Soviet Press*, 45 (44), p. 4.
11. M. Lesage 'The crisis of public administration in Russia' *Public Administration*, 71 (1/2), 1993, pp. 121–33.

the growing independence of enterprises, the gradual emergence of unemployment, the privatisation of housing, and the underfunding of health and education, all mean that regions and districts have increasingly specific local issues to deal with. In the absence of a national social assistance scheme, some regions have responded effectively to this, a good example being Taganrog where a locally organised Social Protection Fund (15 per cent of the city budget) provides a minimum means-tested income, and some basic food assistance to poor families, whether in work or not.[12] However, other areas are struggling to deal with an overwhelming level of need. A conference on the regional situation for social protection in February 1994[13] shows that in many areas, not only are upwards of a third of the population dependent on benefits, but over 50 per cent fall below the threshold set for social protection. The general pattern of poverty is examined in more detail below.

None of this is of course possible without the money to pay for it. The initial reaction, to print money or in effect to allow extended credit to central and local government and to enterprises, has through inflation enabled a rapid and cruel restructuring of incomes. Pensioners and public sector workers, for example, have been unable to maintain their incomes, while others have been able to advance theirs. Thus both the beneficiaries and providers of welfare services have suffered during this phase. Monthly inflation has now slowed considerably to 4.6 per cent in August 1994 compared with 25 per cent a year earlier and 40 per cent in early 1992,[14] and there is a more determined effort to control inflationary credit and non-payment between enterprises.[15] Within the budget there are signs that social spending is rising. Ellman and Layard[16] argued that the figures for early 1992 showed underfunding of social expenditure, for example only 3 per cent of GNP on education and 2 per cent on health, both of which are more than twice this rate in the OECD. By the middle of 1994, when the budget was accepted by the Duma on 24 June, these had risen to 4.5 per cent and 2.8 per cent respectively.[17]

However, these amounts are dwarfed by the costs of income support, which are now technically outside the state budget in four separate funds: employment, social insurance, pension, and social protection. Generated since 1991 by a 39 per cent payroll tax, in 1994 they amounted to 17 per cent of GDP, and ran a massive surplus of 4 per cent of GDP. As in many Western countries this is the area that is most expensive, and is particularly sensitive to two factors: the rate of unemployment, and the level of pensions. Both these figures have been the subject of some debate. The official rate of unemployment as measured by registration with the federal employment service is about 2 per cent, but labour force surveys indicate that for 1994 it is really nearer 6 per cent with a further 2 per cent on involuntary leave and

12. N. Barr *Income Transfers and the Social Safety Net in Russia*, World Bank, Washington, DC, 1992, p. 43.
13. Reported in detail in *Social Security*, 4, 1994.
14. *Russian Economic Trends*, monthly update, 17 October 1994, p. 4.
15. *Current Digest of the Post-Soviet Press*, 1994, 46 (36), p. 8.
16. M. Ellman and R. Layard 'Prices, incomes and hardship' in A. Åslund and R. Layard *Changing the Economic System in Russia*, Pinter Publishers, London, 1993, p. 58.
17. *Russian Economic Trends* 3 (2), 1994, p. 12.

5 per cent of short time,[18] a total of 13 per cent. Although this is double the 1993 figure, it is still quite low – a point taken up later. With unemployment benefit at around 10 per cent of the average wage, pensions take the lion's share of expenditure. The minimum has been indexed to about 20 per cent of the average wage, while the average pension is about a third of the average wage. Thus the pension rate drives the social budget, and will inevitably draw the kind of political fire witnessed in the summer of 1994.

With such a steep payroll tax, the question arises of why enterprises have not slimmed their workforces more aggressively. In fact, of the unemployed in 1994 only a quarter were made redundant, while over 20 per cent of the total workforce moved jobs in 1993. Clearly there is considerable movement, combined with an unwillingness to register as unemployed. For the worker there are strong incentives to accept short-time work. Housing, health care, holidays, food, raw materials, tools, and now share ownership have been and continue to be strongly linked to the job. Employers are also prepared to retain labour (and short time means lower payroll tax) which is beginning to move voluntarily, to retain share owners, and to continue a tradition of paternalistic welfare responsibility. *De jure* privatisation ended on 1 July 1994 with more than three-quarters of the workforce in private firms, spread equally across large and small enterprises. However, *de facto*, management and workers continue their old inter-dependencies.

Privatisation of enterprises in itself does not change social relations unless the financial pressures grow. These will not bite until subsidies disappear, or rather their current manifestation in terms of high levels of non-payment in inter-enterprise trade. The other major sector of the privatisation field, housing, demonstrates this effect. While started in 1992–93 with some vigour, this has now stalled and was running in 1994 at a quarter of the 1993 rate, with only 29 per cent of all flats in private ownership.[19] The main reasons appear to be the burden of maintenance charges and property taxes. With the introduction of a new system of charges for maintenance costs in January 1994, charges are projected to grow from 15 per cent of overheads in 1994 to 100 per cent in 1998.[20]

Clearly, ordinary citizens take a keen interest in these changes. What have been their reactions? It appears that while there is general approval for the new system of democratic government, there is less enthusiasm for the performance of the actual government since 1991. Rose[21] reports that 92 per cent of his respondents in an all-Russia survey in 1993 felt that the new government system was better than the old one. Much of this judgement seems to have been related to increased civil freedoms,

---

18. R. Layard and A. Richter 'Labour market adjustment in Russia' *Russian Economic Trends* 3 (2), 1994, pp. 90–92; G. Standing 'Why measured unemployment in Russia is so low: the net with many holes' *Journal of European Social Policy* 4 (1), 1994, pp. 35–50.
19. *Russian Economic Trends* 3 (2), 1994, p. 84.
20. N.V. Rubstov 'Speech by the Head of the Chief Directorate of the Russian Federal Committee for Municipal Services', *Social Security* 4 January 1994.
21. R. Rose 'How Russians are coping with transition', Studies in Public Policy no. 216, Centre for the Study of Public Policy, University of Strathclyde, 1993, p. 42.

but approval for actual government policies since 1992 was considerably poorer, with 32 per cent not approving at all, and an additional 45 per cent only partly approving.[22] Much of this negative feeling relates to government provision of social benefits, and this judgement has grown stronger since 1991. Surveys in 1991 and 1993 reported in the *Information Monitoring Bulletin* of the survey organisation VTsIOM[23] show that there is a decline from 35 per cent to 26 per cent of people feeling that social rights are partly or fully observed in Russia, and a growth in the proportion who want free schools (41 per cent to 58 per cent), free health care (22 per cent to 46 per cent), and free housing (24 per cent to 32 per cent); for rights to employment and a subsistence income this rate grows to nearly 90 per cent.[24] A survey by Rose for mid-1992 finds that these are not merely wishes, but that more than two-thirds of the sample wanted higher taxes to be levied to pay for better education, health, and pensions.[25] Again, a survey from June 1994, reported in the *Information Monitoring Bulletin*,[26] indicates that a quarter of those families that receive the universally available child benefit would give it up in favour of poor families, and over half of high income (top 20 per cent) families would do this. There is thus still solid support for social protection in Russia, particularly for poorer families, and a strong sense of doubt that the government is effective enough in this area: the same 1994 survey revealed that 78 per cent feel that 'the authorities and the various community organisations in the field of social protection' are doing either practically nothing or 'patently not enough'.[27]

Turning to the other main source of welfare, the enterprise, many people continue to receive substantial benefits, and approve of this arrangement. There is also a clear picture of the enterprise as a multiplier of advantage; those enterprises doing well provide significantly higher levels of help and social benefits than do others. Starting with the population which is urban (about 75 per cent) and thus most likely to work in large enterprises, a survey by Rose[28] suggests that more than 50 per cent of the population have at some time received help with medical care, child care, and holidays, and a third help with housing, food and other goods. A 1993 survey of the total population found that typically 20 per cent of the workforce felt that they could if necessary in the future count on enterprise help with housing, medical care, food, retraining and leisure. In fact those that actually got help in 1993 varied, for medical care and food, from 19–20 per cent in the richer enterprises to 8–9 per cent in the poorer enterprises.[29] And in relation to discounted goods, for example, Gimpelson[30] reports that at AZLK (a large car producer in Moscow) in

22. *Ibid*, p. 37.
23. January 1994, pp. 24–25.
24. *Ibid*, p. 26.
25. R. Rose 'Russians between state and market', Studies in Public Policy no. 205, Centre for the Study of Public Policy, University of Strathclyde, 1992, p. 6.
26. October 1994, p. 45.
27. *Ibid*, p. 36.
28. Rose 'Russians between state and market', *op. cit.*, p. 10.
29. *Information Monitoring Bulletin*, July 1993, p. 33.
30. V.E. Gimpelson 'Labour market and employment in Russia: beginning of changes', in R. Weichhardt (ed.) *Economic Developments in Cooperation Partner Countries from a Sectoral Perspective*, NATO, Brussels, 1993, p. 65.

1992, the total value of consumer goods sold to workers at discount prices exceeded the annual wage fund. There is also a sharp gradient in favour of those on higher salaries within enterprises: the same VTsIOM survey found that for example 75 per cent of high-paid workers received food or cheap goods, compared with 40 per cent of low-paid workers, and housing or medical help was also (at 35 per cent) twice as likely to go to the higher paid.[31] Evidence from repeat surveys by VTsIOM throughout 1993, however, suggests that in all categories of employees there is a small but steady decline in enterprise support across the range of goods and services.[32]

Income: employment, social security, and poverty

The following sections provide a more detailed review of social policy changes on a service-by-service basis. First there is the essential question of living standards, and the mechanisms through which households gain the wherewithal to satisfy their material needs. In industrial societies people generally gain the resources necessary for everyday consumption through either wage labour, family and friends, or state benefits. In post-1991 Russia, all three mechanisms are important, but others, such as growing food, are also important. Nevertheless, employment remains the key. As noted earlier, one of the aims for economic restructuring is the development of a flexible labour market, and new small and medium-size enterprises (SMEs). However, there were significant obstacles to this in 1991 which are now disappearing.

The first obstacle was the attitude to work activity itself. Anyone who stayed in the old Soviet Union for any length of time knows that there was a low commitment to the quality of daily work. As the popular saying went, 'we pretend to work, and they pretend to pay us!'. This was not just a matter of low pay, however, but also the time-consuming nature of goods and service distribution. Many workers had to spend work time each day either shopping, or making arrangements through friends and contacts for the acquisition of everyday requirements.[33] There was also the urgent problem of alcohol abuse in work time that led to great loss of efficiency. Evidence on work attitudes suggests changes here. Gimpelson[34] reports on three surveys, undertaken in 1988 and 1989 after the law on enterprises was adopted, that indicate that there was a marked growth in work intensity, particularly in cooperatives. At that time, however, only about 20 per cent of workers appeared to support the idea of an increase in work effectiveness and efficiency.[35] By 1991, however, Magun and Gimpelson[36] report from a survey of workers in state-run enterprises that the most common reaction to threatened changes in employment is an active response in terms of increasing work effort, retraining, and the desire to retain or increase work status.

31. *Information Monitoring Bulletin*, July 1993, p. 34.
32. *Information Monitoring Bulletin*, October 1994, p. 46.
33. Shlapentokh *Public and Private Life*, *op. cit.*
34. V.E. Gimpelson 'From labour shortage to unemployment: Soviet workers' attitudes about possible changes in labour relations', *Labour* 5 (3), 1991, pp. 63–78.
35. *Ibid*, p. 74.
36. V. Magun and V.E. Gimpelson 'Russian workers' strategies in adjusting to unfavourable changes in employment', *Economic and Industrial Democracy* 14, 1993, pp. 95–117.

Rose[37] found among the urban population that in 1992 just over 50 per cent felt that individuals themselves rather than the state should take responsibility for providing for families, that two-thirds felt that enterprises were better run by entrepreneurs than the state, and that they would on the whole prefer a higher wage combined with the risk of unemployment, than a secure low-paid job. Asked to comment on how other people used their time at work, two-thirds felt that people spent most of their time at work productively, and the rest felt that their colleagues spent at least 50 per cent of their time productively.

A second obstacle to economic change was the absence of unemployment, the result of a right to employment enjoyed since the abolition of unemployment benefits by Stalin in 1930. The situation is changing. As noted above, the labour market shows a substantial minority changing jobs each year now, with only a small proportion being made redundant, and total of unemployment and underemployment of around 13 per cent. Moreover, a study of redundant workers in 1992 by Gimpelson and Magun[38] shows that more than 50 per cent were reemployed within three months, with over a quarter entering the non-state sector. This process has accelerated in 1993, with about one-third of medium-sized industrial firms expanding their employment throughout the year.[39] In some areas this appears to have created a labour shortage in some sectors, particularly for skilled workers.[40]

A third obstacle was the attitude to income distribution. Although Gorbachev[41] repeated his dislike of 'levelling tendencies', using the principle from Marx that under socialism 'from each according to his abilities, to each according to his work', there was widespread support among workers for the principle of wage equality, that is that differential effort should not be rewarded with differentials in pay. Survey evidence suggested that this attitude was deeply entrenched.[42] This is now changing. Rose[43] reports that in 1992 only 10 per cent of the urban population supported in principle the equalisation of incomes, with 90 per cent wishing to link incomes to individual efforts. In terms of how the better off were actually succeeding, however, while hard work was also mentioned by 80 per cent, there was a strong suspicion that luck, connections and dishonesty were almost as significant.

The final obstacle was the attitude to general economic restructuring, particularly price reform. Cumulative all-union representative sample surveys carried out in 1989 and 1990 by VTsIOM[44] showed that there was little public support for the kind of

37. Rose 'Russians between state and market', *op. cit.*, p. 6.
38. V.E. Gimpelson and V. Magun 'Nouvel emploi et mobilité sociale des travailleurs licenciés', *Cahiers internationaux de Sociologie* XCVI, 1994, pp. 57–75.
39. *Russian Economic Trends* 3 (2), 1994, p. 90.
40. A. Solovyev 'The situation in St Petersburg labour market', in *St Petersburg in the Early 1990s: Crazy, Cold, and Cruel*, Charitable Foundation 'Nochlezhka', Petersburg, 1994, p. 167.
41. M. Gorbachev *Perestroika*, Collins, London, 1987.
42. D.S. Mason and S. Sydorenko 'Perestroika, social justice, and Soviet public opinion', *Problems of Communism* 39, Nov/Dec, 1990, pp. 34–43.
43. Rose 'Russians between state and market', *op. cit.*, pp. 5–6.
44. N. Manning 'Social policy in the Soviet Union and its successors', in B. Deacon, M. Castle-Kanerova, N. Manning, F. Millard, E. Orosz, J. Szalai, A. Vidinova *The New Eastern Europe: Past, Present and Future for Social Policy*, Sage, London, 1992.

radical restructuring of prices and ownership proposed in the original Shatalin '500 day' programme. This included a rapid reduction in the large existing subsidies for food, travel, and housing, and the general movement of prices to a level which more accurately signalled the real costs of production. It also planned for the widespread privatisation of enterprises, housing, and land. Public reaction to Yeltsin's actual price reforms, introduced in January 1992, confirms this view. There was growing hostility to such changes, with a large minority of citizens claiming that they would 'actively' resist them. The abandonment in 1990 of this 'shock therapy' in favour of a more gradual programme of price reform and privatisation by Gorbachev may well have been a more democratic decision than was apparent to Western observers.

More specific surveys of particular factories in and around Moscow confirm that there was a clear variation in attitude according to social class: managers supported change, but the shop floor did not.[45] There was also sharp public criticism of cooperative ventures that became legal, since they were felt to be exacerbating supply shortages through their superior purchasing power, and hence became associated in the public mind with unjust privileges. These were in effect the nascent small and medium enterprises (SMEs) of the future, and such antipathy towards them was not encouraging. By 1992 Rose[46] reports that there was still a large majority concerned about price reform, but that anxieties about general inflation had come to the fore. It can thus be concluded that the tension between inherited levels of social justice and attitudes towards work, and a flexible labour market, which may have hampered the introduction of SMEs, is easing off.

Beyond primary employment in the labour market, many people have a mixture of secondary work, friends, family, and unwaged work to maintain their incomes. Shlapentokh[47] and others have shown the importance of these connections under the old regime. Since 1991 they have become if anything more important – at least during the years of acute adjustment of the labour market and consumer prices. Rose[48] distinguishes three types of economic activity: official (employment, or pensions); uncivil (secondary work for money, or exploiting connections); social (non-monetary work, or exchange). He argues that those relying on the first type only are *vulnerable*, on the first and second are *enterprising*, and on the first and third are *defensive*; the rest are *marginal*. In his 1992 survey he found that a distinctive pattern for Russia compared with other East European countries was a higher proportion of *vulnerable* (a third) and a lower proportion of *marginal* (10 per cent).[49] Even so, more than a quarter of the Russian sample of working-age people declared that their main job was not the most important for their standard of living. About the same proportion declared that growing food was their second main source; indeed, overall more than half of the sample grew food, and more than a third reported that

45. Zh. Toshchenko *Izvestiia*, 16/6, 1987, p. 2; V. Chichkanov *Izvestiia*, 4/9, 1987, p. 2.
46. Rose 'Russians between state and market', *op. cit.*, p. 7.
47. Shlapentokh, *Public and Private Life, op. cit.*
48. R. Rose 'Is money the measure of welfare in Russia?', Studies in Public Policy no. 215, Centre for the Study of Public Policy, University of Strathclyde, 1993, p. 25.
49. R. Rose 'Divisions and contradictions in economics in transition', Studies in Public Policy no. 206, Centre for the Study of Public Policy, University of Strathclyde, 1992, p. 21.

they grew most or some of their food during the previous year. Other important activities included exchanging help for house repairs, and using connections for essential services, particularly medical care and medicines (over half the sample).

The third main source of income is, of course, the state. Here the most important activities have been related to pensions, family allowances and unemployment, and a commitment in the first Congress of Peoples' Deputies to monitor the standard of living of poorer groups. As far as pensioners are concerned, evidence about their economic difficulties resulted in the raising of minimum pensions to the level of the minimum wage (70 rubles per month) in October 1989, taking effect from January 1990. This was described as the 'small pension law'[50] since it was a stop-gap to a more comprehensive reform (necessary not least because of the appearance of significant inflation in recent years). The reform of pensions came in 1991[51] when the pension fund was created, financed by a payroll tax of 32 per cent from employers and 1 per cent from employees, relieving the state budget from responsibility, and since 1991 this fund has been generating a large surplus (4 per cent of GDP in 1994). The fund is subject to the control of the Ministry of Social Protection which coordinates policy, and calculates benefits and entitlements. Pensioners are entitled to a minimum, enhanced by the number of years' work, and previous earnings, although there is as yet no retirement test to qualify. In principle the benefit rate should be calculated automatically, but rapid inflation has politicised the rate, as mentioned earlier when the President reduced the State Duma's recommended rise in the summer of 1994 from 50 per cent to 15 per cent, as a result of which the Minister for Social Protection resigned. Current proposals by the Ministry for Social Protection are for a Western-style 'funded' system (such as occupational pensions) based on genuine insurance principles, with a clear relation between lifetime payment and benefit. However this has not been achieved even by the British and United States government schemes, which work on a pay-as-you-go basis, with each generation in effect taxed to pay for the previous generation. A fully funded scheme for Russia would involve the transfer of a massive amount of resources into pension funds, which would have to be built up over many years, in addition to paying for current unfunded pensioners.

Family allowances have almost by default become a significant element in the federal policy for poorer people, since children have become increasingly represented among the poor. A new system has been in operation since January 1994.[52] All children under 18 months are entitled to an allowance of 150 per cent of the minimum wage (up from 60 per cent, and now about 15 per cent of the average wage); up to 6 years of age the rate is 105 per cent (up from 45 per cent), and thereafter 90 per cent of the minimum wage. This is quite high by international standards. It is enhanced for families in the North. The Pension Fund disburses the money, but the funding comes from the state budget. Clearly this benefit is dependent on the political fortunes of the minimum wage level, which has not been stable: between May 1992 and May 1993 this

50. R. Tsivilev and V. Rogogin 'Social assistance for the elderly and the disabled in the USSR', *International Social Security Review* XLIII (2), 1990, pp. 180–188, p. 186.
51. Barr *Income Transfers, op. cit.*, ch. 2.
52. *Russian Economic Trends* 3 (2), 1994, p. 48.

benefit in real terms declined to one-third of its previous value, but the change in 1994 has reinstated it.

There is no doubt, however, that the cornerstone of social security has been the right to work (Article 40 of the old constitution), upon which other policies for income maintenance were based. Therefore the main problem looming on the horizon is the possibility of mass unemployment as the economy sheds the estimated 30 per cent of labour that is economically unnecessary.[53] However it is difficult to decide very clearly what unemployment actually is. For example, Adirim[54] showed that 'joblessness' was in the region of 6 per cent, but that relative 'worklessness' in existing employment which results in incomplete wages might have accounted for another 10–15 per cent, while a desire for a better job had been expressed by the majority of the population.

This problem generated the Employment Law drafted in the autumn of 1990, and formally adopted on 15 January 1991. This officially signalled the end of the right/duty to work by imposing a 1 per cent payroll levy to generate funds to finance unemployment benefit, retraining, public community work, and career guidance.[55] 25 per cent of the funds were earmarked for a central all-union fund available for low-income high unemployment republics, the rest staying at republic level, although the events following August 1991 saw this inter-republic flow disappear. Initially it was feared that there would be insufficient funds generated to pay for benefits set at or near the minimum wage, or to support those who exhausted their entitlements. The latter group were expected to exceed 50 per cent of the future unemployed, and in the absence of a national scheme of income support it was expected that poverty would spread rapidly. Standing[56] argued that only a basic income/social dividend scheme would accomplish both the alleviation of poverty, and the flexibility of labour supply which would dominate social security policy in the 1990s.

However, unemployment benefit has not been as big a cost to the government as was expected in the years from 1991. This is partly because few claimed it, but were voluntarily moving between jobs; it was also probably because the rate of benefit was so low. For the first three months it was 100 per cent continuation of wages, then 75 per cent from the employment service for the next three months, 60 per cent for the next four months and 45 per cent for the next five months. The minimum is equal to the minimum wage (i.e. 10 per cent of average wages). Since this is calculated on the basis of the previous year's wages, and is not indexed, with the high inflation rates of 1992 and 1993 most recipients were in effect on the minimum. However, with inflation coming under relative control, and unemployment rising steadily, if not dramatically, the cost of this benefit may soon escalate. Conditions of receipt include work-seeking, and the acceptance of at least the second appropriate job

53. G.R. Urban 'Introduction – social and economic rights in the Soviet bloc', *Survey* 29 (4), 1987, p. 3.
54. I Adirim 'A note on the current level, pattern and trends of unemployment in the USSR', *Soviet Studies* XLI (3), 1989, pp. 449–461.
55. G. Standing (ed.) *In Search of Flexibility: the New Soviet Labour Market*, International Labour Organisation, Geneva, 1991.
56. *Ibid*, chapter 18.

offer. Benefits are paid from the 1991 Employment Fund. Proposals for a flat rate benefit (to simplify administration), and means-tested unemployment assistance (for those whose benefits are exhausted) continue to be discussed.

The Minister for Social Protection, before her resignation in the middle of 1994, was working on a number of new measures.[57] The first was a proposal for subsistence income guarantee which is not yet available for those poor people who have fallen through other elements of the safety net. While there are number of local and regional funds available for this purpose ('material assistance'), there is no earmarked support across the whole Federation. This relates to her second concern about the demarcation between federal and local government responsibility for public funds for social protection, the targeting of help for poor people, and the coordination of charities with the Ministry's work. The third was, in the context of particular concern over children and old people without families, the development of a long-term anti-poverty strategy as a national policy. As part of the politics of this situation, the Minister wanted to take control of setting the official subsistence level from the Ministry of Labour, and to aim for a national income guarantee of 80 per cent of this subsistence level, until more could be afforded.

Beneath this discussion about incomes is the question of poverty (discussed in Chapter 10 in this volume). In June 1994, using a Ministry of Labour basket of essential foodstuffs for the poverty line, *Russian Economic Trends* calculated that 14 per cent of the population were in poverty – the same as in the mid-1980s.[58] However, calculated on this basis, it had peaked at 36 per cent at the beginning of 1993. Rising average incomes, combined with a slow-down in inflation (which when high particularly affects those on benefits which are only periodically uprated) appear to have resulted in this improvement in 1994, although the new 1994 rates of family allowances must also have helped. Since the minimum pension is currently around 20 per cent of the average wage or half the Ministry of Labour minimum subsistence poverty line, and the average pension around 31 per cent of the average wage or 80 per cent of the subsistence level, the pension rate might be expected to determine the poverty rate. However, average pensions have closely matched the average wage since the mid-1980s, suggesting that the image of impoverished Russian pensioners should be replaced by impoverished children. Surveys in 1992 and 1993 by the Russian Longitudinal Monitoring Survey and Goskomstat respectively, reported by *Russian Economic Trends*[59], show that the composition of the poor was significantly tilted towards children: for both 1992 and 1993 the proportion of children in poverty (at around 40 per cent) was about twice that of men over 60. It may be that the reduction in poverty, reported as halving between January and February 1994, if it is indeed related to the new higher rates of family allowances from January, will mean that children will feature less centrally in the statistics for Russian poverty for 1994.

57. E.A. Pamfilova 'Keynote address by the Russian Minister for Public Social Protection', *Social Security* 4, January, 1994.
58. M. Ellman 'A note on the distribution of income in the USSR under Gorbachev', *Soviet Studies* XLII (1), 1990, pp. 147–48.
59. *Russian Economic Trends* 3 (2), 1994, p. 47.

Health, illness and health care

Here, the main policy problem is the underfunding of the health service, which has been at relatively low levels for many years, as explained earlier in this chapter. Substantial wage increases were granted in 1986 to bring medical staff pay up to average levels, and promises were made in the 12th five-year plan to inject substantial increases in funds for new technology, drugs, and so on. These remained largely unfulfilled. In June 1994 the average wage in the health care sector was 75 per cent of the average industrial wage.[60] The budget for 1994 does seem to have increased the intended allocation to 2.8 per cent of GNP, up from 2 per cent two years before. However, the main source of new money comes from the Federal Medical Insurance Fund set up in 1993, itself derived from a 3.6 per cent payroll tax, although only about three-quarters of this money was spent on health care in 1993, the rest being kept as surplus.[61] By April 1994, a third of the population was covered by this new form of insurance, and this was planned to rise to 50 per cent by the end of 1994. There is also a plan to raise the payroll tax in stages to 8.6 per cent in the future. However, as with the other insurance funds, there is a great deal of uncertainty as to who really controls these huge sums of money, since they are not clearly separated from each other or from state interference. Other sources of new money will in the future be private. There has always been a flow of private money to physicians in the form of tips or bribes to gain access to services, and in more recent years the shortage of medicines resulted in a growing illicit market. Budget caps on hospitals which have now been imposed, combined with an explosion in the price of pharmaceuticals (many of which were in the past imported from Central Europe), have forced health carers to charge for services. In his 1992–93 surveys Rose reported that a half of the population had to use connections to get goods and services difficult to find, the majority of which were medicines and doctors.[62] And with the use of foreign currency growing, again the main use was for buying medical services.[63] An estimated 10–15 per cent of the population have been receiving health care from their place of work,[64] but as mentioned earlier these services are, albeit slowly, on the decline. Should this decline accelerate, it may leave an already stretched health service with a substantial additional burden.

The current proposals, like those on pensions, are thus to extend medical insurance along Western European lines. Starodubov,[65] the Russian Deputy Minister for Health, states that the Ministry of Health is committed to the retention of public ownership of health facilities, most of which have been decentralised to the regions,

---

60. *Current Digest of the Post-Soviet Press* 46 (33), 1994, p. 22.
61. A. Akopyan 'The patient pays three times', *Literaturnaya Gazeta*, 21 September 1994, p. 11, *Current Digest of the Post-Soviet Press*, 46 (38), p. 7.
62. Rose 'Russians between state and market', *op. cit.*, p. 16.
63. Rose, 'How Russians are coping', *op. cit.*, p. 27.
64. A.S. Preker and R.G.A. Feachem 'Health and health care' in N. Barr (ed.) *Labor Markets and Social Policy in Central and Eastern Europe, the Transition and Beyond*, Oxford University Press, Oxford, 1994, p. 309.
65. V.I. Starodubov, 'Address of the Russian Deputy Health Minister', *Social Security* 4, January 1994.

but also to the generation of more money through insurance. However, a 1994 presidential decree suggests that medical facilities should be privatised.[66] If this goes ahead – for example, the proposal to privatise family doctors' offices, under consideration in 1993[67] – it would be likely to have a serious effect on access for poor people. As with the example of the early railway labour shakeout, experiments in service restructuring have been set up. For example, in April 1988 the Leningrad health service was turned over to a strict internal market – well before the equivalent mechanism was even contemplated in the UK. Hospital budgets were set to zero, and polyclinics given the task of purchasing the services that they needed from hospitals, and paying a 'market price' through which hospitals were to earn their revenues. It did not work without major hiccups,[68] but there are some who can see the potential benefits in terms of greater efforts on all sides to think through the consequences of referrals.

However, the main activity in the health field has not been inside the health services, but rather an attempt to remedy the serious stagnation and decline in life expectancy and the increase in infant mortality that developed in the late 1970s.[69] This, without doubt, has been the most serious health problem in recent years, notwithstanding other notable issues, such as the Chernobyl nuclear disaster, AIDS, the disabled, children in care, and environmental pollution.[70] Indeed it was so troubling that the publication of the relevant statistics was suspended from 1972 to 1986.[71] The main reason for this pattern – unique to the industrialised world – was felt to be alcohol abuse, although it is likely that environmental pollution has been an as yet unquantified and underrecognised contributor.

The evidence now is that the poor health record, to which the 1980s anti-alcohol campaign was a reaction, has continued to get worse. For example, by 1992 average alcohol consumption had reached the same level as in 1984 before the campaign. At the same time the increase (from 62 to 65) in life expectancy for men that resulted from the campaign declined to 62 again. By 1994 this had dropped still further to 59 years, directly as a result of alcohol consumption.[72] Price liberalisation has resulted in the comparative decline in the price of vodka, compared with food for example. In addition, new sources of ill health have appeared. Diphtheria, cholera, measles, and general intestinal infections have spread across Russia in higher and higher numbers since 1991. For example, diphtheria cases have doubled annually since 1990, when

66. Akopyan 'The patient pays', *op. cit.*, p. 8.
67. Preker and Feachem 'health and health care', *op. cit.*, p. 301.
68. J. Roberts 'Winter in Leningrad', *The Health Services Journal* 4 Jan. 1990, pp. 18–19.
69. Mezentseva and Rimachevskaya 'The Soviet Country Profile', *op. cit.*
70. J. Dossett-Davies 'Where Glasnost has not yet arrived', *Community Care,* 5 May 1988, pp. 19–20; *Economist*, 22 Sept. 1990, pp. 25–28; J. Harwin 'Glasnost children', *Guardian*, 6 April 1988, p. 23; J. Perera 'The shrivelled sea', *Guardian*, 9 November 1990, p. 29; J. Pierson 'Back in the USSR', *Community Care*, 14 July 1988, pp. 22–24; J. Steele 'Soviet disabled struggle for political recognition', *Guardian*, 7 December 1991, p. 12.
71. A. Trehub 'Social and economic rights in the Soviet Union', *Survey* 29 (4), 1987, p. 13.
72. A. Nemtsov and V. Shkolnikov 'To live or to drink?' *Izvestiia*, 19 July 1994, p. 4, *Current Digest of the Post-Soviet Press* 46 (29), p. 13.

30 people died in a year, to January 1994 when 50 people died in a month, the main reason being a less than 50 per cent coverage of immunisation.[73]

One of the main reasons blamed for many of these illnesses is the pollution of drinking water. An official report by the Ministry for Environmental Protection in August 1994 admits that for almost half of the population, drinking water standards are below official limits.[74] In 1993, 2,992 died as a result of poor quality drinking water, and many more were ill. In the absence of money to invest in cleaning up supplies, the population is urged to boil all drinking water.[75] In a recent survey as part of a project on environmental movements by the author and others, it was found that 80 per cent of the population in Moscow do in fact boil drinking water, compared to 50 per cent in Estonia, and 3 per cent in Hungary.[76] The second main reason for illnesses is pollution in the atmosphere. The Moscow Chief Medical Administration Report for 1993 records that respiratory diseases are the most common illnesses, both among adults and children, and that there was an increase of over 20 per cent for children between 1992 and 1993.[77]

Overall, this increase in illnesses and continued underfunding of health care, on top of the general disruption to people's lives caused by the economic and political changes since 1991, has had an inevitable effect on birth and death rates. In Moscow, birthrates have almost halved since 1989, from 12 per 1,000 people to 7 per 1,000 in 1993. Mortality rates have increased in the same period from 12 to 17 per 1,000. In combination, these rates have thus moved from balance to severe imbalance, with an inevitable decline in the population. Outside Moscow, in 49 regions (about two-thirds of the total country) in 1993 there was a decline in the population, compared with a decline in 41 regions in 1992 and in 33 regions in 1991.[78]

Housing

Housing was a traditional source of dissatisfaction with the old regime, with long queues, small flats, and a monotonous reliance on high-rise architecture. It was very cheap, almost free in fact, but this never generated the gratitude that this 'gift from the state' was intended to. New problems in recent years include homelessness and begging,[79] and the old ones of access, quality, and infrastructure remain. The main effort to tackle them was the commitment in the 1986 Communist Party Programme

73. M. Eratova 'Viruses feast in a poor country', *Pravda*, 13 April 1994, p. 8, *Current Digest of the Post-Soviet Press* 46 (15), p. 24.
74. Y. Shapetkina 'The drinking water situation in Russia is very bad', *Nezavisimaya Gazeta*, 2 August 1994, p. 1, *Current Digest of the Post-Soviet Press* 46 (31), p. 17.
75. M. Yermakova 'In terms of health we are in 68th place', *Rossiiskiye vesti*, 29 April 1994, p. 3, *Current Digest of the Post-Soviet Press* 46 (17), pp. 17–18.
76. N. Manning 'Patterns of environmental movements in Eastern Europe', paper to the University of Cambridge Committee on Russian and East European Studies, 1 November 1994.
77. *Current Digest of the Post-Soviet Press*, 46 (20), 1994, p. 20.
78. Russian Federation State Statistics Committee, *Current Digest of the Post-Soviet Press*, 46 (18), 1994, p. 10.
79. J. Stetina 'When hope hits zero', *Guardian*, 30 November 1990, p. 28.

(27th Congress of the CPSU) to provide all families with their own flat by the end of the century. Since an estimated 20 per cent live in communal flats, this implies a massive increase in housing investment.[80] As noted earlier, half of the stock was enterprise-owned, and some enterprises echoed the Party promise, and also pledged to provide all of their workers with separate flats. Rents, which even together with energy costs rarely absorbed more than 3 per cent of household income, have only just begun to rise as a prelude to a more flexible housing market.

However, an indication of the changes planned for the housing market can be deduced from three important decrees issued in 1988 that gave *carte blanche* (and bank credit) for the expansion of private, and cooperative, housing construction.[81] The final decree, in December 1988, granted the right for organisations and soviets to sell their housing stock, as a result of which the Moscow Soviet in July 1990 decreed that all of its tenants (about 25 per cent of all households) had the right to buy their flats through a complicated formula which entitled families to a basic space allowance, over and above which the price rose steeply. Initially this kind of decree was not, and could not be, effectively implemented in Moscow. However, an example can be seen in pre-independence Estonia, where flats were put on sale in late 1990, and prices were set in the region of 150,000 rubles per flat. The Estonian Academy of Sciences estimated that, with annual salaries at around 5,000 rubles, fewer than one hundred local residents could raise such funds.[82] In 1991, fearing an influx of North American money from returning expatriate Estonians for whom such a price was only $5,000, this market was suspended. The weakening implementation of the *propiska* system of the right to live in a city such as Moscow will heighten this tension between public and private property, since a new influx of hopeful city dwellers will emerge from the satellites and suburbs that have been held at arm's length beyond the city limits.

At first the rate of privatisation was slow. With few buyers interested in the very high prices, and the unattractive prospects of taking on maintenance and other charges, there was little point in householders becoming owners, unless they were leaving the city, or had other reasons to want to move anyway. In 1992 and 1993, however, activity rose, partly as a result of government encouragement, and the setting of apparent deadlines for completing the transaction. By the end of 1993, 25 per cent of flats were privatised, although this now appears to have reached a plateau as the rate slowed considerably in 1994, to an overall total of 30 per cent.[83] Some commentators think that there is little likelihood of this proportion growing much further in the future, and that it will never reach 50 per cent.[84] Unfortunately, since the value of flats (particularly in central locations of use to commercial interests) can be very high, there have been some sharp struggles over ownership. The worst

80. Trehub, 'Social and economic rights', *op. cit.*
81. G. Andrusz 'A note on the finance of housing in the Soviet union', *Soviet Studies* XLII (3), 1990, pp. 555–70.
82. T. Niit Unpublished paper given to the ESRC East–West Initiative Workshop on Social Movements at the University of Kent, 2 October 1991.
83. *Russian Economic Trends* 3 (2), 1994, p. 84.
84. A. Baranov 'The housing situation in St Petersburg' in *St Petersburg in the Early 1990s: Crazy, Cold, and Cruel*, Charitable Foundation 'Nochlezhka', St Petersburg, 1994, p. 159.

examples involve tenants being tricked into moving by threats or promises of non-existent alternative accommodation, or even the murder of tenants (especially the elderly). Property-related murders such as those rose from 17 in 1993 to 50 in the first half of 1994.[85] Another example (which was studied as part of a project by the author and others), was the attempt by tenants of commercially attractive blocks in central Moscow to privatise the whole block collectively, and thus gain control of valuable commercial space on the ground floor and basement. While this was given cautious approval in the democratic atmosphere of 1991, subsequent reorganisation of Moscow local government took these rights away. Local officials had realised the great value of this non-living space which could be sold or let to provide money for the local budget.[86] A long struggle between these housing groups and the local government is continuing.

In any society the high costs of new building and the amount of value locked up in existing property makes the issue of housing finance highly significant. In Russia this issue is being tackled in a rather haphazard manner. Initially, free privatisation to existing tenants, while confirming the existing privileges of favoured occupants, changed the flow of finance very little, and rents, energy and maintenance charges remained nominal. This is slowly beginning to change. A scheme introduced in January 1994 will begin to raise the charges for the running costs of flats, at first to 15 per cent, and by 1998 to 100 per cent of actual costs.[87] In principle this should raise revenue that can be recycled to invest in the improvement of buildings, although it may in reality end up as a means of reducing federal expenditure from other budgets. Two recent presidential decrees (in December 1993 and June 1994) have also tackled the financing of housing by authorising mortgage lending on the value of a property, housing savings accounts, and local government construction funds for low-income housing. However, as is the case in other areas of social policy, the exact mechanisms for actually implementing these decrees are not fully in place, for example the means for an institutional lender to repossess a property in the case of default by the borrower, that is, eviction. The Ministry of Finance has suggested that enterprises may be able to provide guarantees for their employees, but as such enterprise support is run down (as discussed above), or cannot be provided by insolvent institutions, there will continue to be a gap in this part of the financial circle.[88]

As far as construction is concerned, there has been a virtual collapse of state housing starts, with a small boom (from a very low start) of private single family houses. Figures for St Petersburg show a fall of 90 per cent for 1993 over 1989 in state housing construction, but there are 10,000 private houses under construction.[89]

85. I. Savvateyeva 'The housing market: no one sells without risking his life', *Izvestiia*, 12 August 1994, p. 4, *Current Digest of the Post-Soviet Press*, 46 (32), p. 5.
86. N. Manning 'Housing, housing policy, and housing movements in East and Central Europe', *Cuadernos del Este*, 12, 1994, pp. 111–35.
87. Rubtsov 'Speech', *op. cit.*
88. I. Savvateyeva 'New solutions to the apartment problem', *Izvestiia*, 17 June 1994, pp. 1–2, *Current Digest of the Post-Soviet Press* 46 (24), p. 11.
89. Baranov 'The housing situation', *op. cit.*, p. 159.

No doubt the recent presidential decrees will encourage improvement here, but there is a long way to go in terms of total space, public or private.

Two further consequences of the state of Russian housing may be observed. One is the perennial difficulty of matching labour market flexibility and housing market flexibility. As already noted, there is growing evidence of flexibility in the labour market, with approximately 20 per cent of the labour force changing jobs in the last year. Clearly many of these workers can find new jobs in the same city, and with public transport still cheap and effective, this would not require relocation. However, any attempt to move workers around the country, as production needs change, is severely hampered by the lack of anything approaching a normal housing market.[90]

The second consequence is the growth in homelessness. As in Western Europe, estimates for the level of this problem are very difficult to agree on, partly due to the invisibility of the problem, and partly due to disagreements over the definition. Sokolov[91] reports that 525 corpses of homeless people were found on the streets of St Petersburg in 1992; this figure more than doubled for 1993. An estimate of 30–50,000 homeless has been given for 1994 in the city.[92] For Moscow, a similar figure of between 30,000 and 100,000 is reported by Andrusz,[93] 10 per cent of whom are estimated to be the victims of housing transaction crime.[94]

Overall, housing is an important issue, both in terms of its political significance as a continuing source of dissatisfaction, and as site for potentially large flows of finance. As is the case for state industrial enterprises, privatisation has in most instances been a paper exercise. Nevertheless, it is happening, and a small market is emerging, which will no doubt grow in size and effect in the future.

Education

As with health care, the main problem for education has been a shortage of resources, poor wages for teachers and lecturers, and the consequent loss of personnel to the private sector. In June 1994, average pay in the education sector was 75 per cent of the average in industry.[95] The new 1993 constitution makes very clear the state's commitment only up to the ninth grade in terms of free public education. Thereafter there is inevitably going to be an influx of private finance with the consequent growth of social divisions. Privatisation and the effects of markets have thus dominated educational policy discussion. However, there are other important issues. Much educational provision has been decentralised to regional and local control. New curricula with less early specialisation and less ideology are in use.

90. Layard and Richter 'Labour market adjustment', *op. cit.*, p. 88.
91. V. Sokolov 'Homelessness in St Petersburg' in *St Petersburg in the Early 1990s: Crazy, Cold, and Cruel*, Charitable Foundation 'Nochlezhka', St Petersburg, 1994, pp. 161–63.
92. Orebro workshop, 1994, unpublished report, p. 34.
93. G. Andrusz 'The causes and consequences of homelessness in Moscow and Sofia', paper for the ESRC East–West Workshop on the Social Consequences of Marketisation, London, 9–10 December 1994, p. 15.
94. *Ibid*, p. 22.
95. *Current digest of the Post-Soviet Press* 46 (33), 1994, p. 22.

Increased efficiency with higher staff–pupil ratios is planned, but with higher wages so that teachers have less need for second or alternative jobs.[96]

Ironically, one of the main innovations of the Gorbachev era was the radical attempt to match the output of schools to the needs of the labour market. This may now be achieved by more brutal methods than the diversion of the academic streams at the top of the secondary school towards technical training. The 1984 reforms have had little real effect on the opportunities of more privileged children, and hence there has been little opposition. Current changes only add to this process of educational change by further removing the children of the privileged from the requirements of general labour market planning. Three processes can be identified: decentralisation, marketisation, and constitutional change. The first has occurred alongside similar moves in other social services to bring local interests and local budgets together as a reaction to the overplanned and overcentralised character of the old system. However this means greater regional inequalities, since the multiple sources of funding envisaged (federal, regional, local, and commercial) will inevitably vary substantially. Marketisation, then, has been hailed as both a blessing and a curse for education. Certainly, the new higher income groups have expressed a demand for private schools which is being rapidly supplied. By 1994, for example, 140 non-state secondary educational institutions were registered in Moscow. Most of these are designed to prepare students for university entrance – they are similar to British sixth form colleges. Not all are individually owned, but various enterprises and organisations have also set up such schools for the children of their employees or members.[97] However, there are doubts about the quality of the teaching in such schools, which reflects a wider problem of the production of teachers. Proposals in 1993 from the Russian Federation Committee on Higher Education suggested a move of teacher training institutes to local budgets, with federal finance only for those numbers and types of training that were identified as essential for the economy, and with such funds open to competitive bids from institutes. Part of the response from the educational 'market' looks familiar to those in higher education in the UK: there has been a rapid escalation in the number of institutes transforming themselves into universities, in order to enhance their market image. Over 100 new universities have appeared since the middle of 1992, over half of which used to be teacher training institutes.[98]

In general, universities have retained their level of activity in recent years despite fears about falling demand. This has been done in two ways. First is the acceptance of fee-paying students, not only sponsored by enterprises, but also by private individuals. For 1994, 480,000 students have been enrolled for free education, but a further

96. B. Laporte and J. Schweitzer 'Education and training', in N. Barr (ed.) *Labor Markets and Social Policy in Central and Eastern Europe, the Transition and Beyond*, Oxford University Press, Oxford, 1994, pp. 260ff.

97. Y. Bogdanova 'There are more than enough prestigious schools', *Rossiiskaya Gazeta*, 20 September 1994, p. 2, *Current Digest of the Post-Soviet Press* 46 (38), pp. 8–9.

98. A. Baiduzhy 'The collapse of the schools', *Nezavisimaia Gazeta*, 14 December 1993, p. 6, *Current Digest of the Post-Soviet Press* 45 (50), p. 17.

46,000 have been admitted paying full costs.[99] Second is the integration of some universities with the top end of the secondary school system. In some cases this is the establishment of a division for preparing potential applicants, in others there has been an integration of entrance exams with school exams, or in one case an agreement to admit all of a school's graduates without further exams (Moscow State University and the Kolmogorov School of Physics and Mathematics). The State Property Committee now has a draft law on privatising the universities, although there have been assurances that this would be phased in over a 10-year period.

The relationship between the 10th and 11th school grades and universities raises a final matter that caused heated debate in 1994, namely the constitutional guarantee in Article 43 for free and compulsory state secondary education only up to the ninth grade. Initially this was greeted within the educational profession as a drafting error in the constitution, but subsequent consultations in early 1994 confirmed it as correct. The tight hand of the Ministry of Finance is seen behind this move, and the prediction made that it will inevitably disenfranchise most pupils from proceeding to university preparation unless they can get sponsorship, or their parents can pay. In effect it is the achievement of the 1984 school reform by constitutional means. Ministry of Education data for 1994 suggests that there has been a fourfold increase in the number of teenagers without access to grades 10 and 11 in some Russian regions, with a twentyfold increase in Moscow and St Petersburg, on the openly admitted grounds of Article 43.[100]

Conclusion: which way for the Russian welfare state?

In an earlier piece on changes in Soviet and post-Soviet social policy up to 1991,[101] I drew the conclusion that there was little change, and that the welfare state at that point looked stuck in the position of 'authoritarian corporatism'. By this I meant that the question of social expenditure was subject to negotiation between the major power blocks (including enterprises), but subject to still very powerful central direction, and imposed in a relatively uniform manner across the country. This characterisation was challenged by Gotting,[102] for indeed the situation is now patently different. Barr[103] has drawn attention to the distinction between short-term, sometimes emergency, social policy measures forced by events that have developed in the early transition phase (for example the rate of inflation in 1992 and 1993), and the medium-term reconstruction of social policy. In 1991, the former phase

99. I. Prelovskaya 'The kind of students higher schools are choosing in order to survive and not lose face', *Izvestiia*, 17 August 1994, p. 4, *Current Digest of the Post-Soviet Press* 46 (33), pp. 16–17.
100. V. Ignatov 'Russian pedagogical elite sees article 43 of the constitution as educational apartheid' *Sevodnya*, 23 June 1994, p. 9, *Current Digest of the Post-Soviet Press* 46 (25), pp. 20–21.
101. Manning 'Social policy in the Soviet Union' *op. cit.*
102. U. Gotting 'Welfare state development in post-communist Bulgaria, Czechoslovakia, and Hungary. A review of problems and responses (1989–1992)', Centre for Social Policy Research, University of Bremen, p. 25.
103. Barr 'Labor Markets' *op. cit.*, pp. 26–27.

was dominant, but it is now possible to begin to recognise the shape that the future Russian welfare state will take.

The key elements are as follows:

- move from state budget to payroll-financed funding;
- decentralised institutional ownership and control;
- privatisation of housing, and parts of health care and education;
- growth of unemployment and labour market flexibility;
- reduction in enterprise welfare functions;
- future plans for a guaranteed minimum, combined with social and private insurance.

While the new constitution retains national level policy-making in principle for health, education and social security, the plans for private and regional elements in these will slowly pull planning and provision away from central control, and increase regional inequalities. But the tension between presidential decree, and State Duma policy-making, and between policies and their implementation, still make prediction fairly hazardous.

The use of high payroll taxes as the key funding mechanism is reminiscent of the French system.[104] While there remains a strong enterprise commitment to employee welfare, this is acceptable to managers; but strong international competition has forced the French to cut these relatively high additions to labour costs. It may be that in the longer term, Russian managers will come to feel the same. On the other hand, a good example of such enterprise welfare is offered by the United States, where employers provide greater social support than is common in Europe, and where government programmes are much more meagre, and subject to great regional variation. For example the Clinton health security plan was to give employers a key role in health insurance. However, Russian longer-term plans seem to be for a state-regulated national insurance system along German lines, rather than the more minimalist American tradition.

In terms of a model that currently dominates comparative social policy analysis,[105] the Russian welfare state is moving strongly towards social welfare as a *commodity*, towards a sharply graded system of *stratification*, and in favour of a greater role of *markets* rather than state control. In terms of this model, it is moving away from any social democratic tradition towards a mixture of corporatist policy-making combined with a residual minimum for those unattached to the labour market.

104. A. Pfaller, I. Gough and T. Therborn *Can the Welfare State Compete?* Macmillan, London, 1991.
105. G. Esping-Andersen *The Three Worlds of Welfare Capitalism*, Polity Press, Cambridge, 1990.

APPENDIX

Appendix

BIOGRAPHIES OF MAJOR FIGURES

Anisimov, Stanislav Vasilievich

Born 1940. Graduated 1967 Moscow Institute of Steel and Alloys, and 1983 from CPSU Central Committee Academy of Social Sciences. 1957–62 fitter; 1967–70, chief engineer Nikopol South Tube Factory. 1970–82 worked in the State Committee for Supplies (*Gossnab*) Ukraine, and also at the All-Union level. 1983–88 instructor, CPSU Central Committee Department of Economics. 1988 appointed Deputy Chairman and from 1990 First Deputy Chairman of Gossnab USSR: 1991 USSR Minister of Material Resources. November 1991 appointed Russian Minister of Trade and Material Resources.

Borovoi, Konstantin Natanovich

Born 1948 in Moscow in family of professionals. 1970 graduated Moscow Railway Engineering Institute, then a mechanical and mathematical college at Moscow University. Candidate of technical sciences. Career as researcher and university teacher. Since 1987 active in business – published a computer magazine, founded business and charity associations, numerous research, tourist, teaching, wood-working companies. 1989 founded the first Russian Commodities and Raw Materials Exchange, became its manager and president. The Exchange was a basis for many other commercial companies, including the Russian National Commercial Bank, Commercial News Agency, RINAKO Investment Company. Founder of enterpreneurial associations, promoted links with the Industrial Union, formed a Round Table of the Constructive Forces in 1992. Founder and co-chair of the Economic Freedom Party.

Chernomyrdin, Viktor Stepanovich

Born 1938. Graduated 1966 from Polytechnical Institute, Kuibyshev and in 1972 from the All-Union Polytechnical Institute, Moscow (Correspondence). Candidate of Technical Sciences. Member CPSU 1961–91; Full Member Central Committee 1986–90. Deputy USSR Supreme Soviet 1989–91 and RSFSR Supreme Soviet 1991–92. 1957–67 fitter, machine operator, head of technical section, Orsk oil refinery. 1967–73 instructor, deputy head and then Head of Department of Industry and Transport Orsk City Party Committee. 1973–78 Director Orenburg Gas Refinery; 1978–82 Sector Head, CPSU Central Committee Department of Oil and Gas. 1982 USSR Deputy Minister, 1985 Minister Gas Industry. 1989 until June 1992 Chair of

Board of 'Gazprom', a new trust which was set up on the basis of the old USSR Gas Ministry. June 1992, Russian Minister of Fuel and Energy and Deputy Chairman of Russian Government. December 1992–present, Russian Prime Minister.

Chubais, Anatolii Borisovich

Born 1955 in Belorussian town, father in the military. 1977 graduated Leningrad Engineering and Economics Institute, candidate of sciences, professor. 1977–90 engineer, lecturer, professor at the institute. 1990–91 Deputy head, Leningrad City Council. 1991–94 Chair, State Committee for State Property, Minister of Russian Federation. Since 1992 also Vice-Premier of the Russian Federation.

Fedorov, Boris Grigorievich

Born 1958 in Moscow in a workers' family. 1980 graduated Moscow Finance Institute, Department of World Economics. 1980–87 economist, then senior economist of the Central Foreign Currency Office, USSR State Bank. 1978–89 senior researcher, USSR Academy of Sciences Institute of World Economics and International Relations. Doctor of economics 1989. 1989–90 analyst, Socio-Economic Department, CPSU Central Committee. 1990 Minister of Finance, RSFSR. Resigned 1991, in protest at anti-reform Supreme Soviet decision; since 1991 Economics Adviser to President of Russia. 1991–92 Head of Department, European Bank for Reconstruction and Development (London). 1992–93 Executive Director, World Bank (Washington). Since 1992 Vice-Premier, 1993–94 Finance Minister of Russian Federation. 1993 member Security Council. One of the founders of Russia's Choice electoral bloc.

Gaidar, Egor Timurovich

Born 1956. Graduate, Moscow University 1979; Candidate Degree in Economics, 1981, Doctor of Economics 1988. 1981 researcher Economics Faculty Moscow University. 1981–85 senior researcher All-Union Institute for Systems Research. 1987 Chief Research Analyst Institute for Economics and Forecasting, Academy of Sciences, USSR. 1990 Editor and Head Political Economy Department *Pravda*. Autumn 1990, Director Institute of Economic Policy of the USSR Academy of National Economy. November 1991 Deputy Chairman Russian Government and Minister of Economics and Finance. June 1992–December 1992 Chair Russian Government. January–September 1993 economic adviser to the President. September 1993–January 1994, First Deputy Chairman Russian Government. In the December 1993 elections won seat in the Russian Duma as head of Russia's Choice.

Gerashchenko, Victor Vladimirovich

Born 1937 in Leningrad. Father Deputy Chair of the Board, USSR Central Bank. 1960 graduated Moscow Finance Institute, worked as bookkeeper at the USSR State Bank. 1962–65 bookkeeper, inspector, expert, Head of Department USSR Foreign

Trade Bank (Vneshtorgbank). 1965–67 Director of the Moscow People's Bank (London). Held a succession of executive banking jobs in Lebanon, West Germany, Singapore with several USSR foreign trade banks 1967–82. 1982–89 department head, then Deputy Chair of the Board, First Deputy Chair of the Board, USSR Foreign Trade Bank. 1989–91 Chair of the Board, USSR State Bank. 1991–94 Chair of the Board, Russian Central Bank.

Iakovlev, Aleksandr Nikolaevich

Born 1923 in village in Iaroslavl Region in peasant family. 1941–43 fought in Second World War, seriously wounded. 1946 graduated Iaroslavl Pedagogical Institute, 1946–53 instructor, then Department Head at the Iaroslavl Obkom CPSU. 1953–73 career in the CPSU Central Committee propaganda department, up to Acting Department Head, responsible for ideology and culture in the country. Doctor of social sciences. 1966–76 member editorial board *Kommunist* journal. 1972 criticised the growing national-patriot sentiments in the press, 1973 'sent away/exiled' as USSR Ambassador to Canada. 1983 met Gorbachev in Canada, who helped him return to Moscow. 1983–85 Director, Institute for World Economics and International Relations, member of the USSR Academy of Sciences. 1985–86 active in the CPSU Central Committee as a supporter of Gorbachev and, particularly, of *glasnost*. 1987–90 member, CPSU Politburo. 1989–91 deputy, USSR Supreme Soviet. 1991 founder and co-chair of Democratic Reforms Movement. Since 1992 Chair Presidential Commission for the Rehabilitation of the Victims of the Stalinist Repressions. Founding member of the Gorbachev Foundation as well as Russia's Choice bloc. Known as the architect of *perestroika*.

Iakovlev, Egor Vladimirovich

Born 1930 in Moscow. 1954 graduated Moscow History and Archives Institute. 1954–55 second secretary, Komsomol District Committee, Moscow. Dramatic career in big-time journalism; on editorial board of *Pravda*, *Izvestiia* correspondent; several times dismissed from important executive posts in newspapers and magazines for unorthodox ideas and approaches. Member of the USSR and RF Unions of Writers, Journalists, Cinematographers. Written over 20 investigative historical books and 30 scripts, largely about Lenin and the Russian Revolution. 1987 Deputy Head of Novosti Press Agency and Editor in Chief of *Moscow News* which he has radically and democratically reformed. 1991 head of the USSR Radio and TV Company, later renamed Ostankino, but mysteriously dismissed in 1992 by Yeltsin, allegedly for political reasons. 1991–93 member of the Consultative Council with the Russian Federation President. Founder and Editor-in-Chief, *Obshschaia Gazeta* weekly; General Director, RTV-PRESS Publishers' Association. Since 1991 chair of the Glasnost Protection Foundation.

Iavlinskii, Grigorii Alekseevich

Born 1952, in Ukraine, in a military family. Dropped out of school, worked as fitter and electrician at a local glass factory. Finished evening school. 1973 graduated Moscow National Economics Institute. Candidate of economics. Career in economics research institutes 1976–89. 1989 Head of Department at the USSR Council of Ministers and secretary of the State Commission for Economic Reform. One of the authors of the 500 days programme for radical economic reform, RSFSR Vice-Premier in 1990, from which he resigned when the programme was rejected. One of the leading economists and presidential economic advisers in USSR, CIS and Russia. As head of inter-regional centre for economic and political studies, inspired radical market reforms in Nizhnii Novgorod. Gaidar's opponent in economic reform. One of the leaders of Iabloko bloc at the 1993 elections.

Khakamada, Irina Mitsuovna

Born 1955 in Moscow, father a Japanese communist who immigrated to the USSR after the Second World War. 1978 graduated Economics Department of the International Friendship University in Moscow. Candidate of economics. Career in research and teaching. Since 1989 has been active in new business, as deputy head of Systems and Programmes cooperative, responsible for charity work and social protection for the poor, elderly, orphans, and disabled. From 1989, together with Konstantin Borovoi, active in creating the first Russian Commodities and Materials Exchange; on board of directors, Chief Research Expert and Head of Information and Analysis Centre. Director of several joint venture companies. Since 1991 Chief Research Expert of the Rinako Russian Investment Company. One of the founders and Political Council members of the Economic Freedom Party; since 1992 General Secretary of the party.

Khasbulatov, Ruslan Imranovich

Born 1942. Graduated in 1965. Doctor of Economics 1970, Moscow State University. Professor. Member of CPSU 1966–91. 1965–67 Secretary, All-Union Komsomol, Moscow University. 1970–72 Instructor Propaganda and Agitation Department, All-Union Komsomol. 1972–79 Head of Sector in Research Institute of Scientific Information, USSR Academy of Sciences and then in the Department of Higher Economic Studies, Scientific Research Institute for Questions of Secondary Schools. 1979–90 Senior Lecturer, Professor and then Chair, Plekhanov Institute for Economic Management in Moscow. 1990–91 Deputy and then First Deputy Chair RSFSR Supreme Soviet. October 1991–21 September 1993, Chair Russian Federation Supreme Soviet.

Khizha, Georgii Stepanovich

Born 1938. Graduated in mathematics Leningrad Polytechnic Institute, and Academy of the National Economy. Doctor Technical Science. For more than 20 years worked at the 'Svetlana' scientific research and manufacturing association in Leningrad - one of the leading enterprises of the military-industrial complex, Director 1987. March 1989 President of the Leningrad Industrial Enterprises Association. 1990 elected a deputy of the Leningrad City Soviet; from September 1991 deputy to the Mayor of St Petersburg, Anatolii Sobchak. Chaired the Commission of the Mayor's office on economic development. June 1992 appointed Deputy Chair of the Russian Government in charge of industry.

Kovalev, Sergei Adamovich

Born 1930 in Ukraine. 1954 graduated Biology Faculty of Moscow State University. Stayed at the faculty as senior lab assistant, graduate student, and junior researcher. 1961–64 senior engineer, then junior researcher at Biophysics Institute of the USSR Academy of Sciences. 1964 returned to Moscow University, unit head of an inter-departmental laboratory, left 1970 for political reasons. Since 1967 active in human rights work. 1969 met Academician Sakharov, became his close friend. Founding member of the USSR Human Rights Initiative Group, 1969–74 when the group was forced to close down. Since 1974 member of the Soviet Chapter, Amnesty International. Arrested 1974, found guilty of anti-Soviet propaganda, spent seven years in prison and three in exile. 1987 allowed to return to Moscow, with temporary residence permit. Continued human rights work, which cost him job at the Institute of the Issues of Information Transmission of the USSR Academy of Sciences. 1990 member of Democratic Russia Movement, elected People's Deputy RSFSR, member of the Supreme Soviet, Chair of the Committee for Human Rights. Suggested the idea of forming the Russia's Choice bloc of reformist forces. Since 1991 Chair of the International Research Centre for Human Rights, an umbrella group linking 12 human rights organisations. Voted Man of the Year in 1994.

Lakhova, Ekaterina Filippovna

Born 1948. Graduated Sverdlovsk Medical Institute, long career as district pediatrician. Was Deputy Head (Motherhood and Childhood Issues) of Central Health Department of the Sverdlovsk Regional Soviet. 1990 People's deputy (RSFSR, then Russia); since 1991 Presidential Adviser on Issues of Family, Protection of Motherhood and Childhood.

Lobov, Oleg Ivanovich

Born 1937. Graduate Institute Railway Engineers, 1960. Candidate of Technical Science. Member CPSU 1971–91. 1960–72 Engineer, Chief Engineer, Head of Construction Department Urals Chemical Institute and then Deputy Director of Urals Scientific Research Institute for Industrial Construction Projects. 1972, Deputy Head (serving under Yeltsin) and 1975 Head, Sverdlovsk Obkom, Department of Construction. 1976–82 Head of the Main Administration of the USSR Ministry for the Construction of Heavy Industry Enterprises. 1982 Secretary and 1983–87 Second Secretary, Sverdlovsk Obkom (Yeltsin was First Secretary). 1987–89 Deputy

Chairman of the RSFSR Council of Ministers. 1989–June 1991 Second Secretary of Central Committee of the Republic of Armenia Communist Party. June 1991–November 1991 First Deputy Chair of RSFSR Government. November 1991–April 1993 Chief of an expert group in the Russian Government. April 1993–present, First Deputy Chair of Russian Government (and Minister of Economics) and from September 1993 Secretary of Security Council.

Pamfilova, Ella Aleksandrovna

Born 1953 in Tashkent. 1976 graduated Moscow Energetics Institute, trained as electronics engineer. 1976–89 was engineer-technologist, head of the trade union committee at a repair shop of the Mosenergo Moscow energy production unit. 1989 elected USSR People's Deputy on a trade union quota. 1990–91 member of the Soviet of the Union chamber in the USSR Supreme Soviet, secretary of the Commission for Benefits and Privileges. 1991–94 Russian Minister for Social Protection. One of the founders of the Russia's Choice electoral bloc, came third top on the candidates' list to the Federal Assembly after Egor Gaidar and Sergei Kovalev.

Poltoranin, Mikhail Nikiforovich

Born 1939 in Kazakhstan. After school cement worker on one of the big Siberian construction projects, the Bratsk Power Station. 1964 graduated Kazakh State University in Alma-Ata, Journalism Department, 1970 – CPSU Central Committee Higher Party School. Successful career in journalism, was Editor-in-Chief of *Moskovskaia Pravda*, Novosti Press Agency commentator. Member of the Moscow CPSU Committee, one of the very few who did not turn away from Yeltsin after his expulsion in 1987. 1987–91 Secretary of the Board of the Moscow Union of Journalists. 1989 USSR People's Deputy, on Union of Journalists quota. 1990–92 RSFSR (and then Russian) Press and Information Minister. Spring–winter 1992 Vice-Premier of Russia. Since 1992 – Director of FITs (Federal Information Centre) a position which is equal to being a vice-premier and which was designed to support presidential policies in the state-owned media.

Primakov, Evgenii Maksimovich

Born 1929 in Kiev. 1953 graduated Moscow Institute for Oriental Studies. Doctor of economics, member of the USSR Academy of Sciences. 1956–62 correspondent, editor, Editor-in-Chief, Central Department of Overseas Broadcasting, USSR Gosteleradio (State TV and Radio Committee). 1962–70 career in *Pravda* newspaper, as an analyst, correspondent, Deputy Head of Department. 1970–77 Deputy Director, Institute for World Economics and International Relations of the USSR Academy of Sciences, 1977–85 Director of the Oriental Studies Institute of the USSR Academy of Sciences. Successful career in the Communist Party, member of the Central Committee, Candidate member to the Politburo. 1988 member of the USSR Supreme Soviet, 1989–90 Chair of the USSR Soviet of the Union chamber of the Supreme Soviet. 1990 member of the USSR Presidential Council, 1991 member of the USSR

Security Council. After the 1991 coup head of the Central Intelligence Service (formerly the First Central Office of the KGB). Since 1991 Director of the Russian Federation Foreign Intelligence Service. Since 1993 member of the Russian Security Council.

Rutskoi, Aleksandr Vladimirovich

Born 1947. Graduated in 1971 from Air Force School (Altai Krai), in 1980 from Gagarin Air Force Academy and in 1990 from Academy of General Staff in Moscow. Member of CPSU 1970–91. 1990–91 Member of RSFSR Communist Party Central Committee. 1964 Fitter in Aviation plant. 1965–90 Served in Soviet Air Force, rose from pilot to chief of staff of air force regiment, and commander of air force regiment in Afghanistan (1985–86); Deputy then Head of Air Force Pilot Combat Training Centre (1988–90). 1989 Deputy Chair Moscow Branch, 'Fatherland' (*Otechestvo*). 1990–91 Deputy RSFSR Congress, Chair of RSFSR Supreme Soviet Committee 'For Invalids' and Afghan War Veterans' Affairs and for the Social Protection of Army Servicemen and their Families'. Chair Communists for Democracy Faction, RSFSR Congress. 1991 Chair, Democratic Party of Communists of Russia (renamed People's Party of Free Russia in October 1991). 1992 Co-Chair of Civic Union. June 1991–September 1993 Vice President of Russian Federation.

Shumeiko, Vladimir Filippovich

Born 1945. Graduate 1972 from Krasnodar Polytechnic Institute. Member of CPSU 1967–91. 1964 began work as assembly fitter at the Krasnodar Electric Precision Instruments Factory. 1972–90 worked in the Krasnodar Electric Measuring Instruments Research Institute rising to Chief Engineer in 1985 and General Director in 1990. 1990 elected a deputy to the RSFSR Supreme Soviet and November 1991 became Deputy Chair of the Russian Supreme Soviet. 1990–91 member of 'Communists of Russia' faction; April–June 1992 member of factions 'Radical Democrats' and 'Industrial Union'. May 1992 member of the 'Reform' deputies group. President of Russian Confederation of Entrepreneurs' Unions. June 1992 appointed First Deputy Chair of the Russian government in charge of industrial development. February 1994 elected Chair of the Federation Council in the Federal Assembly.

Silaev, Ivan Stepanovich

Born 1930. Graduated 1954. Member CPSU 1959–91; Full member Central Committee 1981–90. Deputy USSR Supreme Soviet 1981–89. 1954–71 Foreman, Chief Engineer, then Director of an Aviation Enterprise. 1974–77 USSR Deputy Minister, and 1977–85 USSR Minister of the Aviation Industry. 1985 Deputy Chair USSR Council of Ministers and Chair Bureau for Machine Building. June 1990–September 1991, Chair RSFSR Council of Ministers. September 1991–December 1991, Chair Committee for the Operational Management of the USSR Economy.

Skokov, Iurii Vladimirovich

Born 1938, graduated 1961. 1961–69 Researcher, Scientific Research Institute USSR Ministry of Defence. 1969–86 rose from Sector Chief to Director of Krasnodar Scientific Production Association 'Kvant'; 1986–90 General Director Moscow Scientific Production Institute 'Kvantemp'. 1989–1991 Deputy USSR Congress of People's Deputies. 1990 First Deputy Chair of the RSFSR Government. 1991 State Councillor Russian Federation for Economic Questions and in 1991 for Security Issues. June 1992–May 1993, Secretary Russian Security Council.

Starovoitova, Galina Vasil'evna

Born 1946 in Cheliabinsk. Completed three out of five years in a military mechanical institute, 1971 graduated Department of Psychology, Leningrad State University. 1966–91 career as a junior and then senior researcher and engineer-sociologist in R&D institutes, production units, and Ethnography Institute of the USSR Academy of Sciences. Well-known academic and mass media writer on ethnosociology, active on inter-ethnic problems and conflicts. Candidate of history. 1989 People's Deputy of the USSR, 1990 People's Deputy of the RSFSR, member of the Democratic Russian and Reform Coalition factions. Declined offer of post of Chair Russian State committee for Nationalities; 1991–92 State Adviser to the RF President on International Relations, unexpectedly dismissed from the post, apparently for her position concerning North Caucasian issues. Since 1990 active in Democratic Russia movement, member of its Coordinating Council.

Umalatova, Sazhi Zaindinovna

Born 1953 in Kazakhstan, where her parents had been deported after the liquidation of the Chechen-Ingush Autonomous Republic, Chechen. After the restoration of the republic in 1957 the family moved back to Groznii. Became manual worker after school, worked her way up to team leader in machine-building plant in Groznii. Often elected member of honorary presidia and committees as representative of the working class, delegate to 26th and 27th CPSU Congresses. Member of the Chechen-Ingush Regional CPSU Committee, and Commission for Social and Economics Issues. Graduated Rostov Higher Party School by correspondence. 1986 deputy USSR Supreme Soviet (ran as candidate from Groznii, then as one from CPSU). A hard-liner, openly criticised Gorbachev for letting the USSR fall apart, supported the coup leaders in 1991. Was elected Chair of the Standing Presidium of the USSR Congress of People's Deputies, set up in defiance of the USSR's liquidation, and, therefore, Acting USSR President.

Yeltsin, Boris Nikolaevich

Born 1931. Graduated 1955 Urals Polytechnical Institute, Sverdlovsk. 1961–90 Member of CPSU; 1981–90 Full Member of Central Committee. 1986–88 Candidate Member of Politburo. 1955–68 rose from Construction Supervisor to Chief

Engineer of a Housing Construction Combine. 1968–75 Head of Department of Construction, Sverdlovsk Obkom. 1975 Secretary, and 1976–85 First Secretary Sverdlovsk Obkom. 1985 Secretary of Central Committee in charge of Construction; 1985–87 First Secretary of Moscow Gorkom; 1987–89 First Deputy Chair USSR State Committee for Construction. 1989–91 Deputy USSR Congress; member of Presidium and Chair of Committee for Construction and Architecture, USSR Supreme Soviet. 1989–90 Co-Chair Inter-regional Group of Deputies USSR Supreme Soviet. 1990–91 Chair RSFSR Supreme Soviet. June 1991 President (and from October 1991–June 1992 Prime Minister) of Russian Federation.

Zhirinovskii, Vladimir Volfovich

Born 1946, Alma-Ata, Kazakhstan. Graduated from the Institute of the Countries of Asia and Africa, Moscow State University, in 1970 and from the Evening School of the Law Faculty of Moscow University in 1977. 1965–67 studied at the University of Marxism-Leninism in the Faculty of International Relations. 1970–72 served in the army in Tblisi. 1973–75 worked in the USSR Peace Committee and from January to May 1975 in the Higher School of the Trade Union Movement. 1983–91 was Head of the legal department in the 'Mir' Publishing House. Founded the Liberal Democratic Party in Spring 1989 and was elected Chair March 1990.

Sources

A.S. Barsenkov *et al. Politicheskaia Rossiia segodnia. Vysshaia predstavitel'naia vlast'*. Moskovskii rabochii, 1993.
A.S. Barsenkov *et al. Politicheskaia Rossiia segodnia. Ispolnitel'naia vlast'. Konstitutsionnyi sud. Lidery partii i dvizhenii*. Moskovskii rabochii, 1993.
A. Vasilevskii and V. Pribylovskii. *Kto est' kto v rossiiskoi politike (300 biografii)*. Vols. 1, 2, 3, Panorama, 1993.
Kto est' kto v Rossii i v blizhnem zarubezh'e. Novoe vremia. Vse dlia vas, 1993.
Kto est' kto v Rossii i byvshem SSSR. Vydaiushchiesia lichnosti byvshego Sovetskogo Soiuza, Rossii i immigratsii. Terra, 1994.

INDEX